Studying History

Jeremy Black and
Donald M. MacRaild

MACMILLAN

First published 1997 by
MACMILLAN PRESS LTD
Houndmills, Basingstoke, Hampshire RG21 6XS
and London
Companies and representatives
throughout the world

ISBN 0-333-68795-7

A catalogue record for this book is available
from the British Library.

This book is printed on paper suitable
for recycling and made from fully managed
and sustained forest sources.

10   9   8   7   6   5   4   3   2
06   05   04   03   02   01   00   99

Printed in Hong Kong

To
Bill Purdue

Contents

PART II

PART III

Editors' preface

IF you are studying history the chances are that you are looking for a book that will not only help you come to grips with the larger themes and issues behind historical study, but also a book that will help you formulate your own ideas in a clear, analytic style. The aim of *Studying History* is to offer you guidance on how to gain both of these important skills by providing the sort of vital information you need to understand history as a discipline and also by providing practical help and tips on how to write about history.

The book is divided into three major sections. Part I deals with the scope of history and the different varieties of history, ranging from the traditional to the new. It provides you with the big picture of history, of how it has been thought of as a subject and how it has changed. Key ideas are explained and explored in a large framework so that you can gain a sense of the overall significance of history as a subject.

Part II is concerned with the sources and methods of the historian, with the sort of theories and concepts historians make use of and bring to bear on documents and evidence. Part II thus acts as a complement to Part I: the move is from the large framework to the detailed work of history and its analytic thinking.

Part III focuses on the practical business of studying history at A level or university. There is advice on how to take notes and organise your reading. Then come chapters on writing an essay and on how to tackle your dissertation. Finally there is a chapter of advice on history exams.

Each part of the book can be read separately or dipped into for information or guidance. In the first instance, however, it may well repay you to read quickly through the book as a whole, so that you gain a sense of what history involves and how the essays you are asked to write grow out of the debates and discussions that characterise history as a subject. At once a guide to current ideas about history and a practical textbook that will develop your skills as an historian, *Studying History* is designed to help you get the most out of your course and to achieve excellent results.

John Peck
Martin Coyle

Preface

Cultures are like individuals: they take on meaning in terms of time passing. Memories of the past are the lodestars of our thoughts, collective and individual. We cannot leave the past: our own present will be someone else's past; our past was once the present. The passage of time, and its important effects, mean that everything will one day be history; that everything has a history.

In this book we examine the multifaceted nature of history. We look at the nature of the subject, the manner in which historians have and do study the past and the way in which you can approach and study it. The book is a considered response of two practising historians, both teachers and researchers, to the complexities of the exciting and enlivening discipline of history. The range of our interests offers a number of complementary approaches and covers the major spheres of historical study. Our proactive text both explains the intellectual milieu of the historian and also supports students pursuing the subject.

The first part offers introductory statements as to the nature of the discipline. It allows students to engage with some of the key terminologies used by historians over the years and provides a clear and comprehensive overview of the discipline.

The second section focuses upon the way in which historians go about the study of history and encourages students to see themselves as engaged in the same process. It discusses the types of documents that historians use and considers the role of theory in the development of the historian's art. This section also considers how students should study themes or case-studies; structures and individuals; ideologies and mentalities. It also considers the importance of such things as facts and narratives in the writing of history. The chapters here also consider the developments of some of the most important schools of history so that students can get a flavour of the diversity of historical understanding. Finally, this section blends the works of some key historians with an articulation of the methods and theories they employ.

The third part sets out practical advice on how to study history. It draws on examples of historical works and explains the way historians analyse and interpret them. It offers students comprehensive guidance on the variety of historical study. It explains how to study documents and texts; how to read effectively; and how to write papers, essays and longer research-based papers, such as dissertations.

Jeremy Black
Don MacRaild

PART I

PART I

1

The scope of history

People will not look forward to posterity, who never look backwards to
their ancestors.

Edmund Burke, *Reflections on the Revolution in France* (1790)

INTRODUCTION

MOST people see history in terms of separate periods (whether,
for example, classical, medieval or modern), with each typified by a
different way of life. At the same time, the study of history is often
characterised as solely concerned with recovering facts about the
past. Seen in this way, history is like a book, with each chapter
charting a different phase or epoch of human development: the rise
and fall of Greece and Rome; the emergence of the Catholic
Church; the heraldry and Crusades of the Middle Ages; the Renaissance and Reformation; or the technology and social change of the
Industrial Revolution. In similar fashion, popular perceptions of the
process of historical change are founded on the idea of progress, a belief
that each new era brings to human society a more sophisticated sense of
being.

History is also about roots. It provides society and individuals with a
dimension of longitudinal meaning over time which far outlives the
human life-span. It connects us with our past. History also allows us to
peer into the future by providing precedents for contemporary action,
forewarning against the repetition of past mistakes. From its sense of
continuity, history offers apparent form and purpose to past, present
and future. There is seen to be a need for history. It has social value,
and its study is both important and rewarding.

The popular view tends to smooth out the contours of the past, brushing away its inconsistencies. As students of history will find out, the past is not simply a collection of distinct ages or a hotchpotch of facts. History is extremely complex and historians disagree on exactly what it is. Since E. H. Carr, in *What is History?* (1961), suggested that history 'is a continuous process of interaction between the historian and his facts, an unending dialogue between the present and past' (thereby implying it was changeable), there has been a steady stream of attempts to provide satisfactory answers. So keen are historians to find new explanations that, though Carr's work remains a masterful exposition on the state of history, it is now some way off the pace of current trends.

Today the very notion that history is a fact-based discipline has come under scrutiny. At the same time, the idea that history is a branch of the humanities has been consistently undermined by its growth as a social science. Over the past thirty years or so, innovative work in sociology, economics, geography and many other disciplines has been brought to bear on the practice of history. The seemingly revolutionary developments in history over the past generation or so have been underpinned further by the systematic development of areas of historical inquiry which might once have seemed marginal: class and gender; ethnicity and race; culture and custom; immigrant or minority groups; women and children. Although factually orientated political history has never gone away (not that it should do so), there has been a decided shift towards what Peter Burke calls 'new perspectives' in historical writing. Historians today are much more receptive to the theories of social science. The methodological implications of new discourses have also been considerable, with historians now looking well beyond the official government-type documents which fuelled most nineteenth-century scholarship.

This book offers students a route across the shifting and often confusing grounds of historical inquiry. The principal task is to present a clear overview of the most important of these changes and to note their impact upon scholarship; equally, however, apparent continuities must also be highlighted. The first part (Chapters 1 to 3) provides a broad-ranging introduction to the study of history. Here we examine the changing nature of historical inquiry, considering how each generation has produced different kinds of history. In so doing, we will see where the major approaches to historical inquiry, which students encounter, actually came from. The second part (Chapters 4 and 5) goes a step further by providing readers with a discussion of the sources and methodologies of historians, as well as an examination of the theories and concepts upon which have been founded the most recent innovations in historical discourse. The third part (Chapters 6 to 9) is much more concerned with the student's own practice of history. It is hoped that by making useful suggestions about reading, preparing papers, writing essays and working on longer research-based assignments, this part of the book will help aspiring historians to engage more clearly, confidently and effectively with their chosen discipline.

Before going on to discuss these issues, this chapter begins with an assertion: that the nature of historical inquiry forces us to understand numerous problems of conception and approach. This chapter challenges the notion that history is simply a neutral discipline founded upon an immutable body of facts. It rejects the idea that historians can claim the same degree of objectivity which Victorian scholars saw as their hallmark. History, we shall see, is far from simple. The past is often contested ground, perceived differently by competing groups and ideologies. In terms of methods of research, we will also discover in later chapters (especially Chapter 4) that history is only as good as its sources, and that no source is ever perfect or impartial.

THE USES OF HISTORY

History clearly has a broader utility and a deeper social meaning than is represented by the writing of books. The past is our heritage; although it is gone, we feel a part of it. Today, historians, students and the lay readership know that there are many kinds of history. Indeed, the sub-division of the discipline is so great that no one could ever master its entire historiography (the systematic study of what historians have written about the past). Currently, professional expertise among historians is actually quite narrow. Doctoral theses are often written around very dense sets of records covering very narrow areas of specialism – 'the Irish in the north of England, 1841–1871'; 'electoral politics in Birmingham, 1867–1884'; 'the English Civil War in Carlisle'. The mystery of huge subjects – as evinced by such great historians as Gibbon, Macaulay, Ranke, Acton or Trevelyan – has largely become lost in the quest to evaluate sources, to know their veracity, rather than to write history itself. Moreover, the development of new technology, by making publishing cheaper, threatens to increase the minute specialisms of academic historians, which will in turn lead to a further separation between the professional writer and the general reader.

Historical scholarship has become an industry that reflects the wider needs and desires of the nation, of the people and of society, as well as those of the practitioners. This need to tell the national story has, however, always been seen as a function of history, and long predates its emergence as an overwhelmingly state-funded profession. Even prior to the mid-nineteenth century, when history emerged as a distinctive discipline in its own right, the writing of history was not simply the remit of gentlemen scholars, clerics, philosophers and Enlightenment thinkers, most of whom were removed from the 'market' pressures of selling books. In the eighteenth century the writings of scholars like Bolingbroke went on alongside the endeavours of a variety of 'hack' historians.

Unlike historical scholarship in many other countries, that in Britain has been dominated by certain key continuities. Since the emergence of the Whig interpretation of history in the eighteenth and nineteenth centuries, historiographical tradition of these isles (though most notably in Britain) has tended to stress a linear notion of historical development. The Whig interpretation, most famously expounded by Lord Macaulay, held that the history of Britain since the Glorious Revolution of 1688 had been the story of continuous progress, the bedrocks of which were constitutional monarchy, parliamentary government, Protestantism, tolerance, freedom and liberty. Moreover, these values were seen, in the eighteenth and early nineteenth centuries, to define British history as different from that of continental countries where Catholicism and absolutism held firm. The key emphases of the Whig view were British distinctiveness and British progress.

Although it is commonly supposed that the Whig interpretation came to an end with the scientific approach to history evinced (as we shall in the next chapter) by Lord Acton (1834–1902), Whiggish attitudes are far from entirely absent from our conception of historical progress. As Raphael Samuel has argued in 'Grand Narratives' (*History Workshop Journal*, 1990), although the Whig interpretation of history has long been removed, 'put to the axe, some sixty years ago by Sir Lewis Namier [1930] ... the idea of progress shows a vigorous after-life in other spheres – the history of the household and family, for instance, as epitomised in the work of Lawrence Stone, or that of welfare, still measured by stepping-stones to social security'. Such approaches are not limited to the field of political history, and indeed derive much of their weight from their wider resonance and applicability.

HISTORY AND THE NATIONAL MYTH

For centuries, history was generally accepted as a morally exemplary tale; a feature of the nation's identity and values that was of
political worth. The first great Whig work was *The Constitutional
History of England* (1827) by Henry Hallam (1777–1859). Never
was the Whig view more clearly expounded, however, than in the
History of England (1848–55) by T. B. Macaulay (1800–59). Politics and
morality were not separated in this approach; the works of Hallam and
Macaulay were a form of party propaganda. Thus the relationship
between politics and history was strongly focused, because of the
obvious political importance of a small number of individuals and
because of the notion of kingship and governance as moral activities.
As the relationship appeared timeless, it seemed pertinent to apply
admonitory tales in a modern context. History was seen as a lesson, a
warning with which to remind politicans and citizens alike of their
responsibilities.

Yet there is an undercurrent to the longevity of this feature of
British historical scholarship. The violence and problematical nature
of recent discontinuties, not least the loss of empire and of relative
power, renders the universally felt need to claim continuity with
the past even more compelling for many. Thus as Britain's world
role diminishes to that befitting a second-rate Euro-nation, so the
desire to cling to images of the past becomes more acute. A society
in the grips of technological change is surprisingly reverential of
and referential to the past. The role of television and the popular
press in presenting symbols of our heritage cannot be gainsaid. In
Britain, a strong Republican movement exists only among the
Catholics of Northern Ireland, and that itself is a consequence of
history. Different historical traditions and myths, kept alive in anniver-
sary marches and regalia, help to define and sustain the warring
confessional groups in that province on which the weight of history is
all too heavy.

In reality, there have been sharp discontinuities in British history,
constitutional, political and religious. The Reformation, the break
with Rome in the sixteenth century, was one such, despite attempts
to disguise it by arguing that it represented a return to the
primitive Church. Similarly the 'Glorious Revolution' of 1688–89,
by which William III replaced James II, was presented as a revolution, in the sense of a return to a desirable past situation after a
period of unfortunate instability and papist despotism. The word

'revolution' did, before 1789, ordinarily bear the connotation of 'wheel-like' motion, a rotation back to the original point. 'Revolution' only came to mean 'overthrow' after 1789. In practice the invasion, and the *coup d'état*, that brought William of Orange to the throne as William III represented a violent discontinuity. His usurpation of the throne was not accepted by many in England and, even more obviously, Scotland and Ireland. It had to be enforced through violence. The 'Glorious Revolution' led not only to civil war, a War of the British Succession (1689–92) and major constitutional changes, but also to a new established church in Scotland and the violent destruction of the Catholic Church and degradation of the position of Catholics in Ireland.

And yet this series of events is perfectly illustrative of the power of historical myth, and its importance for national consciousness. Moreover, every country has its versions of this kind of heroic history, interpreted to suit the apparent needs of the spirit of a nation. The Williamite succession was generally presented, except, of course, in Catholic circles, as part of a progressive move towards liberty, an integral part of a seamless web that stretched back to Magna Carta in 1215, and the constitutional struggles of the barons in medieval England, and forward to the peaceful extensions of the British franchise (right to vote) in the nineteenth century, as well as to the allegedly benign and benevolent acquisition of imperial territories in the same period. This teleological, optimistic and progressive conception of British history was the dominant account in academic and popular circles, a comforting and suitably morally sound historical vision for a nation which, in the late eighteenth and nineteenth centuries, came to dominate the world in terms of commerce and empire. To some extent this publicly held myth of Britain's unlinear historical development is still upheld in the 1990s. The 'Glorious Revolution' is seen by Ian Paisley, a leading spokesman for Ulster loyalism, for example, as not simply a war of succession but as a victory for European religious rights against the authoritarianism of papal dictatorship. For even less extreme camps, these events have a broader utility. Amongst those opposed to the process of European convergence, presented by the growing authority of the European Union, not least in the person of Tony Benn, a prominent socialist, Magna Carta, the historic struggles against arbitrary monarchical injustices and the emergence of an allegedly unique, evolutionary parliamentary democracy are used to counter the seepage of central power to Brussels.

COMPETING HISTORIES

On the Left, historical continuity is expressed largely in terms of a specific view of national history, shaped by changes in productive relations, and expressed through the medium of class-consciousness and struggle. This is a history primarily focused on the last 200 years, on a history that began with the turmoil of the Industrial Revolution, although attempts are made to extend this vista by examining earlier instances of apparent class-consciousness, such as in the case of the English Peasants' Revolt of 1381. This type of history, most obviously seen in the work of the British Marxist medievalist Rodney Hilton, has elicited criticism from the Right on the grounds that it represents a backward projection of later views, and subsequent historical change, on to earlier times. These criticisms are not without foundation. The overriding theme of discussions of class centres on conflict – the vested orders versus the people. It can be applied to past and present, for example, in the search for historical parallel in the debate over the popular hostility aroused by the Poll Tax, introduced by the Conservative government of Mrs Thatcher in the late 1980s. Left-wing opponents of this tax drew attention to past episodes of popular opposition to taxation, all allegedly exemplifying the ongoing struggle between popular will and abusive power. This interpretation is both historical, in that it looks for evidence of continuity, and ahistorical, in that it underrates, if not denies, the specificity of particular episodes. This question of relativism (which is discussed later in this chapter) – of time frozen or time in continuum – might be seen as a metaphor for problems of historical inquiry. Thus a sense of the past, as constant reference point, is of major importance. History is a battleground; an ebbing and flowing of styles, approaches and ideologies; a metaphor for 'this' or 'that' cause; a sharp and at times dangerous tool.

This competition for the past can be seen clearly in a number of fields. It might appear to have but a minor role in international relations. Britain's position in the 1990s is very different from that of thirty years ago, let alone sixty years ago. The empire is lost, and the nature of military strength has altered dramatically with the development of nuclear weapons. Even within the life-span of an adult of fifty the changes have been dramatic. And yet, the continued historical references in modern debates over foreign policy are very obvious. The parliamentary discussion over the likely response after the Argentinian invasion of the Falkland Islands/Malvinas in 1982 included numerous references to appeasement and the Munich Agreement of 1938. The

Foot's view of Thatcher during Argentian invasion [margin note, handwritten]

then leader of the Labour Party, Michael Foot, who had bitterly criticised Tory appeasement of Hitler in 1938, was undoubtedly influenced in his response to the invasion of 1982 by earlier formative experiences. Suspecting that the government of Mrs Thatcher would appease the Argentinian dictatorship – that, in short, the Conservatives could not be relied upon to stand up to right-wing aggression nor to defend national interests – he called for firm action and thus divided his party when Mrs Thatcher did indeed respond firmly.

HISTORY AND IDEOLOGY

Political history [margin note, handwritten]

The past has considerable political leverage. For this reason history is a contested terrain: between 'high' historians and the 'low'; Whigs against Tories; the Left versus the Right; nation against nation. History is not a subject to be trifled with or taken lightly. It is extremely dangerous in the wrong hands, though a source of enlightenment too. In the political arena, history's worth is well known. Political parties are aware of their own past, and are usually anxious to conceptualise the collective past in their own vision. Each party has its favourite historians; many politicians, from Lord John Russell to Spandolini, have written histories.

Politics, of course, has many meanings; its definitions certainly go beyond mere political parties. For the purpose of opening up a discussion of the role of history as politically charged, the definitions offered by Joan W. Scott, the prominent feminist historian ('power', 'the strategies aimed at maintaining power' and 'ideology') will suffice. Those who reclaim aspects of that past, historians, are themselves both the perpetrators and, at times, the victims of the ideological battles that consume their chosen subject. The past is an inheritance that we all share, but its interpretation varies according to how it is viewed in terms of political and social utility. It is naive, for example, simply to see history as an accumulation of facts and figures, or as a series of colourful little stories which enliven human knowledge. Instead, political suppositions have often played a major role. In the Soviet Union history was shamelessly and repeatedly rewritten. As crucial figures, such as Trotsky, were expunged, so their part in the Communist Revolution was at first written down, then written out, and later written back in some negative, counter-revolutionary role. In Nazi Germany, history was utilised as a tool of social control (defined broadly) in an attempt to sharpen the masculine, heroic history of the Fatherland and of the German *volk* (people), evinced in the propaganda of Goebbels.

Great store was set by the fables of German history and so emerged a renewed and reinvigorated imagery of Valkyrie and German eagles; a mytho-history in which the characters of the *Nibelungenlied*, such as Siegfried, who played a major role in Wagner's operas, took centre stage. This was the equivalent of drawing direct analogies between modern English history and Arthurian legend.

The ideological importance of history is not only rooted in the machinations of men like Joseph Stalin (1879–1953), Adolph Hitler (1889–1945) and Francisco Franco (1892–1975). The implications for history of an ideological treatment of the past are not solely the remit of undemocractic or authoritarian societies. History, as was argued above in the case of the 'Glorious Revolution', is often about the creation and perpetuation of national myths. Once in the realm of myth-making, we perhaps approach an ideological treatment of the past. Therefore, the ideal of students and scholars might be to study history by endeavouring to separate myth from reality; to clear the ground of the dead wood of many disingenuous interpretations and to develop a more meaningful, systematic and less biased assessment of what constitutes a reasonable knowledge of the past. Yet certain attitudes to the past are welded on through common sense or by personal development and experience. While no one can objectively know all of the past, the incremental development of skills, and a simultaneous awareness of pitfalls, might improve the kind of history we write. In the eyes of some critics, however, such a view is a positivistic myth that exaggerates the potency of historians, and 'postmodernist' writers argue that myth is central to the historical process and cannot be separated from reality. These questions of 'bias' and 'objectivity' in the study of history will crop up time and again throughout this book.

The frequent controversies in states which have national education systems over what consitutes a proper national curriculum in history, indicate the contentious nature of the subject and its importance as a tool for politicans' use. No other subject arouses the passions like history; when it comes to deciding what our children should learn about the national past, debate can be zealous. In Britain in the 1980s and 1990s questions arose about the future of history teaching: should we teach a national history, or does membership of the European Community require a European dimension to the child's learning; does the nature of Britain's economic heritage necessitate exhaustive treatment of the Industrial Revolution; are the towns in which most of us live suitable vehicles for learning about past societies; should the National Curriculum primarily concentrate on the greatest examples of British endeavour – Kings and Queens, eminent statesmen and great generals as well as scientists, entrepreneurs and national heroes? Debates over such subject matter are history themselves. Today, the National Curriculum reflects a broad range of interests, from the Greeks and the Romans, through Antiquity and the Middle Ages, to modern British, European and American history. Politicans still habitually pop up with suggestions as to what constitutes proper history, and some would say they should, because politicans are the elected representatives of the people. Politicians and leaders in any country, then, have a vested interest in the past. Whether driven by a self-serving or narcissistic desire to connect themselves to the glories of their predecessors in high office, or by a need to revive and mould the national spirit, politicans use history.

IDEOLOGY AND THE HISTORIANS

The charge of making ideological use of history does not only rest at the door of politicans or those who design curricula. Historians themselves are often driven as much by considerations of ideology as by the nature of historical evidence, although it can be argued that the attempt to distinguish them is naive. This division between theoretical and empirical approaches is considered in later chapters in greater detail. For now, it will suffice to sketch out some of the main arguments concerning the way in which historians' ideological positions might affect the history they produce. In the nineteenth century, when the empirical mode and positivist ideology (with their emphasis on facts or grand scientific explanations) were ascendant, historians, driven by the desire to use sources objectively and impartially, sought to appear neutral and unbiased. By contrast, Marxist historians, with their concentration upon historical materialism (the changing history of an evolving world), with its primacy placed upon the rise and fall of productive systems, seemed, to some traditional historians, to offer a teleological and ideological type of history. However, not all those seduced by Marxism were left-wing; nor were (or are) all left-wingers Marxists. Empirical approaches are sometimes criticised from the left as outmoded. In addition, it is suggested that objectivity is a myth and that empiricism was just as ideological in its own way as other approaches.

For the most part, controversial areas of historical study are always the most likely to elicit charges of ideological bias. In recent years, feminist historiography – a development in historical writing which has in many respects mirrored the emergence of the women's movement since the 1960s – perhaps provides the most salient example. Today, women's history is very much at the vanguard of the 'new history'. As the question of women's equality is being addressed by women's groups, women have begun to conquer the traditional male preserves of many professions, including academe. At the same time, developments in women's history are marching alongside other non-traditional histories, for example, those of class and labour. As is the case with most new developments in history, women's history has surfaced out of some perceived inadequacy in existing arrangements for historical study; women's history, unlike many new developments, claims to represent the largest chunk of the past (50 per cent or more of the population) which has remained, to borrow Sheila Rowbotham's phrase, 'hidden from history'.

At the same time as women's history has broken new boundaries, and women have entered universities in large numbers, so also much controversy has surrounded the rewriting of history from women's perspectives. Joan W. Scott's logical interpretation of what women's history is about, presented in her essay, 'Women's history' (in P. Burke (ed.), *New Perspectives in Historical Writing*, 1993), seems self-evident and acceptable: 'Most women's history has sought somehow to include women as objects of study, subjects of the story. It has taken the axiomatic notion that the universal human subject could include women and provided evidence and interpretations about women's varied actions and experiences in the past.' At the same time, however, some women's history has been tendentious, and it is here that the question of ideology is again raised. This is the case, Scott argues, because traditional historians exercise powers of guardianship over history, by which is implied their 'mastery of history'. This they do, she says, by 'invoking an opposition between "history" (that knowledge gained through neutral inquiry) and "ideology" (knowledge distorted by considerations of interest)'.

IDEOLOGY AND SOURCES

Many of the problems associated with this question of ideology stem from the sources which historians use, for many of the things historians wish to write about are not well documented. The comparative dearth of sources for the everyday history of ordinary women in the Middle Ages is one example; indeed, the further back we go, the harder it is to find material on any aspect of popular life. The picture, of course, is not all bleak; indeed, historians 'from below' such as George Rudé, and members of the *Annales* School, such as Emmanuel Le Roy Ladurie, or cultural historians such as Robert Darnton, have long argued that creativity and immense hard work can reap rewards. We shall say more about sources in Chapters 4 and 5.

For now, let us consider one final illustration which is addressed much more directly at this question of ideology. Even when writing of comparatively modern times, historians face a struggle with the documents. It is common, for example, for historians of the nineteenth and twentieth centuries to make much use of newspapers, for the advent of the popular press has left for posterity a huge amount of material concerning the way in which contemporaries saw their world. Newspapers, then, are both makers and reporters of opinion; yet even in times of sharp media polarisation, we know very well the limitations of newspapers as purveyors of bias, rather than recorders of news. Questions of efficacy and veracity, questions of historical 'worth', can be asked of newspapers reporting any historical event. Take, for example, the observation of George Orwell (1903–50), the writer and critic, on reportage of the Spanish Civil War (1936–39). His words, first published in 'Looking Back on the Spanish Civil War' (*New Road*, June 1943), are a savage indictment of the newspaper's worth as an historical artefact, although, like most critics, Orwell underrated the problems of reporting war. Orwell knew that newspapers often published things which were incorrect, but it was in Spain in the 1930s that he noticed for the first time publications which bore no relation to the facts as he knew them. 'I saw,' he alleged, 'great battles reported where there had been no fighting, and complete silence where hundreds of men had been killed. I saw troops who had fought bravely denounced as cowards, and others who had never fired a shot hailed as heroes of imaginary victories.' Even back in London, Orwell recounts, there were newspapers 'retailing these lies and eager intellectuals building emotional susperstructures over events that had never happened'.

HISTORY AND TIME

What is time – whether past, present or future? This question is central, on many different levels, to our understanding of what history is. The historian who fails to conceptualise time, its variable speeds in different contexts, and its varying impact upon past or present societies, will be somewhat disadvantaged. Students must not view time as an inflexible or unchanging entity but as a relative phenomenon. Certain things about time do, of course, remain static. However, when we as historians concern ourselves with time it is not to ask: has the number of hours in a day changed over time? Time itself is an interesting category of historical inquiry. As a measure of work, or as the perimeters of a task, time already has a sizeable literature associated with it.

E. P. Thompson's essay 'Time, work-discipline and industrial capitalism' (*Past and Present*, 38, December 1967) is about time, or, more properly, the way in which perceptions of time changed over time. As Thompson tried to show, time came to mean something different with the emergence of factory labour and industrial capitalism (athough critics have said that much of Thompson's work revealed a limited grasp of pre-industrial society that reflected his own critique of society). Time altered from something that was measured by the seasons, or the sun and the moon, to another that was harshly prescribed by the foreman's fob-watch or the chimes of the factory bell. Notional time became regimented time. With industrial modernity, time came to have new meanings. For late medieval society, time was wholly different from our own notion of time. For example, J. R. Hale tells us, in *Renaissance Europe, 1480–1520* (1971), that in the late fifteenth and early sixteenth centuries, 'Emotionally, the year began with the first flowers, the lengthening of the day, the first judgement on the winter-sown grain', while 'Only those concerned with legal or diplomatic documents thought of the year as beginning on an official rather than a seasonal date.' Equally, as Carlo M. Cipolla has demonstrated in his *Clocks and Culture* (1967), while timekeeping and clocks have heavily influenced the nature of life in Europe, not all societies have clocks; not all societies follow the chimes of bells as the West has done.

Our concern here, though, is not with the way that historical actors understood their own time, interesting though it is. Instead, we must focus on time in relative perspective: the relationship between past time and present time; the number of things, for example, that historical and contemporary actors could do in the same time; our time versus theirs. How far could they travel and how much work could they do; how many people could their communications reach? We are concerned to ask: how far could an Elizabethan travel by road in one day, given that we can cross the Atlantic in hours? This is the point about the variability of time and it is worth bearing in mind, for such things are crucial for us to frame the past.

Seen from the perspective of contemporary society, history is commonly characterised by the increasing number of tasks which can be completed in a given amount of time. The people of today believe that their stressful, fast-moving world of new technology and high-speed communications differs greatly from the languid and slow-moving character of life in past ages. Today, we think of telephones, supersonic air travel, space missions and the Internet; 200 years ago, when the first canals were being built, people travelled by horse-power, under sail or else on foot; and they communicated by word of mouth or by letter. The contrast, then, seems clear. It is not for nothing that historians have traditionally emphasised the role of change in history. For to understand, or even to discover, change, from era to era, is to understand how we are different from past peoples.

THE RELATIVITY OF TIME AND CHANGE

How far is our analysis based on a conception of time that is anachronistic when applied to the past? Herbert Butterfield wrote in *The Whig Interpretation of History* (1931) that 'The study of the past with one eye, so to speak, upon the present is the source of all sins and sophistry in history, starting with the simplest of them all, the anachronism.' The charge of relativism, or 'present-mindedness' (sometimes called 'presentism'), is often levelled at historians, and it is worth some consideration here. Keith Wrightson, in *English Society, 1580–1680* (1982), tells us that 'social change in late sixteenth- and seventeenth-century England was slow. Nevertheless contemporaries knew that they lived in a changing world, however blurred might be their perception of the nature and cause of social change.' The further back we go in time, the slower change seems to us, and the more people found unremarkable things (to us) remarkable (to them). Jan Huizinga, in the preface to his classic study, *The Waning of the Middle Ages* (1924), offers posterity this reminder of the nature of the medieval world: 'We, at the present day, can hardly understand the keenness with which a fur coat, a good fire on the hearth, a soft bed, a glass of wine, were formerly enjoyed.'

Such perceptions seem to set us apart from past societies. At the same time, what Wrightson or Huizinga convey are taken for granted by a society like ours which is driven by consumerism and supplied by mass production of just those items. Yet features of our own society, parts of our own lived experiences, are comparable to those of the past.

Take, for example, warfare. Those who do not know the past would, not unnaturally, consider that the Middle Ages (*c.* AD 400–1500) were bloodier and more violent times than our own. Perhaps in many ways they were. Sickness, disease, even the mere thought of dental work, struck greater fear into the medieval person than it does into us; and were there not many wars waged in the Middle Ages, across the world, from Scotland and Ireland to the Holy Lands? Yet our own century, which saw the deaths of 50 million people in the Second World War alone, is the bloodiest on record. Try to imagine the changes witnessed – even only at at second hand – by someone born in 1900, who lived a long and healthy life: two world wars, the rise of Communism and Fascism, the invention of the atom bomb, the first man on the moon – the list is endless. Then let us cast our minds back to the seventeenth century, a time when, historians admit, social change was slow but events (like the English Civil War) had a deep effect on society. Take the example of John Okey (1608–84), cited by Jim Sharpe in *Early Modern England: A Social History 1550–1760* (1987). When Okey died in Bolton his friends, rather unusually, recorded the key events through which Okey had lived. Germany, they reported, was 'wasted 300 miles' and Ireland witnessed the murder of 200 000 protestants. England, they averred, saw 'the crown or command' changed eight times between the 1640s and 1680s, while the Great Fire of London, they believed, had been caused by 'papists'. These were indeed troubled times: even Okey's own town of Bolton was 'thrice stormed' during the Civil War.

These things are, of course, relative; but perceptions of change can be compared between one generation and another. There are continuities in history which must not be ignored. When we consider, for example, the notion of the rise or emergence of different ways of life, we are then very close to the periodisation of the past with which historians seem so concerned. George Orwell's remembrance of childhood experiences, in 'The Rediscovery of Europe' (1942), makes a useful, if tongue-in-cheek, point about his childhood classroom experiences which made him 'think of history as a sort of long scroll with thick black lines across it at intervals. Each of these lines marked the end of what was called a "period", and you were given to understand that what came afterwards was completely different from what had gone before.' Orwell likened each change of epoch to be like a clock striking. Thus, in 1499, Orwell exclaimed, 'you were still in the Middle Ages, with knights in plate armour riding at one another with long lances, and then suddenly the clock struck 1500, and you were in something called the Renaissance'.

This emphasis upon seemingly overnight change is common. Orwell's sardonic rendition of the transformation from one age to the next, or one century to another, is important. The idea that each age is unique and different is called Historicism (from the German *Historismus*), and has been very popular among writers of all hues and tendencies since the nineteenth century. Historicists emphasised this idea that time changed society; that, as John Tosh writes in *The Pursuit of History* (2nd edn 1991), 'each age is a unique manifestation of the human spirit, with its own culture and values'. He adds: 'For one age to understand another, there must be a recognition that the passage of time has profoundly altered both the condition of life and the mentality of men and women.' This succinct statement seems to stand as the ultimate warning against 'present-mindedness', or anachronism. However, it also represents a secularisation of history, and a susbstantive shift from providental ideas which dominated the Middle Ages, wherein history (in this sense human development) was the expression of God's (unchanging) will on earth.

Benedetto Croce (1866–1952), the great Italian liberal historian and social theorist, once wrote that 'all history is contemporary history'. In other words, each generation rewrites history in the light of its own time and experiences. These prescient words are still relevant. For historians and students of history today, the point about the passage of time – and with it, the charges of anachronism and historicism – is that we must strike a balance between judging the past by our own standards and entirely stranding the past in its own frozen compartment of history. The problem, then, is one of extremes. If, on the one hand, we adopt a present-minded stance in our approach, we risk overplaying continuities, or indeed manufacturing continuities, between us and our past which do not actually exist. If, on the other hand, we adopt a historicist position, or posit the hermetically sealed epochal approach to history (as evinced in Orwell's telling passage), we risk removing any thread which might connect our past and our present. This notion of time, of change and continuity, or similarity and difference, is the hardest balance to achieve; yet it is central to our understanding of the nature of history and the dynamics of social developments.

HISTORY AS 'PROBLEMS'

The preceding discussion clearly suggests that the past is problematic. The fact that history is difficult should lead historians to address challenging questions. At the same time, historical inquiry should be problem-orientated. In the 1920s, Lucien Febvre of the French *Annales* School (which is discussed at length in the next chapter) highlighted what he dubbed 'histoire-problème' as the way forward for all historians. While Febvre was reacting against history written as a sequential story (narrative), it is arguable that all history − short of propaganda, of course − is concerned with problems. Thus Gibbon's eighteenth-century classic, *The Decline and Fall of the Roman Empire* (1776–88) was as much problem history as *The Mediterranean and the Mediterranean World in the Age of Philip II* (1949), which was written by Febvre's disciple, Fernand Braudel. Both men were concerned with the 'problems' of great empires; each wanted to explain historical change and process through the particular vehicle they chose, whether the Roman or Spanish empire. In addition, even seemingly straightforward textbooks − a history of America or of France − are at root concerned with problems: how did the American people develop; what were the dominant ideas of France under the *ancien régime*; which controversies dominate those countries' historiographies? Even the simple stories of the past, which the *Annalistes* decried, uncover problems and perspectives which are often difficult to resolve, or which throw light on unknown areas of knowledge.

Equally, however, historians only know a limited amount about the past. Very little of all that happened in history is known to our contemporary world. Even that which we do know is often debated furiously. Apart from a few uncontentious dates, for example, little of the past is definitely known or agreed upon. Even dates become problematic as soon as we add texture to them. If we say that Harold was shot in the eye at the Battle of Hastings in 1066, most historians would concur, and only a pedant would point out that Harold's demise occurred at nearby Senlac Hill. This, of course, hardly constitutes a debate. If, however, we ask 'what is the significance of Harold's death?', then a debate might well begin.

The problems of historians' approaches are, of course, analogous with students' experiences as they struggle to get to grips with new material in their studies. The dynamics of history, once we move from the listing of a few unquestioned facts, are considerable. Let us consider some examples.

THE PROBLEM OF DESCRIPTION AND ANALYSIS

Important questions in history are not centred around description, but concern analysis. When Lawrence Stone's *The Family, Sex and Marriage,*

1500–1700 was published in 1977, it received critical acclaim in some fields, vitriolic attacks in others. Stone's book has been attacked as a 'Whig history' in which the family is the hero. Stone argues that family life shifted from the deferential, distant and patriarchal ways of medieval times to what he sees as the more 'affective individualism' of emerging capitalist relations. Stone also writes of the flourishing of the patriarchal nuclear family in this period, with a concomitant decline in communal ties and increased allegiances to the nation, monarch and Church. He notes that, from the mid-seventeenth century, there emerged a 'closed domesticated nuclear' family which eventually became dominant in the eighteenth century. The emphasis of Stone's work is upon the development of individualism and the recession of more communal forms of social organisation.

Stone's work is in some ways related to the earlier work on family and personal role by Philippe Ariès, *Centuries of Childhood* (1961). Ariès, whose main interest was in the relationship between nature and culture, argued that a sense of childhood did not exist in the Middle Ages, that children went from infants to miniature adults at the age of seven or so. Ariès also wrote about death and was generally concerned with cultural representations of natural phenomena. Both Ariès and Stone challenged demographers with their sentiments (non-statistical, non-quantitative) approach to family and social roles. Little they wrote, however, has gone unchallenged in recent years. Meanwhile, demographers have consistently challenged the notion that families changed over time with the rise of capitalism (for this seems central to the sentiments approach). Applying complex and painstaking quantitative methods of family reconstitution to a breathtaking array of long-run records (from parishes and the poor-law guardians, etc.), they have demonstrated that the family remained overwhelmingly nuclear in the early modern period, and argue that the idea of the communalistic extended family network, while relevant in eastern Europe, was largely a myth in western Europe.

THE PROBLEM OF CONTROVERSY AND DEBATE

Historical debate is rife, and historians generate much heat in their disagreements. Stone's work is still many students' starting point, and has been pivotal to the history of the family – sentiments versus demographics – debate. Subjects such as 'the family' (like other features of social organisation) are, in a sense, bound to generate controversy

because they are so important. The Industrial Revolution, the crisis of
the sixteenth century in England, American slavery – all have raised
much controversy.

Population history, for example, is one of the most debated areas of
historical inquiry. Historians, like contemporaries at any given time in
the past, are concerned with the progress of population. Marx said
population was central to history since it charted the most basic of
social experiences: human reproduction. Looking back on population
profiles in the past, we can see that from the eighteenth century the
number of people in Europe began to rise dramatically. Why, then, did
population stagnate, fall or else grow slowly in the Middle Ages and
grow (with notable exceptions like France, where it grew slowly) on a
steep upward curve in the nineteenth century? Schoolchildren's textbooks of twenty years ago, still driven by the 'Great Men' approach,
tended to stress human endeavour and scientific improvement. Thus
the health of nations and the growth of population was seen in terms of
this or that medical improvement: smallpox vaccines, antiseptics, X-
rays, the fight against tuberculosis.

Later generations of historians have moved away from this
approach, again using sophisticated quantitative techniques, to look
at mortality and fertility patterns, age-cohort performances – measur-
ing, therefore, not simply growth but the velocity of growth across
different regions, nations, occupations and age-groups. As a result
of such work our understanding of human performance has been
changed.

The great fertility decline after (approximately) 1870 is another
instance of huge endeavours shedding new light on the old problem
of population performance. Once it was presumed that the fertility
decline – the reduction in the number of live births and/or family
size – was a uniform experience which began with the middle classes
and trickled down to affect working-class sexual practices. A recent
study by Simon Szreter, *Fertility, Class and Gender in Britain, 1860–1940*
(1996), has radically changed accepted views of a fundamental feature
of human life. Szreter's book examines an area of interest to historians
which was no less important or debated at the time. The fertility
decline led to great anxiety among commentators and politicians, and
poor population growth rates were seen to threaten the position of one
nation against another. Thus, the French feared that the newly unified
Germany, with its greater and growing population, would outstrip
France in both economic and military terms, and such fears were
duplicated elsewhere.

Something as crucial as population inevitably affects other facets of life. Falling fertility in the later nineteenth century, for example, led to debates about migration being reopened. Whereas in the period 1820 to the 1870s British political economists had believed migration was a panacea for overcrowding, unemployment and population boom, the fall-off in fertility rates prompted a return to the eighteenth-century idea that migration was a drain on human resources because it prompted only the industrious and intelligent to leave. On the eve of the First World War, the fertility decline was tied into wider pessimism about Europe as a spent force, and has been linked by historians to increased militarism and aggression among European nations on the eve of the war.

The related questions of family, fertility and population are obviously of enormous importance. Although they cannot be adequately covered in just a few words, the impression of their importance can still be gleaned. Historians are concerned with problems and debates in the field of population history; at the same time, the magnitude of this phenomenon suggests it will always be a contentious area.

Even in less controversial waters, few books are ever published without some recourse to a literature of controversies and perspectives. It is standard practice for historians to ask their students to consider debates – whether about falling prices or changing mentalities – for a number of reasons. In the first place, debates are usually important, or else no one bothers to disagree. Secondly, they are interesting. Thirdly, reading about them gives scholars insights into both the practice of history and important episodes and trends in our past. Finally, we can say that controversies, debates, problems – call them what you will – provide young historians with certain skills. Debates usually explode on to the page in a flurry of theory, historiography and empirical content. They are a microcosm of the historian's work of reconstruction/deconstruction. Debates between historians, which are usually conducted through the pages of a journal, give readers a sense of participating in something important. Watching historiography in the making is never quite as exciting as when it takes the form of debate.

CONCLUSIONS

We have seen from this opening chapter that there is much controversy over what constitutes historical inquiry. The value of history, its roles and uses, have also been the subject of repeated debate. At the same time, it is important to note that history is part of our culture; it is something we all share and no individual or group owns it. Consequently, tensions often arise over what might be termed the utility of history. People from different interest groups and classes, regions and localities, religions and cultures, have seen (and will see) history in contrasting ways. Often these differences are as much concerned with ideology as with knowledge. The question of what constitutes national history was discussed because this is one of the key areas in which controversy and disagreement arise. There are particular tensions, for example, attached to the histories of peoples or nations with their emphases upon distinctness and uniqueness. The Whig view of English history is a fine example of this.

This chapter also discussed how scholars and students of history must come to terms with a number of key ideas if they are to understand the past more effectively. Historical studies are crucially shaped by the conception of what we call 'historical problems'. Using the concept of time itself, we argued that academics today see themselves not simply as story-tellers, but as problem-solvers. We can thus conclude that without an understanding of the problematical nature of historical inquiry, and in the absence of a questioning approach to historical sources, historical inquiry lacks a crucial dimension of rigour.

In the coming chapters, when the emergence of history as a distinct discipline and the importance of methodology and theory are considered, we will see that the observations of this chapter are central to our understanding of the past.

2

Varieties of history (i): 'traditional history'

INTRODUCTION

MODERN historical scholarship emerged in the nineteenth century, although the history written during this period was of a very particular sort. In France, Germany and Britain, the principal mode of operation was empirical, by which is meant the scientific interrogation of sources. Prior to this period, history writing generally took on grand themes, written from the perspective of charting human progress or the emergence of civilisation. History was the remit of a variety of thinkers, writers and commentators, but, in the eighteenth century and before, it was based more on creative observation, or some master plan (such as the presence of God's will on earth and the improvement and perfectibility of the human spirit), than upon the rigorous interrogation of primary materials. During the twentieth century, the empirical school of historiography – personified by Ranke, the nineteenth-century father of this approach – came under fire. The period from the 1880s in Britain saw the growth of an embryonic interest in social and economic history. From about the same time, on the Continent, the theories of Karl Marx, and later those of Max Weber and Emile Durkheim, influenced the reassessment of history, and its shaping into a social science, rather than humanities, discipline. In Britain, however, despite the work of many historians and social commentators, the empirical mode continued to flourish.

The period after 1914 witnessed the fragmentation of the discipline as the notion of a 'universal' or 'ultimate' history diminished in the face of pressures from new techniques of inquiry, new theoretical developments and the emergence of a sub-disciplinary approach. This period also saw the formation of the *Annales* School (1929), arguably one of the most important occurrences in twentieth-century historiography. After the Second World War, the ideas of the *Annales* School began to spread around Europe, and even in Britain, where empiricism maintained a dominant position, a new style began to emerge. At the same time, Marxist theory took on an even greater importance than it had done before. British writers like Christopher Hill and Eric Hobsbawm and, later, E. P. Thompson – all one-time members of the Communist Party of Great Britain Historians' Group – emerged as major players on the world scene, with their radical overhaul of Marxist approaches to history. Since the 1960s, the break-up of history from its position as a unified single entity – the development and redefinition of the discipline – has moved apace. Computers have significantly increased the amount of data which historians can handle, and this has had an enormous impact on the methodological possibilities for the discipline throughout the world. At the same time new developments in ideas, methods and contemporary circumstances encouraged the fragmentation even of sub-areas like social and economic history, with the arrival on the scene of labour history, history from below, gender and women's history, and local and regional history.

The pace of change in historical inquiry has been great; indeed, at times the transformation from one assumed norm to another has been breathtaking. Where once history was a distinctive compartment in human knowledge, it now has blurred edges which run into other disciplines and across national boundaries. From the eighteenth-century Enlightenment (when philosophy emphasised reason and rationalism rather than tradition or providence), with its development of the idea of progress, through the nineteenth century and the primacy of the fact, to our own century of innovation and radical change, the emergence and re-emergence of history have been phenomenal. This chapter seeks to outline some of the key developments in pre-twentieth-century modes of operation and to explain their significance. It provides a sequential analysis of the major developments in historiography from the medieval period to the late nineteenth century. The chapter attempts to show how different history was before its 'professionalisation' in the Victorian age; at the same time, it picks out the key continuities in historians' attitudes and approaches to the past which the reader needs to be made aware of. This chapter and the next are contiguous, one leading on from the other. To help the reader through the sometimes bewildering array of historical approaches, this chapter and the next have been organised around the themes of 'traditional' and 'new' history which dominate the most recent writings.

The contrasts between 'old' and 'new' will become apparent as the chapters unfold, although continuities must also be noted. As will be argued, history in the twentieth century, in all four corners of the globe, has been perceived as a reaction against those 'old' or 'traditional' forms of history practised by the dominant scholars of the Victorian period. While this chapter outlines some of the major features of the traditional approach, and considers the main weaknesses of the genre, two points must be borne in mind. First, although historians tend to chop historiography (like their history) into manageable chunks of chronology, no single, dominant style of historiography was ever without an opposing camp offering different approaches to the past. Social and economic history, for example, did not appear overnight; they evolved slowly, even as Ranke and Acton were dominating the profession in Germany and England. Secondly, while the traditional form has its critics, not everything that came before the present century was intellectually poor or scholastically weak – far from it. In fact, some of the older forms of historical writing are simply old-fashioned, but not inferior for it.

EARLY HISTORY

The writing of history in any age reflects the mores, beliefs and purposes which contemporaries invested in their own society. Thus, medieval writers, living in an age before reason and rationalism dominated social thought, believed that the course of history, and thus social change, were direct consequences of God's purpose. The Middle Ages were more deeply religious than European society today, and it is important to understand that religion played a part in ordering people's world-view, as well as affecting their everyday beliefs and judgements, in the period up to the Enlightenment. At the same time, it is also important to notice that the Enlightenment did not lead to the secularisation of history overnight: religion remained deeply important in the scheme of things, even in the Victorian age, and any notion of secularisation even in the contemporary world appears problematic in, for example, an Islamic context.

This notion, that God's hand could be divined in the actions of Man, is known as Providence, and this has influenced historical writing at various times in the past. Medieval scholars, for example, believed that human life was moving inexorably and unswervingly towards the Last Judgement, as prophesied by the teachings of the Bible and the Catholic Church. Thus, the belief in secular progress appeared of no value. While no medieval writer ignored the hand of God, there were, however, other strains to historical writing at the time, one of the most important of which was the development of the national myth, whereby European writers tortuously traced their own country's origins to the classical civilisations. One of the classics of this genre is Geoffrey of Monmouth's *The History of the Kings of Britain* (1136), although Monmouth's account hardly measures up to modern standards of scientific accuracy. His main focus is upon King Arthur, connecting the kings of Britain, through the house of Constantine, to the great Trojan civilisation. This national 'story' became known as the Albion Myth and was commonly employed by writers up to the sixteenth century. In general, medieval scholars formulated the recent history of their countries and monarchs in chronicle form, narrating great deeds or else casting in a bad light those who fell out of favour.

Each medieval nation captured its spirit of being, its sense of historical place, in fantastic fables, like Monmouth's work. The Frenchman Chrétien de Troyes is one of the most famous examples. He, too, wrote about Arthur, as well as Launcelot du Lac, and inspired later writers, like Guillaime le Clerc, whose *Feargus of Galloway* (*c.*1200) was a significant improvement on earlier works in the romance genre, for it displays greater geographical precision as well as stylistic nuance. Such works were often written to promote a particular claim to the throne, although this is not in evidence in le Clerc's writings.

Gerald of Wales's *History and Topography of Ireland* (1185) is, as the title suggests, more historical. Like Monmouth, Gerald's work contains a fantastical element, tracing the Irish kings back to near-biblical times and writing as though myth and legend were history. At the same time, however, Gerald's *History* covers wide aspects of Irish life — from eating and costume to culture and religion — in an often disdainful manner. However, his book remains one of the principal texts for Ireland in the Middle Ages. The fictional, romantic history should not be dismissed as simply unhistorical. It was part of a thriving literary tradition which flourished in the Latin world of Europe. While the genre tells us little about actual historical events, it does inform us on medieval states of mind.

While Monmouth, Chrétien de Troyes, Guillaime le Clerc and others were part of the popular consciousness of the Middle Ages, they were not without critics who could see through the transparent mythology of their style. Medieval chroniclers were acidic about Monmouth's work, for example, describing it as 'the fables about Arthur which he took from the ancient fictions of the Britons and increased out of his own head'. Geoffrey would not be the last 'historian' whose powers of historical imagination were brought into question.

BEYOND EUROPE

Historical writing in imperial China and in the Islamic world of sub-Saharan Africa, the Middle East and the eastern Mediterranean was, in many ways, much more advanced than in medieval Europe. The great imperial Chinese dynasties had long known the utility of history. Since the days when most of Europe was ruled by the Romans, Chinese scholars bolstered the idea that history was about truth, morality and education. Each emperor set great store by the work of historians, realising the utility of the past for present purposes. Historians were part of the court system in China and produced histories of dynasties which reflected their elite position. In Africa, the great civilisations of Egypt and Carthage had been considered part of the story of civilised history by Greek and Roman historians since Herodotus's day. Many Greek and Roman scholars visited North Africa and wrote of their experiences with the traveller's eye. Herodotus's *Histories* in fact devotes considerable space to the manners, customs and life of the Egyptians. In the enormously powerful Arab world of the Middle Ages Ibn Khaldun (1332–1406) played an important role in collecting the history of African and Middle Eastern peoples. Khaldun, dubbed the 'Arab Toynbee', constructed his histories primarily from the oral tradition of the Islamic world, for Africa and Eastern recollection was primarily relayed by word-of-mouth in this period. The tradition of writing in the monasteries of Europe should not be allowed to obscure the fact that an oral tradition was also fundamental to Western history. Latin scholars were often simply chronicling what they had heard, just like Homer had done with the *Iliad*. By contrast, Indian history is noted for its range of written texts, in Sanskrit and Persian. Few in Europe could compare with the works of Khaldun, whose comparative studies of cultures, it has been argued, tried 'to give causal explanations of historical processes' (T. Büttner, 'Aspects and roots of African historiography', *Storia Della Storiografia* [*History of Historiography*], 1991).

Western students today know very little about the historiographical traditions of the Islamic, Indian or Chinese worlds. Yet these were the great centres of ancient and medieval culture. The main problem for

African civilisation has been the relative and growing strength of European powers since the high Middle Ages. As E. J. Alagoa writes: 'In the Egypt of Herodotus, the Greeks came as respectful visitors to do business, live, see sights, or to learn. In the Africa of Western expansion, European visitors came with derogatory concepts, and often to trade with Africans' ('African and Western historiography before 1800', *History of Historiography*, 1991). Thus by the late eighteenth century, attitudes to Africa had so changed that G. W. F. Hegel (1770–1831), the German philosopher, and writers like him, gave no credence to the role played by African civilisation.

While African scholarship was well established by the early Middle Ages, principally through Islamic historians, European historiography was bitty by comparison. The Renaissance saw a revival of the cyclical view of history which had been popular with the Greeks and Romans. Behind the cyclical interpretation of history was the idea that great civilisations – for example Greece, Rome and Egypt – rose and fell, with new ones rising in their place. The important point about this view is its pessimism: for here civilisations, or nations, were destined to rise and then to fall; there was no prospect for continued improvement. Effectively, decay was part of the natural order of things. The Renaissance sense of cyclical development accorded with a more general medieval sense of the circularity of life that can be seen in the role of the seasons. It also reflected the Christian sense that life on earth could not be perfect.

THE ENLIGHTENMENT AND HISTORY

The Enlightenment, with its emphasis on individualism and reason, changed this emphasis. Many of the features of historical inquiry which dominated the modern world began to develop in the eighteenth century. With the emergence of rationalism, the cult of secular reason, and the greater store that was set by humans' own ability to affect their own fate, the notion of decay as an inevitable consequence of civilisation came to be replaced by the idea of progress – the belief that historical change was ever improving human society. The medieval position on historical change died in the eighteenth century. Indeed, many of the *philosophes*, the leading French intellectuals of the eighteenth century, disparaged much of the past – the Middle Ages for being barbaric, the age of the Reformation for being fanatical and the reign of Louis XIV (1643–1715) for its supposed obsession with *gloire* – and found that history could not provide the logical principles and ethical suppositions that were required to support the immutable laws they propounded.

Despite the Enlightenment's strong interest in the future, there was also an interest and sense of continuity with the past. Giambattista Vico (1668–1744), Professor of Rhetoric at Naples, emphasised the historical evolution of human societies in his *Scienza Nuova (New Science,* 1725). Like his Renaissance predecessors, Vico also advanced a cyclical theory of history, underpinned by a sense of progress through stages of development. Vico saw three ages of progress which the Egyptians had handed down to contemporary Europeans:

(1) The age of the Gods, in which the gentiles believed they lived under divine governments, and everything was commanded them by auspices and oracles, which are the oldest things in profane history.
(2) The age of heroes, in which they reigned everywhere in aristocratic commonwealths on account of a certain superiority of nature which they held themselves to have over the plebs.
(3) The age of men, in which all men recognized themselves as equal in human nature, and therefore there were established first the popular commonwealths and then the monarchies, both of which are forms of human government.

Within this framework, and perhaps more historically, Vico noted particularly different linguistic traits that characterised the three ages: first, a mute world of symbols and signs; secondly, a language of 'heroic emblems, or similitudes, comparisons, images, metaphors and natural descriptions'; and, thirdly, 'human language using words agreed upon by the people'. These ages were also marked by different governments and legal systems, each representing gradual progress from 'mystic theology' to 'natural equity'. The key to Vico's overall view is progress and perfectibility; unreason to reason; irrational to rational.

The cyclical vision of history, first re-enlivened by Vico, could still be noted several generations later in G. W. F. Hegel's (1770–1831) advancement of the idea that each age of development was dominated by 'world-historical peoples', whether the Greeks, Romans or (as Hegel thought of his own age) the Germans. One of Vico's greatest ideas, however, was developed to challenge earlier scientist–philosophers, such as René Descartes (1596–1650), who had claimed that only the world of natural philosophy (science) was knowable by man because only it could be tested empirically. Whereas, before Vico, philosophers argued that only God could understand the laws of social change because He had made the world, Vico turned this on its head, arguing that because God had made the natural world, only He could know its true meaning, whereas because men had made human society, it was possible for them to understand that society, past, present and future.

Like Vico, the German philosopher Immanuel Kant (1724–1804) also formulated philosophies of historical development. Kant's essay of 1784, 'Idea of a Universal History from a Cosmopolitan Point of View', was typical of eighteenth-century designs for an overall plan of historical change. Kantian perspectives would influence social theorists and historians up to the present day, including those who try to formulate 'societal history', a long-run forecast of social development. Kant believed in the idea of progress and desired to find the scheme of history – what made history develop in the way it did. He argued that mankind had to assume some kind of 'secret plan', a teleological principle to history, because only then could the immediate horrors of history be explained in the overall scheme of cultural improvement.

At the same time, in the eighteenth century there was widespread interest in history. In the Empire (Germany), historiographical traditions of imperial reform, imperial history and Latin humanism were very much alive. The Sicilian cleric Rosario Gregario used scholarly methods to challenge false views of the medieval past of the island. In Sweden, Olof von Dalin wrote a scholarly *History of Sweden*, which was commissioned by the Estates and refuted the Gothicist myths of Sweden's early history. Sven Lagerbring introduced a criticism of source material into Swedish history. In France and Britain, Voltaire (1694–1778) and Viscount Bolingbroke (1678–1751), respectively, propounded the notion of history as *belles-lettres*, of 'philosophy teaching by example'. They did so to great commercial success, reflecting the growth of a reading market interested in history. Authors wrote for a large and immediate readership, producing a clearly commercial product, in contrast to the classical model of history for the benefit of friends and a posthumous public. In 1731 Voltaire brought dramatic near-contemporary history to a huge readership, his *Histoire de Charles XII* being printed ten times in its first two years. His *Siècle de Louis XIV* was similarly successful. There was also a strong interest in the idea of an impartial inquiry into the past, an emphasis on history as scholarship. Historical research was well developed in England, where scholars studied both the Anglo-Saxon period as well as the more recent past, the seventeenth century being a particular focus of discussion and research.

THE EIGHTEENTH-CENTURY BRITISH TRADITION

During the eighteenth century, many of the greatest historians were British. The Scottish cleric William Robertson (1721–93) acquired a European reputation with his works, which were praised by Catherine the Great, D'Holbach and Voltaire, and he was elected to academies in Madrid, Padua and St Petersburg. Robertson was a thorough re-searcher, noting in the preface to his *History of the Reign of Charles V* (1764), 'I have carefully pointed out the sources from which I have derived information.' The Scottish philosopher and Tory historian David Hume (1711–76) was best known in his lifetime as the author of *The History of England* (1754–62), a six-volume work of enormous popular appeal which earned him considerable royalties. Hume's great work of history was primarily a synthesis, although he did conduct research in documents he felt to be relevant to his arguments and he employed explanatory notes; nor did he avoid critical controversy. His work was marked by the moral lessons which each age of history might teach to posterity, and also contained appendices on the 'social' aspects of his-tory. By the mid-eighteenth century, God was less prominent in social thought, but it would be wrong to say that historical writing at this time was entirely without some kind of religious plan. This can be seen in Hume's rationalist *Natural History of Religion* (1758) and, for example, in the work of the great critic of the French Revolution, Edmund Burke (1729–97), who wrote an unpublished *Essay towards an Abridgement of the English History* (1757–60), which ascribed the development of human society to Providence's role in providing suitable conditions.

The eighteenth century, then, gave us texts of great importance which, unlike many of their medieval predecessors, were recognisably history in the way we know it. The greatest historical work of the century was Edward Gibbon's *The History of the Decline and Fall of the Roman Empire* (1776–88). This was a book of ambition, range and scholarship that had a very favourable critical and commercial recep-tion. A master of irony, Gibbon offered an exemplary tale that ex-plained the history of Europe until it reached its contemporary state of multiple statehood and Italian decadence. He presented in a clear, narrative form, interesting people and events, dramatic occurrences and often theatrical details to the domestic reader. History as an exemplary tale was generally accepted because politics and morality were not differentiated, either on the individual or on the communal scale. As with other works of history of the period, Gibbon offered essentially a political account, and the notion of rulership, governance and political life as moral activities were such that history was seen in that light by Gibbon, other historians and their readers. Morality served to provide both an instructive story and an enlightening approach to the complexity of the past.

THE WHIG TRADITION

It is commonly considered that the Whig interpretation of history – with its nationalistic and myth-making tendencies – was essentially a nineteenth-century phenomenon. Indeed, it was then that the leading historians associated with this view – Lord John Russell (1792–1878), Henry Hallam (1777–1859), William Lecky (1838–1903) and T. B. Macaulay (1800–59) – wrote. Other prominent Whig historians of the period included E. A. Freeman, J. A. Froude and G. O. Trevelyan. However, the roots of the Whig approach are buried in the previous century; understanding of its evolution can only be gleaned by first referring to the role history had played in the eighteenth century. The Whig view is clearly linked to the wider eighteenth-century idea of progress.

Debate in eighteenth-century British politics was firmly anchored in a recent and tumultuous history, both because of the continuing political significance of the events of this period, especially the 'Glorious Revolution' of 1688 (when the Protestant king, William of Orange, later William III, deposed the Catholic king, James II), and because the political culture of the age was one in which legitimacy was derived from the past. It was from this series of events that Whig politicians, and thus Whig historians, claimed the legitimacy and liberty of the English constitution was derived. Whig history was a clearly political form of history; one which embodied the national myth which Victorians were to promote with such vigour. At the same time, a number of eighteenth-century writers sought to legitimate the political system, the rule of the Hanoverian dynasty and therefore the exclusion of the Stuarts, and the dominance of politics and government after 1714 by men who called themselves Whigs, by producing works which stressed the beneficial nature of the changes that had occurred. The historians of the following century inherited this legacy, and we shall examine them presently.

THE FRENCH REVOLUTION

The international turmoil of the French Revolutionary period in many ways encouraged British scholars to look to continuity and stability in history, as a panacea against the troubles abroad. In his *Reflections on the Revolution in France* (1790), Burke argued that developments in France were harmful because they were unrelated to any sense of continuity, any historical consciousness, whereas in the Restoration of the Stuart dynasty in 1660 and the 'Glorious Revolution' of 1688, the English 'regenerated the deficient part of the old constitution through the parts which were not impaired. They kept these old parts exactly as they were, that the part recovered might be suited to them. They acted... not by the organic *moleculae* of a disbanded people.' This view of what was then relatively recent history was related to a more general interpretation of English history. Citing Blackstone's edition of Magna Carta, and quoting the texts of the Petition of Rights of 1628 and the Declaration of Rights of 1689, both already classic texts of English liberties, Burke argued:

> It has been the uniform policy of our constitution to claim and assert our liberties, as an entailed inheritance delivered to us from our forefathers, and to be transmitted to our posterity.... This policy appears to me to be the... happy effect of following nature, which is wisdom without reflection, and above it.... People will not look forward to posterity, who never look backwards to their ancestors.

In his *Appeal from the New to the Old Whigs* (1791) Burke sought to show that it was his views, as expressed in the *Reflections*, that were consistent with the 'Glorious Revolution'. He quoted from the 1710 prosecution case against the Tory cleric and ideologue Dr Sacheverell in order to clarify what Whig principles had been in the reign of Queen Anne, and how the 'Glorious Revolution' had been interpreted then. Burke felt that the events of 1688 could only be appreciated in the light of the assumptions to which they had given rise. These were seen as a crucial part of the legacy of the 'Glorious Revolution'. Moreover, a century later these events were still perceived as crucial, instead of being a dead monument of constitutional progress. The detail of Burke's use of historical examples can be challenged, especially in the light of his failure to accept that the 'Glorious Revolution' marked a major discontinuity in English history and was only enforced in Ireland and Scotland after considerable bloodshed. However, the polemical purpose of Burke's philosophical discussion of historical development made such an interpretation necessary. To insist upon his historical errors is to miss the point of history, and to criticise him for thinking of the past as a divinely intended teleological order – while literally correct – is to dismiss most eighteenth-century history as well as the attitudes that illuminated it and gave it both meaning and impact. Burke struck an echo not only thanks to his ability to write powerfully, but also because his understanding and use of history were far from marginal.

'HISTORY *FOR* BELOW'

History writing in the eighteenth century was not solely the remit of theorists and philosophers; nor was all history intended purely for elite consumption. In fact the division between 'high' and 'low' history which has been popularised since the 1960s actually has deep roots. In the eighteenth century, however, the distinction was not so much of 'history from above' versus 'history from below' as between 'history for above' and 'history for below'. That is, there was a strand of history in this period that, while concentrated upon 'high' topics, like national history, was meant for popular consumption and enjoyed significant sales.

Much history in this period was designed to serve a political or polemical purpose – unsurprisingly so, given the role of the past as a source of legitimacy. Parliament, pamphlet and newspaper writers made ample use of historical examples. Pressing the Crown to take parliamentary advice, John Cockburn MP told the Commons in 1734, 'Our histories will inform us, that where they have done so, they have generally done well, and where they have done otherwise, they have had but little success.' Both modern and ancient history were discussed in order to illuminate contemporary developments, and were plundered to make points. History at the time also played a major role in the education both of the influential and of the political nation. In 1730, Viscount Perceval's son, later 2nd Earl of Egmont and a prominent politician, wrote to his father: 'I have read very nearly three volumes of Tyrell's history of England, and one of Wicquefort, besides a great deal of Livy and another Roman historian.' The utility of this history for the nation's future leaders was summed up in a letter of 1744, written by Benjamin Holloway, tutor to John, later 1st Earl Spencer, to the latter's grandmother, Sarah Duchess of Marlborough: 'A large and comprehensive knowledge of history seems expedient for a person of quality. This contributing to lay a good foundation for a superstructure, not of political wisdom only, but of a common prudence also, with great and ready insight into affairs and events public and private.' The interest in history, both popular and elite, made it profitable to write such works. The subject's undoubted and wide-ranging popularity also made it useful to apply historical analogies in political debates. Indeed, in the eighteenth century the use (and abuse) of history to score political points led to considerable argument in Whig and Tory circles. It was common at the time, for example, to use historical works to debate such points as the legitimacy of the Jacobite Pretender's claim to the throne. This manifested itself in radically different readings of the recent history of the 1715 and 1745 Jacobite Rebellions. Thus, the dominant mode of writing at the time remained narrative and Whiggish in approach.

It is all too easy to assume that all historians of the eighteenth century shared the methods and values of the writers who have received most scholarly attention: Bolingbroke, Gibbon, Hume and Robertson. This, however, was far from the case. Enlightenment history, with its stress on dispassionate inquiry, was also matched by popular xenophobia. Works by historians who displayed the latter characteristics, such as those of Richard Rolt, are commonly ignored by today's historians. Dependent on his writings for a living, Rolt adopted a polemical style and a didactic method. Anti-clericalism and xenophobia can be found throughout his books, as the title of one work, published in 1759, illustrates: *The Lives of the Principal Reformers, Both Englishmen and Foreigners, Comprehending the General History of the Reformation ; From its beginnings in 1360, by Dr. John Wickliffe, to its establishment in 1600 under Queen Elizabeth. With an Introduction wherein the Reformation is amply vindicated and its necessity fully shown from the Degeneracy of the Clergy and the Tyranny of the Popes.* This book was a brilliant example of the linking of history to current political events. In 1759 Britain, at war with France, was in alliance with Frederick the Great of Prussia. Rolt's work explicitly presents the position of Protestantism *vis-à-vis* Catholicism as one of continuing struggle, and the Seven Years War in terms of the conflict between the powers of darkness and light. Frederick was extolled as a Protestant champion, 'the appointed guardian-angel of truth and liberty', and a religious teleological explanation of recent history was advanced. The 'Glorious Revolution' of 1688 was termed a religious revolution, just as the Reformation was seen as having established 'liberty...the mind was no longer chained down in intellectual darkness'. This, then, is a classic example of history as a national enterprise, a tool for divining the unique cultural characteristics of a people, the English, and linking them to a providential mission and a cosmic struggle.

At the same time, 'hack' and 'high' history were matched by the writing of urban histories. Between 1780 and 1820, for example, over 100 histories of English towns were published, which demonstrates the growing importance of local centres of commercial and political power, and the emergence of local–municipal–urban identities. These histories were not simply studies of the flavour or character of localities, but often carried political or religious messages. J. Baillie's *Impartial History of the Town and County of Newcastle-upon-Tyne* (1789) united a full history of commercial activity with a fierce assault on local oligarchies. Similarly, Joshua Toulmin's *History of the Town of Taunton* (1791) was a proud pronouncement of religious liberty and independence, again focusing upon the oligarchical nature of local politics. Such histories were not uncommon.

If the vitality and prejudice of much popular historical work in the eighteenth century is neglected, then a misleading picture, both of the writing of the period and its historical consciousness, is created. To suggest a crude contrast between 'enlightened', 'rational' history for an elite readership, and xenophobic, hack-written history for a mass readership would be misleading. The works of Gibbon, Hume and Robertson were all extremely popular, and Gibbon certainly was very concerned about his sales. It is wrong to assume that hack history was necessarily of poor quality because it was based on the works of others, written for profit and written fast. Enlightened history was not without its own prejudices, and the principal difference between hack and 'enlightened' history lay in the latter's tendency towards sceptical and critical judgements in the use of sources.

CONNECTING THE EIGHTEENTH AND NINETEENTH CENTURIES

History as the embodiment of the spirit of the nation did not die with the eighteenth century. This is clearly shown by the career of Edward Nares (1763–1841), Regius Professor of Modern History at Oxford, 1813–41, who, in common with many writers of the period, combined a nationalistic perspective, born of Protestant zeal and hostility towards foreign developments, with an interest in history. For Nares, as for many others, the French Revolution awakened a sense of British uniqueness. Typical of historians at the time, Nares was an Anglican cleric. He made a powerful case for the value of history in a sermon preached in 1797, on a day of 'public thanksgiving for a series of naval victories over France. He presented history as of value because it displayed the providential plan, and he contrasted the historical perspective with the destructive secular philosophy of present-mindness that he associated with the French Revolution and British radicals, coming to the reassuring conclusion that British victories proved divine support: 'From the first invention of letters... it has ever been the wisdom of man, under all circumstances of public and general concern, to refer to these valuable records as the faithful depositaries of past experience, and to deduce from thence, by comparision of situations, whatever might conduce to his instruction, consolation, or hope.' From these sources, Nares avers, statesmen draw inspiration from past political actions, and religious men look back to trace the actions of 'God in all concerns of importance to the good and welfare of man, is pleased to discover, in the course of human events, a direction marvellously conducive to the final purpose of Heaven, the constant and eternal will of God.' Thus it was that Nares used his account of Tudor England to defend the establishment of the Church of England as 'Catholic Christianity restored', in other words, cleansed of papal accretions. In his last work, *Man as known to us Theologically and Geologically* (1834), Nares sought to reconcile theology and geology and to ensure that the discoveries of the latter did not invalidate the historical framework of the former.

Despite the emphasis placed upon God and religion by this important early nineteenth-century historian and his ilk, scholars argue that the writing of history underwent something of a revolution in the second half of the nineteenth century. History, as the discipline we know today, developed during the Victorian period. It grew as a response to three perceived failings of history writing in the previous century. First, it was argued that historians of the Enlightenment failed to place sufficient emphasis on human development, and thus did not see change as central to historical development. This, of course, led to a much greater concentration upon human history in nineteenth-century circles, and a focus upon politics and diplomacy and the role of 'Great Men' in particular. History, it can be said, became less obsessed with the 'hidden hand' of God and more interested in human affairs. Secondly, it was claimed that the scholars of the eighteenth century gave little or no credence to facts; indeed Voltaire had dubbed them 'confused detail', and the men of the eighteenth century tended to concentrate on interpretation. This quest for facts reflected the nineteenth-century prestige and example of science, and led to the evolution of an empirical *modus operandi* and great emphasis upon the historical record. Finally, nineteenth-century historians also reacted against the fact that history, as a discipline (unlike the natural sciences, philosophy and other subjects), was not taught systematically in schools and universities. The Victorian period, then, saw the emergence of recognisa-

ble history curricula up and down the country, along with the establishment of Chairs of History at a number of key universities, including
Oxford and Cambridge.

THE AGE OF RANKE

It was in a tide of reaction against eighteenth-century thought that
Leopold von Ranke (1795–1886) began to re-create the way history was
conceptualised. Ranke, a conservative Protestant German, was driven
by a desire 'to show it how it actually was' (*Wie es Eigentlich Gewesen*).
Although this is a gross oversimplification of what Ranke stood for, it
was his central tenet. For him historians were to understand, not merely
interpret, the past. And the way to achieve this, Ranke believed, was to
uncover as many past documents as could be found. In this sense,
Ranke was developing a hermeneutical approach to history, by which
is meant the science of correctly understanding texts. Ranke, however,
also believed in narrative: he was the master story-teller, and was no
theorist. His basic premise was not to say of the past what the evidence
would not allow. As a result of his seemingly unquenchable search for
facts, Ranke's works, like his multi-volumed *Histories of the Latin and
Teutonic Nations* (1824), show immense erudition and a vast array of
factual knowledge. Moreover, his hermeneutical approach was in many
ways new.

Typically, we learn from the history of historiography, Ranke, in fact,
was acting only partly from original ideas. Many of his basic values had
been learned from the Danish historian B. G. Niebuhr (1776–1831),
who was the (admittedly now less well-known) pioneer of text-based
histories. The importance of Ranke is that he took Niebuhr several
steps further. The school of documents-based history owed much to
the seemingly revolutionary growth of state bureacracy in Ranke's
age. In Germany in the 1820s, for example, the *Monumenta Germaniae
Historica*, a collection of national records, began to appear. Similar
developments occurred in Britain and elsewhere. In France, under
the auspices of the French historian and statesman François
Guizot, the period between the two French revolutions (1830 and
1848) saw the publication of thousands of volumes of manuscripts
and documents.

Aside from the mass production of offical archive material, the most
important feature of Rankeian approaches was their collegiate mentality. Ranke did not keep his techniques to himself; instead he spread

them throughout German academe, holding innumerable seminars on research methods. His encouragement of historians received much praise and he became an important symbol of scholarship, helping to anchor the prestige of German historical writing. From the publication of state papers and through the historian's pen, the formalisation of history in Ranke's generation saw the foundation of important national journals, dedicated to the history of politics and state. Among the most important were the *Historische Zeitschrift* (Germany, 1856), the *Revue Historique* (France, 1876) and the *English Historical Review* (1886).

Traditionally, there are, however, a number of criticisms of the Rankeian approach to history. Despite his claim to 'simply tell it how it was', Ranke's work inevitably entailed judgement. His own views and values, like those of any historian, influenced the work he produced. Ranke was a German conservative and a Lutheran Protestant, and this imbued his work and ideas with two fundamental characteristics. First, in a continuation with earlier forms of historical scholarship, Ranke believed that God's actions could be seen through the lives of men and, therefore, in the course of history. Secondly, he believed that the development of modern Germany, its unification by Bismarck's Prussia in the 1860s and the proclamation of the German Empire in 1871 were manifestations of God's intention for that nation. As a result, Ranke has been accused of being historicist, for stressing the differences between the past and the present, and for seeing history as a process which links the two. Others, especially American and English scholars, have called Ranke an old-fashioned positivist (see below). Ranke's hermeneutical approach has also been criticised as too obsessive. Although even today historians decree that facts are important, the huge amount of evidence available for certain types of history (or their absence in others) means that historians must interpret. Empiricism, though, was the dominant form of historical scholarship for much of the nineteenth century, and it produced a rash of huge books, or multi-volumed series, displaying a breathtaking amount of reading and research.

Although Ranke was criticised for many years, there has been something of a rehabilitation of him in recent times. Marwick, for example, acknowledges the biases of the German school, but argues 'nationalism was a major impulse, but scholarship was a main outcome' (*The Nature of History*, 1989 edn). Indeed, few historians today could match Ranke's industry or insight. The charges of historicism or positivism levelled at Ranke have been challenged. Fritz Stern, in *The Varieties of History: From Voltaire to the Present* (1978), argues that Anglo-American criticisms of Ranke (and especially of his claim to show history 'simply as it happened') were misguided. Ranke emphasised the need for a universal history, one which transcended nations, and he set more store by an honestly conceived impartiality than have most historians since. In the preface to his *Latin and Teutonic Nations*, Ranke places his desire to show what actually happened in context – a context which his critics have subsequently expunged: 'To history,' Ranke considered, 'has been assigned the office of judging the past, of instructing the present for the benefit of future ages. To such high offices this work does not aspire: I want only to show what actually happened.' Thus we can see that Ranke was not claiming his history was absolute; only that he wanted to tell what happened rather than imposing some grand design on history. Thus, he was surely taking a step back from those who would use the past for their own designs? This is clearly a renunciation of positivism, anachronism and most other 'sins' of historical reconstruction.

NON-EUROPEAN EMPIRICAL TRADITIONS

A key problem with historiography is that, rather like with history itself, writers sometimes invest too much explanatory force in revolutionary change. Ranke was undoubtedly a European path-breaker, but many of his basic assumptions about the centrality of evidence had been employed in China in the previous century. In the same way, the stages of development proposed by Vico during the Enlightenment were already well known to Chinese and Islamic scholars. Q. E. Wong, in his 'History in later imperial China' (*History of Historiography*, 1992), tells us that for nearly 1500 years dynastic histories had been much concerned with the lessons that history could teach to present generations. In the eighteenth century, under the Qing dynasty, source-evaluation became pronounced, although historians did not seek to rewrite history as such, but to balance competing views – a feature which Wong attributed to the privileged position of the historians. Why, he asks, should historians change a history which had provided them with wealth and prestige? Nevertheless, the emphasis upon evidence can be seen most clearly in the works of three historians: Wang Mingshen (1722–97), Qian Daixin (1728–1804) and Ahao Yi (1727–1814). Wang, for example, produced *A Critical Study of the Seventeen Dynastic Histories*, with an emphasis on balancing differing interpretations in an historiographical fashion. This might be loosely compared to the textbook evaluations with which students are familiar today.

POSITIVISM

In Europe, the nineteenth century was also the age of positivism as well as of empiricism. This philosophy of positivism rests on the confident assertions made by social scientists, central to which is the idea that sociologists – like natural scientists – could, by taking empirical data, produce the link – the causality – between past, present and future. To the most strident positivists, the application of scientific methods to the study of human society could lead to the formulation of perfect laws of human development and social change. In other words, if Man could understand the laws which governed social change in the past, he could understand where the future would bring change. The father of this approach to social science was Auguste Comte (1798–1857), who coined the term 'sociology' for his new-found discipline. Comte saw history as divided into three stages: the Theological, when God's hand was seen to be everywhere; the Metaphysical, when Man began to seek alternative views of the world; and the Positive (the nineteenth century), when Man had the rational method (empiricism) to approach the study of society in the way scientists understood the natural world. The emphasis, then, was on the comprehension of social phenomena by discovering the laws which governed progress. Comte's thesis reflected the sway of scientific method and ideology.

THE VICTORIAN TRADITION: MACAULAY TO ACTON

How did these developments in history and in the social sciences affect the way the past was written by British academics? Gareth Stedman Jones, in an influential article, 'History: the poverty of empiricism' (in Robin Blackburn (ed.), *Ideology and the Social Sciences*, 1972), argues that the important continental developments, like those in sociology, were rejected by British (or more properly English) historians in favour of rigidly empirical methods, which, Jones argued, maintained an ascendant position in official circles until at least the Second World War. In many ways this was true. Those who held positions of power in the English historical hierarchy were indeed hostile to theoretical history. T. H. Buckle, Britain's leading nineteenth-century sociologist, and a disciple of Comte, was attacked mercilessly by Lord Acton (1834–1902), Regius Professor of History at Cambridge, and Britain's foremost supporter of Ranke, for what Acton saw as Buckle's positivism. Acton claimed that positivism subjected 'men and men's actions to the crucible of induction'. In other words, men were reduced to the role of scientific data and were allowed no independence of thought or action.

Stedman Jones argues, however, that this does not mean that men like Acton were not positivists; it merely means that *they* saw *themselves* as empiricists, which is quite a different thing. Jones claims that although historians like Acton did not subject humankind to the causal theorising that exemplified positivism, they did see history as a progression from the inferior to the superior – a Whig interpretation of the progression of the English national spirit which, naturally enough, put the Victorians at the top of the pile of human development. Jones argues, therefore, that British liberalism – and a concomitant belief in the uniqueness of British liberty, church and constitution – imbued British historiography with a positivist methodology. Acton and his ilk were not out to show history simply how it was; like Ranke, they believed they could justify their social systems and could establish links between, say, the Reformation, the 'Glorious Revolution' of 1688 and the freedoms of the British people in 1900. These events were thus presented as linked historical phenomena that related directly to the present. This is what the Victorians meant by the idea of progress. These were traits shared with eighteenth-century writers. The legacy of 'Englishness', and the Whiggish acceptance of the progression of a democratic and free Britain, were enforced by strong emphasis upon a Protestant identity, respect for property, the rule of law, and a nationalistic self-confidence that combined a patriotic sense of national uniqueness and qualities with a xenophobic contempt for foreigners, especially Catholics. Present-mindedness (which was discussed in the last chapter), analysis of the past in terms of the present, was a characteristic of their work.

Thus, Stedman Jones claims, all British history in the nineteenth century was concerned with moral lessons. For T. B. Macaulay (1800–59), who was the last of the great literary historians, history was about charting continual improvements in life – again, the idea of progress. Macaulay's *History of England* (1848–55) was a work of immense knowledge, but it was what would later be dubbed 'Whig History' by Herbert Butterfield. In Macaulay's work, all the heroes are Whigs and the villains are Tories. It was also an act of justification for Britain; for Protestantism; for Parliament; for the great British institutions and traditions. Macaulay first linked Britain's greatness to the exclusion of Catholicism and the creation of constitutional monarchy in the 'Glorious Revolution' of 1688. 'The history of our time during the last 160 years', Macaulay wrote, 'is eminently the history of physical, of moral and of intellectual improvement.'

Despite the positivism of Macaulay's assumptions, empiricism remained the most obvious feature of British historiography. In fact, from the 1880s there was something of a reaction to the Whig interpretation, which was born partly from the professionalisation of the discipline. Certainly, Acton, who was greatly influenced by German scholarly methods, was less obviously 'Whig' than Macaulay before him. Such historians' works entailed a less overtly nationalistic approach to the past and one that was more scholarly, more critical towards sources and methods. Acton was also suspicious of interpretation. Political history remained the dominant type, but was less exclusively constitutional. Instead, there was a greater interest in administrative history, a subject especially appropriate for the new professional historians with their strong archival bent. More generally, historians displayed a greater concern with the political reality that underlay past constitutional settlements. Present-mindedness was attacked. The opponents of royal power in the Middle Ages and the Tudor and Stuart periods were no longer accepted uncritically; either as heroes or progenitors of modern reformers. Magna Carta (1215) did not prefigure the nineteenth century for all scholars as it had done for Whig historians.

Acton was a historian of immense erudition: indeed, F. W. Maitland argued that Acton had the knowledge to write the *Cambridge Modern History* (12 vols, 1902–10) on his own. In fact his death meant he only planned and began what was a collaborative project under his editorship. Acton's concern with historiography as well as history is unquestionable. So is his historicist approach to the past. The letter he wrote to potential contributors to the *Cambridge Modern History* evinces some of his most basic philosophies:

1. Our purpose is to obtain the best history of modern times that the published or unpublished sources of information admit.
   The production of material has so far exceeded the use of it in literature that very much more is known to students than can be found in historians, and no compilation at second hand from the best works would meet the scientific demand for completeness and certainty.
   In our own time, within the past few years, most of the official collections in Europe have been made public, and nearly all the evidence that will ever appear is accessible now.

Evidence for what? Administrative and political history; a history of great events. The claim for the primacy of facts, which Acton held so dear, did not extend to the vast majority of the population, the working class. British historians continued to tell the story of monarchs, prime ministers and great battles. In 1861, Charles Kingsley, Regius Professor of History at Cambridge, attacked the idea of studying the 'little man' as 'no science at all'. Over fifty years later, this theme was reiterated when H. W. C. Davis, Regius Professor of History at Oxford, argued that there was no sense in studying the 'little man'. 'Our common humanity', he proposed, 'is best studied in the most eminent examples that it has produced of every type of human excellence.' Again, this is history with moral lessons to be learnt: while politicians could gain from Peel, Disraeli and Gladstone, engineers might take their lead from James Watt or Isambard Kingdom Brunel. This is history with the essence of a supposed national spirit at heart. The emphasis upon empirical methods and what Stedman Jones calls 'liberal-moralism' was bolstered by the strength of the philosophical liberalism of nineteenth-century Britain. It was also harnessed to the self-confidence and national and cultural self-opinion which governed the way Victorians saw their special place in the world.

The apparent stagnation of much mainstream historical scholarship in Britain as the nineteenth century progressed was made more apparent by the sub-current of new developments in social and economic history. The ideology of Rankeian scholars like Acton appears somewhat conservative when it is contrasted with the intellectual revolution occurring between 1880 and 1920 on the Continent. After years of positivist–empiricist domination, the Europeans left Britain lagging sadly behind with the speed of new developments in the social sciences. During the period encompassing the First World War, British universities all but ignored the contribution to new debates provided by such influential progressive thinkers as Sigmund Freud, Max Weber and Emile Durkheim and by the universal spread of Marxist and anti-Marxist ideas.

CONTINENTAL INNOVATIONS

There were, by contrast, many instances of European scholars opening up new avenues of historical inquiry. Even in Ranke's time, writers like Jules Michelet (1798–1874) and Jacob Burckhardt (1818–97) had a much broader conception of history than the empiricist political historians. Burckhardt's histories concerned the interaction of religion, culture and the state, while Michelet's appeal for historians to study 'those who have suffered, worked, declined and died without being able to describe their sufferings' is, Peter Burke argues, 'what we would now describe as "history from below"'. The major work of Fustel de Coulanges (1830–89), *The Ancient City* (1864), also focused on religion, family and morality, rather than politics and statecraft. Thus it would be an error to see British and German traditions as uniform or without alternatives.

Acton's great collaborative vision, *The Cambridge Modern History*, had parallels in the deeply empirical tradition which also dominated German historical inquiry. In France, however, collaboration tended to be much broader in conception. In 1900, for example, Henri Berr (1863–1954) founded the journal *Revue Synthèse Historique* to encourage the participation of others, particularly psychologists and sociologists, in the field of historical inquiry. Berr also originated a massive series of monographs, *L'Evolution de L'Humanité* (65 vols, 1920–54), which, as the title might suggest, was intended to address human development since prehistory. Berr's aim was for a scientific history, and his interest in 'historical' or 'collective psychology' influenced later *Annales* historians and can be seen as a forerunner of what the Americans have called 'psychohistory'. Berr saw his plans beginning at the more abstract theoretical level before focusing on more specific issues. Rather like a painter, he saw the need to block out the canvas, to set the composition, before the detail could be added. The introductory statement for the *Revue Synthèse Historique* carried these words:

> Our project is very broad, some will say excessively so.... Studies in theory will perhaps abound to begin with: but unless we repeat ourselves, this is a vein that will not be slow to exhaust itself. Furthermore the world 'theory' should not give alarm: it does not presuppose, it absolutely does not presuppose, vague, excessively general speculations put forth by thinkers who have never been working historians. We should particularly like to have...a series of articles on the methods of the various historical sciences.

Berr, then, was appealing for a new approach; expressing a broad-church desire to encompass learning and scholarship from disparate histories as well as far-flung disciplines. His aim was a far cry from that which dominated the Anglo-Saxon world at the time.

At the same time, Berr's efforts did not exhaust the French capacity for innovation and methodological leadership. By the later nineteenth century, scholars in France and Germany were also developing schools of historical geography and historical cartography, which brought the study of the environment, climate and the physical world to bear on the history of human society. The Frenchman Paul Vidal de la Blache (1843–1918), who founded a new journal, *Annales de Géographie* (1891), is one of the finest examples. Trained as an historian, Vidal de la

Blache played a major role in the development of French geography, which, as we shall see, maintained close links with history through the work of successive generations of historians. Vidal de la Blache argued that the environment created a context for human development, which was a view contrary to that of his great contemporary in Germany, Friedrich Ratzel (1844–1904), whose *anthropoéographie* (as he dubbed the link between geography and history) stressed that physical environment was central to human destiny (a determinist approach). In Vidal de la Blache's case, geography was a factor that set the scope for socio-cultural developments, rather than *the* central issue in history. Through his work we can see that in France history was not viewed as entirely separated from geography. At the same time, therefore, this interest in geographical regions – the *pays* – was readily translated into major themes for progressive historians. In 1910 Vidal de la Blache's work on French historical geography led him to propose the division of France into new *pays*, based upon the spheres of influence of the large urban centres. This idea was rooted in history, geography and methodology as well as in contemporary observations concerning the changing face of French life.

THE NEW WORLD

In America, history was, perhaps, more positivistic than anywhere else. Unlike in Britain, the purpose of history was not primarily about training. Instead, it was meant to capture the moral direction of the nation, a perhaps unsurprising state of affairs given that immigration, urbanisation and westward expansion were all playing a part in defining American-ness in the nineteenth century. Thus when American history became professionalised (1880–1920), like its European counterparts, the task of ascertaining the very nature of American society – past, present and future – had become the domain of historians. Protestantism, nationalism, and the founding spirit dominated the way many Americans and most American academics saw the past. American history in the nineteenth century was like British history under the Whigs a century earlier.

Of all the American historians of this period, one man stands out. Frederick Jackson Turner's (1861–1932) highly acclaimed work on the importance of the frontier in American history (1893), with its central thesis concerning the 'Manifest Destiny' of the American people, was taken as an emblem of the national spirit: the idea that Americans were the new chosen people of God. It marked a decided shift away from political history, and towards a much broader conception of the culture and character of the American people. Turner's argument was that the American institutions were shaped by the expansion and by 'winning a wilderness', the growth outwards of an evolving new country. Turner harnessed geographical imperatives to discuss the complex evolution of the American nation. For Turner, America was like a speeded-up Europe: in the states of east and west could be seen examples of the juxtaposition of primitivism and social complexion: from California to New England, log cabins and city tenements were a way of life. Turner, who rejected European perspectives on historical development, and expounded the uniqueness of the United States, argued that the map of the USA could easily represent future national and ethnic claims, a division into new countries. This geographically determined sectionalist argument caused uproar, but Turner's socio-psychologic of American development has affected American scholarship ever since. Turner and his followers were advocating a 'new history' which did not neglect key aspects of the American experience, although it was later, in 1912, that James Harvey Robinson (1863–1936), a contemporary of Turner, raised a clarion call for historians to consider every aspect of human development, calling his chosen emphasis 'The New History'.

In South America, the changing political scene naturally affected historiography, just as it did in Europe and America. By the 1830s Spanish colonial rule had been shaken off in most regions of the continent. The problem that faced the new polities of South America was to balance the Old World origins of the elites with what N. K. Vallenilla, in 'National identities and national projects: Spanish American history in the nineteenth and twentieth centuries' (*History of Historiography* 1991), calls 'the need to create a new civic consciousness'. The task of historians was thus to ally 'History', 'enlightenment' and 'virtue', for these formed 'the holy trinity of an acquired civic morality'. As one early history of Venezuela (published in 1858) argued, 'The republic must draw lessons from history, for only by being enlightened and virtuous will they [the people] become patriots.' Spanish South America, therefore, demanded *historia patrias* (national histories) to unite the present population in a common bond with the past. In this project, Vallenilla argues, the discontinuities of history were smoothed over in preference for an emphasis upon the connections between the contemporary world and, if necessary, the pre-Columbian one.

Spanish-American historians knew of the great European writers of history: Thiers, Guizot, Michelet, Fustel de Coulanges, Carlyle and

Ranke. They looked intellectually to Europe, especially France. However, Vallenilla states that it is wrong to assume that the newly emancipated South Americans simply appended themselves to the stream of European developments: 'Historiography does not necessarily follow the path of imitation set by fashions for women's dresses or men's hats.' Instead, Vallenilla argues that Spanish-American writers learned from methodological advances in Europe and used them to answer the pressing question of their own society: 'Where are we headed? What are our national goals?' It is not unusual to see Europe as the epicentre of intellectual life; but this is as erroneous as it is narrow-minded. The citizens of the United States neglected European perspectives that saw the New World as a 'discovered' appendage, or as a colonial outpost; why, then, should the new nations of South America accept these perspectives?

THE INDUSTRIAL WORLD

Socio-economic and political fortunes in Europe and the Americas played a major role in determining the character of historiographical traditions. The period down to 1914 was one of crisis in Europe, with the emergence of socialism, anarchism and, later, of a bloody and brutal world war. Britons, Stedman Jones argues, saw themselves as separated from the troubles of the Continent; free of an oppressive Catholic Church, secret police or peasant insurrection. Victorian and Edwardian scholars could conveniently ignore the crisis in Ireland, 1886–1923, when formulating their 'High' histories of kings and queens, which consciously or unconsciously reflected what they perceived to be the peace and stability of the United Kingdom. Failure to lose the Boer War (1899–1902) and, more significantly, the First World War ensured that the core habit of nearly a century of fixed attitudes to the past was not broken. Without revolution or significant social upheaval in Britain, the academic world of historical scholarship continued to produce books which meant little or nothing to the majority of Britons and bore no resemblance to their lives.

CONCLUSIONS

We have noticed that the key emphases of history have been determined by the dominant cultures and ideas of given periods. Thus, before the Enlightenment, early scholarship was concerned primarily with Providence, and God's role, as the organising themes of historical development. In Asia and Africa, pre-modern historical inquiry was often more advanced than that in Europe: even there, however, God and God's actions remained dominant. From the Enlightenment, in the eighteenth century, we argued, history began to mature into the discipline that we know today, although the main impulses for modern scholarship – not least the emphasis upon facts and documentary analysis – came in the nineteenth century. Throughout the periods in question – whether medieval, early modern or Victorian – there was a tendency to concentrate on the notion of one history, the idea that national histories, however written, were dominant. This became especially the case under Macaulay and Ranke, because unity of purpose either typified the age or reflected the political objectives of the Whig historians. However, as we go on to show in the next chapter, the unity of the nineteenth century was broken by war and social decay; the assumptions of the Victorians were sorely tested in the age of Communism and Fascism. Although British academia maintained a traditionalist perspective on the past, historians elsewhere were beginning to shake off the limitations of narrow empiricism. We have already seen how, on the Continent, new modes of inquiry were springing up next to the old. This trend grew in the twentieth century. The grand vision of the Victorian ruling elite, moreover, was not matched by a similar state of mind among socialists, trade unionists or new liberals. As the British began to suffer relative decline next to the United States and Germany, while poverty still accompanied progress, the past was bound to excite new interest. Thus it was that even in Britain historical inquiry before the First World War was marked by distant rumblings: new questions, new approaches and new ideologies. One of the key features of historical inquiry, it seems, is that whenever the contemporary world develops a fault, historians look at the past to seek its origins.

3

Varieties of history (ii): 'the New History'

INTRODUCTION

IT is fallacious to see historiography as falling into sealed chronological units in which can be found just one 'style', 'school' or history. While certain eras were dominated by certain assumptions about the past, other modes of operation still went on in tandem, although perhaps below the surface and away from the public eye. Thus we saw in the previous chapter that, although empiricism represented the *modus operandi* of Victorian scholarship, there were other strains of opinion – alternative ideas and agendas – floating around the university-based orthodoxy of Ranke, Mommsen and Acton. The Victorian age might have been characterised by 'Great Men' and administrative–political subject matter, but it was also the time when many other practitioners began to ply their alternative trades. In France, we have seen, there was the invitation for historians to write synthesised histories issued by Henri Berr, as well as the geopolitical method encouraged by Vidal de la Blache. In Germany and Britain, concerns with the social world were beginning to emerge long before Acton edited his *Cambridge Modern History*. In America, Frederick Jackson Turner's 'Manifest Destiny' was capturing imaginations and exciting responses. The maturing South American polities were coming of age with their own nationalist (as opposed to Europeans' national-type) histories. At the same time, local historians were co-operating to chart their own communities' development, sometimes in puff-chested displays of civic pride. We might look to Ranke or Acton for the emblems of this grand and self-referential age, but theirs were not the only stars in the constellation.

As if to prove the point that historiography, like history, comprises structures which move at different paces, this chapter, although concerned with the most recent developments, begins our examination of 'The New History' with the eighteenth century, where the true roots of social and economic history are to be discerned. We will notice that the Enlightenment ushered in the earliest forms of cultural history. At the same time, it should also become clear that significant new directions in socio-economic historical inquiry were only made when postwar practitioners combined the structural overview and organising principle (provided by nineteenth- and early twentieth-century social theory) with the empirical, records-based precision of the great Victorian scholars. Only then could social and economic histories be taken seriously.

History is not such a battleground that the majority of practitioners – however diverse in outlook – cannot agree on certain fundamentals. One of the most basic shared beliefs is that historical inquiry is rooted in the artefacts – the records – that past societies have bequeathed to posterity. Consequently, throughout this chapter we will notice a constant interchange between seemingly different and diverse schools of writing.

History has changed much since the 1880s: the scale of activity has increased, the range of inquiry has been broadened. Over the past century or so, perhaps the most important development has been the integration with historical method of the theories, practices and ideas of other disciplines. History today is not as isolated or singular in the way it was for Acton. Geographers, sociologists and all manner of 'others' have things to contribute to our ability to scrutinise and understand the past. These developments may have begun earlier, but it was in our century that they became the orthodoxy. This chapter, therefore, concerns the period when 'alternative' histories rose up and seized the epistemological high ground (epistemology is the philosophy of knowledge). First, it considers the reaction against dominant and elitist nineteenth-century forms of inquiry, examining the emergence of social and economic history. It then goes on to look at the formation of the *Annales* School (1929), one of the most important and influential developments in modern historiography. We then go on to examine the intellectual ferment of the 1960s, and the way in which *Annales-* and Marxist-inspired approaches came to dominate the discipline. The central purpose of this chapter is thus to consider the advent and influence of what James Harvey Robinson in 1912 called 'The New History'.

THE HISTORICAL ANTECEDENTS OF SOCIAL AND ECONOMIC HISTORY

Economic and social history have their roots in the Enlightenment. It is certainly worth stressing the role of continuity and connection in historical inquiry, because links between seemingly older and more modern forms of knowledge crop up time and again. Whereas social history clearly began life as cultural history, as part of the cyclical conception of social and cultural development, the philosophical precursors of economic history lie in attempts to rationalise and understand the nature of the economy and the processes by which agricultural forms were being eroded by spreading industries. In eighteenth-century Europe, as mercantilism (an economic theory that money is the only form of wealth) declined, the origins of money and capital wealth assumed an important position in philosophy. This, too, can be seen as a forerunner of economic history. At the same time, however, it must be remembered that economic history of the kind we recognise was not being produced in the age of Voltaire or Gibbon; nor, in fact, was it being written in the age of Acton. As we have noted, figures like Comte, Marx and Weber expressed an interest in structures, rather than events, but the broader academic community of historians in most countries drew little inspiration from these thinkers.

As the seventeenth and eighteenth centuries progressed, social and economic change prompted interest in that change. Classic among efforts to explain the nature of economy and society at the point where they were linked was Adam Smith's *Wealth of Nations* (1776), which provided a study of economic development – what Marx called inquiry into the nature of wealth. With Smith, we can argue, began the discipline which became known as political economy. From this basis, political economy developed into the modern discipline of economics, from which in turn economic history splintered. The so-called Scottish School, of which Smith was a part, provided what Christopher Lloyd in *The Structures of History* (1993) called an 'embryonic historical materialism' with which to frame the nature of social change. At the same time, in France, A. R. J. Turgot formulated similar accounts of economic development and social structures, and further ideas about the organic nature of historical development. The background to the growing interest in economic and social change, then, is provided not just by Enlightenment thought, or the formulation of political economy, but by much more pressing questions about the impact of modernisation. The eighteenth century witnessed a decidedly quickening pace of economic modernisation, the roots of the Industrial Revolution. These changes were not of a scale or a pace that we would recognise; but they were, nevertheless, both real and substantive.

In France, positivism, historical sociology and early socialism came together in the ideas of Saint-Simon (1760–1825), who formulated a series of ideas about the social laws which govern social change and development, and the need to harness the power of the emergent working class to realise them. In Britain, in the middle of the nineteenth century, economics developed as a discipline, but moved away from genuine efforts at historical understanding, departing from the 'totalism' propounded by eighteenth-century theorists like Smith. Instead, utilitarian classical economics became individualised, ahistorical and increasingly divorced from the historical past. This is one of the reasons why economic history emerged from economics in the 1880s, attempting to explain contemporary socio-economic experience by reference to historical understanding.

Even by the later nineteenth century social and economic history was not as we know it now. It remained a curious hybrid, constructed of positivist theory and Enlightenment philosophy. Historians of the social and the economic were not really historians (as now understood) at all; they were more like philosophers. They did not engage actively in empirical research, because they were not empiricists, and, instead, they tried to make scientific the understanding of the social and economic world, using classical economics, Enlightenment thought and abstract social scientific notions of what constituted the laws of the social. They were more concerned with the laws that governed change – perhaps societal history – than they were with social or economic aspects of the past at any given time.

SOCIAL HISTORY: GREEN AND TREVELYAN

On a less abstract though, perhaps, more comprehensible level, historians were beginning by the mid-Victorian years to think about the social dimension of the past. Compared with the writings of Marx or Adam Smith, however, these earlier works seem turgid and limited. The first work in Britain to challenge the idea of E. A. Freeman (onetime Regius Professor of History at Oxford) that 'history is past politics, and politics is present history' was J. R. Green's *Short History of the English People* (1874). Green argued that his book was a departure from 'drum and trumpet' history; an attempt to write history from a perspective other than that of monarchs, statesmen, generals and battles. As Green himself wrote:

> The aim of the following work is defined by its title; it is not a history of English Kings or English conquests, but of the English people. . . . I have preferred to pass lightly and briefly over the details of foreign wars and di-plomacies, the personal adventures of kings and nobles, the pomp of courts, or the intrigues of favourites, and to dwell at length on the incidents of that constitutional, intellectual, and social advance, in which we read the history of the nation itself. It is with this purpose that I have devoted more space to Chaucer than to Cressy [the Battle of Crécy, 1346], to Cax-ton than to the petty strife of Yorkists and Lancastrians, to the Poor Law of Elizabeth than to her victory at Cadiz, to the Methodist revival than to the escape of the Young Pretender [Bonnie Prince Charlie].

However, for all Green's new ideas and high ideals, he was not really departing from the dominant historiography of his day. He used the same official, state-generated records as the constitutional–political historians and was essentially an institutional historian, and has been since accused of anachronism. As Marwick argues, and as the above passage demonstrates, Green was at heart a Whig historian. In his *English People*, 'the men of the middle ages speak with the accent of Victorian reformers'. In fact, British scholarship, and thus the reading public, had to wait nearly seventy years for a social history of note or merit – George Trevelyan's *English Social History* (1941) – where the author famously declared that social history is 'history with the politics left out'. This dictum is one which many academics still tout as the basic definition of social history. Trevelyan, writing at a time when economic history was growing apace as a distinctive sub-discipline, was aware of the connection between the 'social' and the 'economic'. His introduction to *English Social History* also displays a nuanced apprecia-tion of the parallel existence, at any given time, of continuity and change. For Trevelyan, both 'old' and 'new' elements of society needed to be borne in mind. 'Sometimes,' he wrote, 'in forming a mental picture of a period in the past, people seize hold of the new feature and forget the overlap with the old'. For example, Trevelyan continued: 'students of history are often so much obsessed by the notorious poli-tical event of the Peterloo massacre that they often imagine the Lanca-shire factory hand as the typical wage-earner of the year 1819; but he was not; he was only a local type, the newest type, the type of the future.' Like many in the great British tradition of Acton, Trevelyan had a massive, encyclopedic knowledge of history; yet it is flawed for all that. Trevelyan underscored his writings with a Whiggish sentiment, shaped around a story of improvement and the idea of progress. He wrote about religion and values rather than kings and their politicians, but his *English Social History* avoids the darker side of history. The concept of class struggle, an idea beloved of the generations of social historians writing after the Second World War, is entirely absent from his work.

A TIDE OF REACTION? THE EMERGENCE OF MODERN SOCIAL AND ECONOMIC HISTORY

Despite the limitations of these famous, early attempts at social history, however, a concern with the social and the economic *does* represent the first and clearest move away from events-based history and the related obsession with the political activities of elites. These new developments can be explained by one major impulse in historians' thought: namely, a shift in interest from the individual to the masses. Yet, when in the 1880s economic history emerged, it was indistinguishable from social history. To understand why questions were asked of social and economic life from the late Victorian period, we must understand something of society itself. The years 1880 to 1939 were ones of great change. Equally, then, these changes impacted upon the intellectual terrain. Broadly, the generation after 1880 saw the emergence of democracy in western Europe; and the starting point of working-class groups which remain with us today: the SPD in Germany, the American Federation of Labor and the British Labour Party. In a broad sense, the period from the 1880s up to the outbreak of the Second World War marked the beginning of the age of labourism: genuinely 'mass' trade unionism in Britain, a strong Communist Party in Germany and industrial militancy, such as Syndicalism, in France and America.

The erosion of Britain's once seemingly unassailable world prestige made this age simultaneously reflective and self-conscious. The once unique Industrial Revolution in Britain had reached Germany, America, France, Belgium, and was rousing in Japan. The development of modern economies, however, had social costs – and orthodox theories like political economy and *laissez-faire* neither explained nor ameliorated those costs. Liberal individualism – the philosophy whereby individuals were encouraged to pull themselves up by their bootstraps – was placed under threat in the years up to the First World War by the emergence of the interventionist state and the popular quest for social reform and political participation. This was an age when social theorists asked why, if the Industrial Revolution had produced so much wealth, was there still so much poverty? In the 1830s and 1840s, the rigours of industrialisation had seriously undermined the way of life of certain 'old' trades: domestic spinners and handloom weavers; men in the handicrafts, whose jobs were falling to mechanisation. The year 1848 heralded the final explosion of Chartism and revolutions in Europe, but still there remained a mood of optimism: industrialism would improve living standards; the majority would benefit.

THE INFLUENCE OF THE INDUSTRIAL REVOLUTION

Indeed, the period 1850–75 seemed to bear this out. New technology spread and unemployment fell; moreover, living standards improved and the struggles of the 1840s faded in the memory. Yet, by 1880, three things had happened: first, British industrial pre-eminence had been challenged and was eroding in the face of stiff competition; secondly, the boom of the mid-Victorian years had collapsed; and, finally, the social problems of the early industrial period had not been removed, but were exacerbated by recurrent economic slumps and the impact of migration and urban population growth. The conflation of these factors led to much criticism from the intellectual Left, advanced most clearly by the Fabians, the reformist group founded in London in 1884 by Sidney and Beatrice Webb.

Concurrently, the discipline of economics had been taking shape. Anyone reading early economic histories of Britain will realise one thing above all others: that the whole sub-discipline has emerged and changed through differing interpretations of the Industrial Revolution. In its infancy, then, economic history was driven forward by concern about social problems. The term 'industrial revolution' was first used by the French socialists to delineate the difference between the upheavals in France and the quickly changing social and economic climate in early nineteenth-century Britain. The whole question of the social utility of the Industrial Revolution was given new importance in 1884 by an influential series of lectures by Arnold Toynbee, published as *Lectures on the Industrial Revolution*. For Toynbee, the Industrial Revolution was 'a period as disastrous and terrible as any through which a nation ever passed; disastrous and terrible because side by side with a great increase in wealth was seen an enormous increase in pauperism; and production on a vast scale, the result of free competition, led to a rapid alienation of classes, and to the degradation of large bodies of producers. Notice Toynbee's emphasis here: not on machines, technology or productive capacity; not on empire and trade. But, instead, on the impact of the Industrial Revolution: on the alienation of the working class and an increase in pauperism; and a consideration of the existence, side by side, of wealth and poverty. Toynbee's view of the British Industrial Revolution was apocalyptic; it pinpointed the drudgery of industrial life and marked up the sharply differentiated society that industrial change had produced. Toynbee's lectures were followed by a generation of pessimistic assessment of industrialism's impact: from the works of Sidney and Beatrice Webb (who founded the London School of Economics (LSE) in 1895) and J. L. and Barbara Hammond, to the social surveys of London and York carried out by Charles Booth and Seebohm Rowntree. This school spawned a series of influential books, including the Webbs' *The History of Trade Unionism* (1894) and *English Poor Law History* (1927) and J. L. and B. Hammond's *The Village Labourer* (1912) and *The Town Labourer* (1917), which were all attempts to analyse the Industrial Revolution in terms of its impact upon the standards of life and organisations of the working class. They almost uniformly declared that the Industrial Revolution was a bad thing for the working class. This was the beginning of the standard of living controversy, which still rages on today, as a glance at many issues of the *Economic History Review* will show. In essence a new condition of England question, like the one that dominated social thought in the 1840s, had been born. At the same time, pessimistic assessments of industrialism were bolstered by government surveys which pointed to the abject position of a large part of the working class, while a gloomy outlook for the political consensus of the time was highlighted much later in George Dangerfield's *The Strange Death of Liberal England* (1935), which neatly summarised the introspection of the ruling classes. The problems of industrial Britain were also highlighted by a blaze of social comment novels, such as Mearn's *The Bitter Cry of Outcast London* (1883) and Jack London's *People of the Abyss* (1903), which captured the poor living conditions and low wage levels of a disconcertingly large part of the British population. This body of work, of course, was not economic history as we know it; but was, instead, what G. N. Clark, in his *The Idea of the Industrial Revolution* (1953), described as 'a social concern with economic conditions'. These early studies were overwhelmingly inductive in approach, in that they attempted to derive general laws from specific instances. Nevertheless, they did offer a genuine attempt to tie together economic processes and social consequences, and attempted wholeheartedly to understand the impact of industrialisation.

J. H. CLAPHAM

This predominantly 'social' vanguard, with its deeply pessimistic tone and qualitative source-base, was savagely attacked in the 1920s by a growing body of professional economic historians with their stress on statistics. Pre-eminent among these was J. H. Clapham, whose *Economic History of Britain* (3 vols, 1926–38) shifted the emphasis on the history of industrialisation away from cataclysmic upheaval, or revolution, to gradual, organic change. Clapham also attributed less social dislocation to this process than did his pessimist opponents. His attacks signalled the beginning of the economists' counter-attack in the standard of living debate. Under Clapham's aegis, the emphasis shifted from the social impact of industrialisation, to looking at the emergence of the great staple industries – cotton, coal, iron and steel and shipbuilding. Clapham was concerned with the origins of the Industrial Revolution, not its social impact.

This period also saw the birth of an obsession with the technology of the Industrial Revolution – one which still holds a powerful place today. The names Richard Arkwright, James Watt, Henry Bessemer, George Stephenson and I. K. Brunel – the spinning-jenny, steam engines, steel smelting, railways – these heroic inventors, entrepreneurs and machines of energy, force and power came to the fore in the 1920s as they had never done before. The famous quotation of a schoolchild's remark about economic development by T. S. Ashton, in his *The Industrial Revolution, 1860–1830* (1948), summed up the new approach to the Industrial Revolution: 'after about 1760 a wave of gadgets swept over England'. Clapham and his colleagues thus emphasised the economics of innovation, while terms like 'speculation' and 'entrepreneur' became familiar to readers for the first time.

Clapham, more than any other economic historian, was rooted in the nineteenth century. He was a connection with the world of Acton. Clapham produced work that is still recognisable as the kind of economic history – with its emphasis on production, industrialisation, money and exchange, innovation and entrepreneurship – that was taught to schoolchildren until the later 1970s. A revolutionary in his own way, Clapham was a founding father of the academic economic history that came to feature prominently in universities such as those of

Manchester and London. Clapham's methodology was directly linked with that of his mentor, Lord Acton, and the empiricist school. As Clapham himself asserted: 'Economic history is a branch of general institutional history, a study of the economic aspects of the social institutions of the past. Its methodological distinctiveness hinges primarily on its marked quantitative interest; for this reason it is or should be the most exact branch of history.' Clapham invested much faith in the quantitative aspects of his work; he could not tolerate the guesswork of the previous generation of untrained social writers, like the Hammonds. For him, 'Every economic historian should have acquired what might be called the statistical sense, the habit of asking in relation to any institution, policy, group or movement the questions: how large? how long? how often? how representative?'

The antagonism between these earlier forms of social and economic history, concerning the question of whether or not industrialisation was a good thing, continued throughout the inter-war years. With their recourse to statistical material, the economic historians of the 1920s and 1930s were seemingly in the ascendant. Although their work represents a more upbeat interpretation of the economic past than was true of the period up to the First World War, there still lurked in the inter-war years a pessimism driven by the socio-economic and political turmoils of the rise of Communism, Fascism and the Great Depression. Government policy failures, such as the 'Geddes Axe' (swingeing economic cuts of early 1922) and the flawed return to the Gold Standard (1925) in Britain, and the economic-political scandals in France, further eroded economic confidence and seemed, symbolically at least, to drive a wedge between contemporary society and the glories of the Victorian past. By the eve of the Second World War, Clapham may have enforced a greater judiciousness upon social historians, but the latter still had points to make about the limitations of industrialism. Even in the 1960s, when the fourth edition of G. D. H. Cole and Raymond Postgate's hugely popular social history, *The Common People 1746–1945* (1938) was published, the authors were questioning the material circumstances of the working class. Their tone was not apocalyptic, as Toynbee's had been, but their claims were still sharp, even for the very recent past. Despite all improvements of the twentieth century, they were still able to characterise 'two nations' standing against each other after the Second World War. The contrast was not as stark, the authors accepted, as had been portrayed in Disraeli's *Sybil* or in Dickens's works, but in those post-war years, and despite the collectivist interventions of the Labour administrations of 1945–51,

Cole and Postgate argued, 'The great majority of those who died still had almost nothing to leave to their successors.'

LEWIS NAMIER AND R. H. TAWNEY

The inter-war years also produced Lewis Namier, whose systematic reinterpretations of eighteenth-century English politics established him as one of the pre-eminent scholars of the period. His two main works (*The Structure of Politics at the Accession of George III* and *England in the Age of the American Revolution*) were published in 1929 and 1930, and by the 1950s his reputation was enormous. Employing new methods, particularly those of psychoanalysis, to understand his subject matter – the politicians of the Whig oligarchy – he was dubbed the English Freud. Namier offered a non-idealistic account of Whig politicians. However, for a number of reasons, including his personality, his eastern European accent and possibly his Jewish background, Namier for long found it difficult to gain a permanent academic position and, though he eventually gained a Chair at the University of Manchester, his dreams of a post at Oxford went unrealised.

Most of the great historians are also philosophers: writers who capture the essence of their age. R. H. Tawney (1880–1962), Professor at the London School of Economics, was, during the inter-war period, such an historian – one whose influence was to be great, especially in left-wing historical and political circles. More famous today as the Labour Party's chief philosopher of social democracy, and the man whose ideas the 'Gang of Four' claimed to take with them when they broke away from the Labour Party to establish the Social Democratic Party in 1981, Tawney was in fact a social theorist and economic historian of some vision. He wanted to find answers to the problems of inter-war Britain; he desired to know why wealth-making had failed to deliver social harmony; and he turned to the past to help in this.

Although many of Tawney's works were concerned with medieval and early modern history, his key interest was in the way modern society had emerged; his writings were invested with contemporary relevance. His first major work, *The Agrarian Problem in the Sixteenth Century* (1912), an economic history examining the impact of enclosures on peasant life, set the historical scene for his emerging critique of contemporary society. *The Acquisitive Society* (1921) outlined his thesis that society was morally 'sick', again capturing the pessimistic mood of his age. Here he argued that the emergence of liberalism and secularism had freed capitalism from the shackles of moral obligation. Modernisation, Tawney believed, had seen the demise of social unity and collective purpose and the emergence of acquisitive individualism and the creed of private property. This was, he argued, the basis of a functionless and amoral society. Tawney bewailed the fact that economic life had been removed from its correct place within the moral scheme of social being. Modern societies, he argued, were governed solely by the desire to acquire wealth; and in such societies, Tawney claimed, crucial components of a pre-capitalist social ethic were eroded with acquisition and individual rights replacing giving and mutual obligations. Crucial to this interpretation was the argument that human beings, as members of society, became the means to an end, rather than an end in themselves. With this transformation was promoted, in Tawney's view, a society of misery, despair, inequality and moral malaise. In lacking a sustaining social ethic, capitalism had undermined society.

Tawney's next and perhaps most famous work, *Religion and the Rise of Capitalism* (1926), was the sum of his attempts to understand the historical context of the sick society of which he was so despairing, and its central theme was not simply the rise of capitalism but, crucially, the withdrawal of past Christian ethics from social and economic life. This book drew inspiration from, but was not simply a reworking of (as some have said) the famous study, *The Protestant Ethic and the Spirit of Capitalism* (1904–5), by the German sociologist and social theorist, Max Weber (1864–1920).

Tawney, as well as describing the moral malaise of modern British society, also suggested remedies. It was to this end that he wrote *Equality* (1931). His biographer, Anthony Wright, highlights three central principles of Tawney's social theory: the existence in social and economic life of 'function', 'freedom' and 'equal worth'. Each of these was crucial if society was to be reinvigorated. A functional society, Tawney believed, was antithetical to an acquisitive one. His measure of function was neither authoritarian nor pluralistic, but was founded on a medieval ideal linking social harmony and moral rectitude. In a correctly functioning and moral society, common purpose and mutual obligation must replace individual rights. The absolute measure of moral decay, for which there must be a practicable solution, was the seemingly unassailable position in society of essentially functionless private property. It was in adopting this position that Tawney most obviously inherited the nineteenth-century tradition of Ruskin and Morris. Tawney viewed political freedom as a fact in British society: what he lamented was the lack of freedom in the economic sphere. He argued that capitalism was irresponsible, arbitrary and tyrannical; in its presence workers were powerless. Unlike some of his socialist colleagues, Tawney was neither a general critic of the British political system nor a proponent of change by political means alone. His key concern was with obligations and the rejuvenation of society through the creation of participatory citizenship. This earned Tawney the label 'guild socialist' and was seen to separate him from Fabianism, with its statist and bureaucratic emphases. In Tawney's vision, the state was not a living thing, naturally centralising and authoritarian; it was an instrument that could be mobilised for the common good. Tawney desired to see capitalism controlled and deployed for social utility; he wished to invest it with function.

Tawney exercised enormous influence on left-wing and liberal British individuals and movements during the twentieth century. Dubbed the English Marx, Tawney was neither a Marxist nor an anti-Marxist, although his *Religion and the Rise of Capitalism* is cited as a key influence upon Maurice Dobb, the Marxist economist and economic historian. Tawney's influence was not restricted to the academic world but extended to Parliament, especially leading members of the Labour Party, such as Hugh Gaitskell and Michael Foot.

RUSSIA AND THE USSR

Tawney's conception of history as a lesson for the present, as a gauge of the progress of human society, characterised the crisis of left-leaning social democracy in an age of totalitarianism and world crisis. However, while Tawney's Britain may have indeed been in the doldrums, there were more cataclysmic problems emerging elsewhere. The October Revolution (1917), for example, ushered in a completely new era in Russian life. The Bolshevik seizure of power, and the establishment of the Soviet Union, had a profound impact upon historiographical traditions. The main problem for Bolshevik historians was to fit previous history into a Marxist framework – to rewrite the past with reference to present political/ideological considerations – because the non-Marxist view was regarded as a bourgeois 'falsification' of history. Anatole G. Mazeur, in his *The Writing of History in the Soviet Union* (1971), tells us that major Bolshevik historians of this period were N. N. Baturin, M. S. Olminskii and, particularly, M. N. Pokrovskii. Despite their establishment of research centres, and the training of new generations of historians, their history was stuffed with Marxist ideology. Indeed, these writers are noteworthy more for their contribution to the Party than to historical knowledge. This, it seems, is a recurrent theme in Soviet historiography, and typical of scholarship under totalitarian regimes. Pokrovksii, nevertheless, was noted for his attempts to frame Russian history in terms of Marxist approaches. His *Short History of Russia* (1920) was approved and commended by Lenin himself, while his later work, *A History of Russia from the Earliest Times* (2nd edn 1932), was the first full-scale attempt to apply Marxist economic imperatives to the formation of Russian society and culture. Early writings, under Pokrovskii, took as read the idea that Lenin had 'already suceeded in formulating with relative finality the basic periodization of history... [with] scientific accuracy'. This was the foundation of Bolshevik traditions of historiographical endeavour; history was to be rewritten.

In this early period, institutional structures were put into place to promote the Marxist–Leninist perspectives on the past. In 1918, for example, the Socialist Academy of Socialist Science was formed to teach this kind of Communist history. Later, Pokrovskii oversaw the foundation of the University of Sverdlovsk, *Ispart* (an institution dedicated to Communist Party history) and the Institute of Red Professorship. These organisations, Mazeur writes, were meant to impress the Marxist view at the expense of other Marxists, revisionists, old guard, diversionists and 'all manner of renegades and heretics within the ranks of fellow-travellers and even among full-fledged members of the party'.

During the 1920s, however, Moscow had nearly 100 independent publishers, which, despite the attentions of Bolshevik censors, still managed to produce anti-Marxist literature, including histories. Even in the universities, there was dissent from the official line. Mazeur argues that because Soviet–Bolshevik historians were overwhelmingly concerned with modern Russian and European history, a void existed in earlier periods: for example, classical, antique and medieval. Consequently, it is perhaps to the credit of the Bolsheviks, or a sign of wider problems in the 1920s, that they employed archaeologists and historians to teach these periods and cultures even though many were non-Marxist and often anti-Marxist. Throughout this decade, Pokrovskii campaigned against the dissenters, and, by 1930, greater internal stability enabled the Party to implement plans for the eradication of non-Marxist histories. During this phase of development, uniformity of practice and ideology was coming into place.

Although the 1920s were marked by some degree of variety in historical inquiry, this finally ended with the tightening of Joseph

Stalin's hold on authority. Pokrovskii died before this could happen, and by the mid-1930s his works were being attacked by his own former pupils. Stalinists claimed that Pokrovskii had placed too much emphasis on Russia, ignoring wider national imperatives within the Soviet Union. They also claimed that his work over-stated the importance of material development – that he was an economic determinist – which was seen to strengthen the claims of German racial theorists that Russia was a backward 'cultural and political vaccum'.

While Soviet historians began to stress national issues as a challenge to the growing menace of Nazi Germany, the unassailable position of Stalin (especially after the brutal purge of Communists he disapproved of in 1937–38) also fuelled a bizarre interest in the 'cult of personality'. This led historians to look back on great Russian hero-leaders, especially tsars of infamous reputation like Ivan the Terrible and Peter the Great. The analogy with the personality of Joseph Stalin was all too clear.

It is perhaps ironic that, during the crisis of the inter-war years, Chinese scholars should look to the West for the secrets of modernisation, as part of a growing interest by progressive Chinese circles in Western models. However, like their European and American counterparts, Chinese historiography also changed in the inter-war years, prompted partly at least by the growing influence of Western historiography. Quinjia Wang, in his 'Western historiography in the People's Republic of China' (*History of Historiography*, 1991), points out that Chinese scholars believed that their country's traditionalist culture was holding up the pace of progress, and that this could be counteracted by studying Western models of development. Thus, in the same era when James Harvey Robinson was appealing for a revolution in American history writing, Lian Qichao (1873–1929), the Chinese historian, was also calling for a 'New History'. In the 1920s, Hu Shi and Fu Sinian, who both spent time studying in America, were at the vanguard of the push to study Western development. The formation of the National Studies movement, under Ku Chieh-Kang, was indirectly influenced by Robinson's exhortation for a new direction in historical writing.

A CONTINENTAL REVOLUTION? THE EARLY *ANNALES* SCHOOL IN FRANCE

While Britain was slow to shake off the shackles of the nineteenth century, on much of the European continent the situation was quite different. The *Annales* School was founded in 1929 by two French historians, Marc Bloch and Lucien Febvre, as a result of their strong reaction against nineteenth-century historiographical traditions, including empirical methodology and subject-specificity as well as intellectual isolation from other disciplines. Since the 1920s, when the first of their works appeared, Bloch and Febvre came to be known as the founding fathers of a revolutionary movement in France, which now has disciples across the world. In terms of its breadth, its important journal, *Annales d'histoire économique et sociale* (as it was first called, although the subtitle has changed frequently), its esteemed followers, and because of its sometimes breathtaking range and methodological innovation, the *Annales* School is widely regarded as the most important development in twentieth-century historiography. In some senses, at the outset, Bloch and Febvre's mission was part of a worldwide trend among young scholars to achieve what the Americans dubbed a 'New History'. These two young men were 'problem-orientated' historians who eschewed traditional narrative forms. They also attempted to answer big questions by thematic examination of structural change. Hugh Trevor-Roper, in his 'Fernand Braudel, the Annales and the Mediterranean' (*Journal of Modern History*, 1972), posits three features which connect the work of Bloch and Febvre and later *Annalistes*, like Fernand Braudel. First, he argues, the *Annales* tried to 'grasp totality' and 'the vital cohesion of any historical period' by delineating its structures, whether social, economic, mental or physical. Secondly, that the *Annales* approach is 'deterministic', in that it espouses a belief that 'history is at least partially determined by forces which are external to men'. Thirdly, that the *Annales* constructed an 'intricate web of method, theory and philosophy [which] give coherence to French social history'. The *Annales* represented the first systematic attempt to theorise a new way of understanding the past. In the early years, Bloch and Febvre tackled history with fresh methodologies, building in new conceptual models, and borrowing freely from other disciplines. At the same time, Bloch and Febvre demanded that other historians should follow their example and work out the ways in which the traditional bastions of history could be broken down. The implications of these new approaches were to emerge into something of a philosophical system.

The force that united Bloch and Febvre was an understanding that if sociologists' knowledge of the present could be harnessed by historians, then human knowledge of the past would grow. In this sense these young scholars were rounding on the historical establishment, criticising traditionalists for their limited outlook and atheoretical minds. Thus, too,

Bloch and Febvre shared the view that politics was less than central to historical understanding. The *Annalistes* disapproved of narrative histories (what Braudel later dubbed *l'histoire événementielle* – 'the history of events'), and argued anyway that such history was the consequence of structural features. Bloch, Febvre and their followers had long opposed the idea that history can be re-created accurately or satisfactorily from a patchwork of facts. For the *Annales* tradition, analysis was the key to understanding the past; events, they argued, are 'particular', not 'essential', features of the past. While the *Annales* called for interdisciplinary approaches, and denounced narratives, they also suggested ways in which observation might be improved. In other words, they sought new methods and sources as well as new theories. The *Annalistes* opened up the idea of using legal and other records, not meant consciously for posterity, to uncover the lives of peasants. This was done, for example, by using monastic records in which the lives of the state and real people intersected – usually briefly, sometimes brilliantly – as during inquisitions and court cases. These innovations raised eyebrows, of course, but nobody could question the scholarly approach of the *Annalistes*. In fact they shared previous historians' concern with documents: indeed, Bloch, with all the high-mindedness of an Acton, described the difference between amateurs and professionals as being about 'the struggle with the documents'. In other words, he viewed amateurs as submitting, uncritically, to the documents, never questioning why they exist, or who wrote them and with what agenda.

Febvre, the older man, shared his younger colleague's zest for new approaches. As a student, Febvre had freely attended the lectures of geographers, iconographers, sociolinguists and others. He had notably catholic tastes. He acknowledged the influence of intellectuals like Jakob Burckhardt and Henri Berr, and he also read Marxists, like Jaurès, developing an interest not only in economic struggle, but also in past ideas – the collective mentalities of past generations. In this, he was heavily influenced by Emile Durkheim. Like Febvre, Bloch indulged in a broad interdisciplinary undergraduate programme, and drew similarly from sociology, geography, psychology and economics. At Strasbourg, which was regained by France after the First World War, these early interests continued to grow. Bloch and Febvre met up with eminent scholars in many fields and continued to develop their history in a broad way. Strasbourg provided the young men with what Peter Burke, in *The French Historical Revolution* (1990), describes as 'a milieu [which] favoured intellectual innovation and facilitated the exchange of ideas across disciplinary frontiers'.

The study of geography, in particular the work of Vidal de la Blache, had an enormous impact on Febvre. Febvre was suspicious of the notion that geography determined Man's existence and was fiercely critical of Friedrich Ratzel's deterministic approach. Febvre preferred to think in terms of interaction between the physical and social worlds, rather than the domination of the latter by the former. He also directed attention to the problematic nature of sources of environmental determinism that were all too often presented in simplistic terms, referring, for example, to the 'complexity of the idea of climate'.

In 1924, with these broad influences shaping his research, Bloch published his seminal work – *The Royal Touch*, one of the classics of this century. It is a study of mentalities, ideas and beliefs – a classic *Annales* subject area. In it Bloch examines a belief, held in France and England down to the eighteenth century, that the king could cure the skin disease scrofula ('the king's evil') just by touch. In three ways, *The Royal Touch* was path-breaking. First, it did not conform to rigid periodic boundaries and crossed the traditional divisions between medieval and early modern where necessary. Secondly, it was perhaps the first truly comparative history. By using comparison Bloch was formalising what he believed to be the way forward for all history. Finally, it was a study of 'religious psychology', an attempt to give meaning to the dominant beliefs and actions of real people. As such it shattered the mould of standard political histories of the medieval period. At this time, Febvre too was developing his interest in ideas, plainly influenced by psychology. *Martin Luther* (1928), for example, was far from just a biography, but was, instead, a study of 'social necessity', of the links between men and groups. The new trend was set. Bloch and Febvre continued to spread the word, writing books like Bloch's *French Rural History* (1931). In 1933 both men moved from Strasbourg, where they had met, to Paris – Bloch going to the Sorbonne and Febvre to the Collège de France. At this point they were at the centre of French intellectual life and were taking over the major institutions. Some would say that the *Annales* had become French history; like all successful revolutionaries, Bloch and Febvre *were* the historical establishment! But the innovative work went on. In 1940, Bloch produced his *Feudal Society*, the book for which he is now most famous. It is a broad-ranging study and even contains sections on Japan. Two years later, Febvre produced *The Problems of Unbelief in the 16th Century*, a study of the religious milieu of Rabelais which is also a classic. Along with Bloch's *Royal Touch*, Febvre's *Martin Luther* and *Problems of Unbelief* were to stimulate the 1960s generation of *Annales* members to study the history of mentalities. Bloch met a tragic end. When war broke out he joined the army and then the resistance to the German occupation, even though he was in his fifties. In 1944, he was captured and executed, although Febvre lived on, in Rio de Janeiro, until the 1950s, and inspired later historians, like Braudel, who followed the *Annales* tradition.

DEVELOPMENTS AFTER THE SECOND WORLD WAR

Whereas the cessation of previous wars involving Britain (1793–1815 and 1914–18) had juxtaposed great optimism with biting recession, the end of the Second World War was very different. Instead of being optimistic, people were trepidatory; yet instead of announcing high unemployment and social hardship, the period after 1945 delivered unparalleled growth and opportunity. The 1950s and 1960s saw the development of a truly international economic system; the growing co-operation of the European states; the development of mass consumerism: in a sense, ideologies and theories were themselves swamped by a wave of optimism. This was the era summed up in a phrase by Harold Macmillan, British Conservative Prime Minister, 1957–63: 'you've never had it so good'. While the same issues of poverty and progress, industrialisation and modernisation were raised, the post-war climate fostered a belief that inequality might be overcome and that industrialism was, on the whole, a good thing. This optimism and the climate of economic growth also led to many more universities, books and a greater emphasis upon the leisure aspect of human life.

David Cannadine, in an important article, 'The present and the past in the English industrial revolution, 1880–1980' (*Past and Present*, May 1983), argued that this mood of optimism gave rise to a new economic orthodoxy, which in turn influenced the direction of economic history. The once fatalistic acceptance of the inevitability of the trade cycle – boom followed by slump – was replaced by a belief in growth and prosperity. At the same time, another important influence was the emergence of independent Third-World economies in a world affected by decolonisation. Economic historians, like W. W. Rostow, in *The Stages of Economic Growth* (1953), argued that Third-World economies could use Britain as a model for their own industrial development. As a result, a school of thought developed that the job of the economic historian was the measurement and explanation of economic growth. The emphasis, then, was on progress, with the real danger that history was being used as a prescriptive. Rostow said his writings offered a 'non-Communist manifesto' for growth; in fact, he seemed to be arguing that he had discovered the secret of Western economic growth and that he would share the elixir with the southern hemisphere. Rostow's ideas, however, proved to be a long way wide of the mark; his argument that the developing world was like Britain in the eighteenth century proved both naive and erroneous. His work failed to allow for the fact that when Britain was industrialising it did not have to deal with avaricious multinational companies, or dogmatic left-wing governments which, in the 1950s, dominated the fledgling Third-World economy. Throughout this period, despite the emergence of the Third World, Britain remained central to studies because it was the 'first' industrial nation, the original theatre of modernisation. Irrespective of the impact that this had on the Third World, the notion of progress, of organic development and of growth influenced very clearly the way in which the British Industrial Revolution was studied.

COMMUNIST PERSPECTIVES

The age of Stalin saw and enforced uniformity of Soviet historiography; he became General Secretary of the Communist Party in 1922 and died in 1953. Under totalitarian regimes, the historian's freedom of speech is no more guaranteed than that of the ordinary person. Russia's entry into the war in 1941 encouraged her historical interest in conflict. After the war, the spread of Communism to what we now refer to as the Eastern Bloc – Poland, East Germany, Yugoslavia, Romania and Bulgaria – led to historical works in related areas. The spectre of the Cold War (the international stand-off between the Communist and 'Free' worlds), says Mazeur, led Soviet historians into a fierce reiteration and re-examination of what they termed the 'foreign falsification of history'.

Following the war, similar attitudes were being evinced as Communist governments gained power elsewhere. China provides one of the most telling case-studies. Given the great traditions of eastern historiography in China and the Islamic world, it is perhaps sad to note that the greatest developments in historiography in the twentieth century have come from the West. There are, of course, exceptions, but the Chinese case, to take one example, is typical of the historiography of totalitarian regimes. The days of the dynastic historians, which date at least to the fifth century, are long gone. In general terms, in the years immediately after the Communists took control (1949), Chinese historians were called upon to provide a new history to complement the new culture that was being forged. For this purpose Russian historiography appeared to provide the best model, argues Quinjia E. Wang in his 'History in late imperial China' (*History of Historiography*, 1992). For this reason, the number of Chinese scholars employing Western techniques, or writing histories of the West, went into sharp decline. For thirty years from its publication in the 1940s, Yiliang and Yujin's *Outline of World History* was the standard school textbook. Wang tells us that, although the authors had been trained in America, this four-volume tome was based closely upon a much larger Russian version. This book 'demonstrated that, though China had broken out with its Soviet older brother [from the imperial Western world], Chinese historians had not yet generated their own interpretation of world history'. Subsequently, in the process of creating their own world history, Chinese historians stuck faithfully to Marx – even though Marx either modelled his perceptions of Asia on Europe or else was ambiguous in reference to the Asiatic world. The writing of a Marxist people's (proletarian) history also resulted in traditional culture being downplayed or expunged. From the 1960s, however, there was evidence that certain Western texts were being rehabilitated, through translation, in certain Chinese circles, although Mao Tse-tung's xenophobic 'Cultural Revolution' of the later 1960s circumscribed some of these efforts.

Today, Chinese students are forced to take compulsory courses in the history of the Chinese Communist Party and, in the worst cases, the history of all else is subsumed within that. The writing of the Korean War (1950–53) is a good example of the limitations of this approach. Western historiography on this war is considerable, yet in China only recently has the full picture of the involvement of the People's Army begun to emerge. Liangwu Yin-Shiwei Chen, in 'Forty years of the Korean War research in China' (*History of Historiography*, 1994), notes with great sorrow the lack of knowledge of the Chinese dimension of the Korean conflict, which, it is argued, stems from the way in which history is taught in China, and from the closure of crucial government archives. Chen also claims that this cover-up served the ideological purposes of the Chinese government. Maintaining a vague recollection of these events strengthens the war's utility as a symbol of American imperialism, which is especially apposite given recent controversies over the future of Taiwan, whose independence from China is protected by America. At the same time, Chen argues, uncovering exact details of many thousands of Chinese deaths in the war might be counter-productive to the Communist Party's cause.

In China, historians under the Communist regime still display an interest in long-range notions of history. In fact, their aim is often to conceptualise total world history of the most breathtaking scope. Dorothea L. Martin, in her *The Making of A Sino-Marxist World View: Perceptions and Interpretations of World History in the People's Republic of China* (1990), argues that the Chinese quest for world history is Marxist in origin and ideology. Many Chinese historians view the social world in the way Darwin saw the natural one – as an evolutionary development. The desire to write world history is essentially positivist in conception.

INDIA

Elsewhere, the break with Western orthodoxies was not always so complete. In post-colonial India (after 1947), historiographical trends have been similar in many ways to those of the West. According to Sumit Sarkar, in 'Many worlds: the construction of history in modern India' (*History and Historiography*, 1991), Indian professional historians work in universities modelled on those of the West and teach predominantly in English. At the same time, 'Their conscious methodological assumptions also derive from the West – with a certain time-lag characteristic of under-development.' Thus, Sarkar argues, Indian writing has 'grown up in the distant shadow of Ranke' and has been mediated through 'Anglo-Saxon positivism'. In the 1950s and 1960s Marxist approaches became popular in India. The sources for Indian scholarship of the ancient world or the Middle Ages were often great Sanskrit and Persian historical texts (like the *Mahabharata*), evaluated with the same hermeneutical verve that characterised Ranke or Acton. At the same time, the rise of Indian nationalism in the 1920s led to a new kind of history, at root concerned with identity in the pre-colonial world. This was partly in reaction to the writings on India perpetrated under British rule in the nineteenth century. The nature of Indian geopolitics before and after the period of British rule has necessarily fostered a strong tradition of local/regional history writing to match that concerned with religious or national destiny.

FRANCE AND THE POST-WAR *ANNALES* SCHOOL

In post-war France, where an interest in regions has also traditionally been strong, the torch of the *Annales* was passed to Fernand Braudel, a protégé of Lucien Febvre. Braudel's classic book, *The Mediterranean and the Mediterranean World in the Age of Philip II* (1949), came closer than any other to total history. Perhaps more than any other French book, even Bloch's *Royal Touch*, this study can be regarded as the greatest historical work of the twentieth century. It is an enormous study, crammed with masses of material, which Braudel assiduously pieced together over twenty years. *The Mediterranean* was Braudel's attempt to reverse the increasing fragmentation of history – which had been a feature of the 1920s and 1930s outside the *Annales* School – and to halt 'thematic specialisation', in other words, to depart from 'prefix' history and to look at whole problems. Indeed, Braudel's vision was, Tosh says, to meet the *Annales*' key challenge: 'to recapture human life in all its variety... – to write "total history"'. Bloch and Febvre had done this for parts of the past – but never for whole ages. Bloch's *Feudal Society*, for example, was concerned not only with the whole medieval world, but the key aspects of its social structure. James A. Henretta, in 'Social history as lived and written' (*American Historical Review*, 1979), aptly describes *The Mediterranean* as 'a comprehensive, multi-dimensional cubist portrait of the society'. The key problem with 'total history', Braudel argued, was that time was multi-layered, that the history of different aspects of the world changed at different paces. In wrestling with the immense problem of writing the history of Philip II's empire, Braudel organised his book, and with it his overarching conception of history, into three phases. The first, *la longue durée* (the long run), spanned the seemingly timeless phase of human interaction with the natural world. At this level, the effects of the passage of time, Braudel argued, were slowest. In the second phase, Braudel framed the quicker-moving medium term in which political, social and economic structures – states, nations and economic systems, for example – were formed. Finally, the third part of *The Mediterranean* tackled the fast-flowing short term: peoples' actions; the narratives of events; political and diplomatic history.

Braudel's *Mediterranean* has been likened to Gibbon's *Decline and Fall of the Roman Empire*, in that both authors display a vast historical knowledge to conclude that the empires they studied, Spanish and Roman respectively, were limited by their own scale. In writing his masterpiece, Braudel captured a variety of interdisciplinary procedures. Braudel was more than just an innovative methodologist; his work, like Gibbon's, has style – a literary force expressing the author's eye for detailed observation. In any age, Braudel would have been a great historian. He shared the 'totalist' vision of sociologists, but did not write in that dry, social science language: he had the turn of phrase of a Macaulay, a Ranke or an Acton. His history is creative, and the third section moves at great pace.

Braudel, of course, was criticised, as would anybody be for such a vast plan. He was accused of determinism, of reducing men to inevitable defeat in their natural world. Moreover, it is not always apparent that there is a link between his three-tier conception of time. Others argued that 'total history' was impossible beyond the local level (something which influenced later *Annales* writers) – and claimed that something as big as the Mediterranean world cannot be treated inclusively. Furthermore, in trying to offer an alternative conception of historical change to Marx, Braudel failed to integrate political history with the environment and demography. Nor does Braudel's work have the dynamism of Marx's base-superstructure philosophy. The American humanist–socialist historians Eugene and Elizabeth Genovese condemned Braudel for failing to allot people their correct place in his histories: 'the people who inhabit this earth do not fare so well in the story', going on to say that Braudel's great work, with its 'structural interpretation, with its anthropological, ecological and archaeological predilections, implicitly negates the historical process itself'. Thus geography – the Mediterranean itself – was the crucial component of his history. Braudel may have had his critics, but his work provides a crucial stepping-stone between the first generation of *Annales* scholars, Bloch and Febvre, and those, like Emmanuel Le Roy Ladurie, who came later.

THE 1960S: 'REAL' NEW DIRECTIONS IN HISTORY?

During the post-war period, and particularly from the early 1960s, there have been a number of important developments in social and economic history around the world. From that time, social history, in particular, began to assume a new complexion. In Britain, many new societies (and with them periodical publications) emerged, dedicated to all manner of sub-disciplinary and interdisciplinary histories, including the study of population, the family, labour and oral history. The 1960s also witnessed the emergence of a clearly articulated 'history from below', as well as numerous pioneering scholars dedicated to women's history, subaltern studies (from the word meaning 'rank below captain', a 'history from below' which makes especial overtures to India, but also to Africa and South America) and a host of interconnected yet distinctive areas which marked a decisive shift from crown, constitution and politics.

These changes were derived partly by the new social histories, of the *Annales* School in France and elsewhere, and partly by the implementation of new interpretations of Marx's writings. The development of a new cultural–Marxist approach resulted in a number of important works of social history, including E. P. Thompson's *The Making of the English Working Class* (1963). The strengths of this book are numerous – it is theoretical, yet it is rigorously researched. It is a study of working-class culture, politics and economy, but it is also a work of social anthropology. It is important because it offered a new focus to social history. Society and class are not static things, argued Thompson, they are dynamic processes. Thompson's influence on European and American labour history has been considerable. Thompson's study is also important because it connected scholarly approaches with what in the 1950s were called 'amateur historians'. Much of the inspiration for *The Making of the English Working Class* was derived from Thompson's time as tutor for the Workers' Education Association in the West Riding of Yorkshire. Other works with 'amateur' connections at this time were Maurice Beresford's *Lost Villages of England* (1954) and W. G. Hoskins's classic of *Annales*-type historical geography, *The Making of the English Landscape* (1955).

One of the problems with British social history before the 1960s was the absence of an *Annales*-type school to fight its corner, to promote uniformity of good practice or to disseminate new methods and ideas. However, groups like the Cambridge Group for the Study of Population and Social Structure and the History Workshop, which emerged in the 1960s and 1970s, sought to assume this role. Some of the most important debates in feminist, Marxist and theoretical history have taken place within the pages of the latter group's periodical, the *History Workshop Journal*.

In the broadest sense, among middle-of-the-road historians, British social history has never really rid itself of the ghost of Trevelyan. In other words, much social history in Britain is not 'social history' but some smaller fragment that does not merit survival on its own; a history so defined because, for instance, it simply misses out the politics. Yet no 'proper' social historian would study the social composition of popular radicalism without reference to the political events against which the various movements are set. The inherent conservatism of British historiography and the remaining power of empiricist traditions have made most British social history that way.

LATER *ANNALES* AND 'NEW ECONOMIC HISTORY'

The third generation of the *Annales* School innovated in three principal ways: first, they developed a microhistory approach to the study of regions; secondly, they made inroads into using quantitative techniques; and, thirdly, they built on Febvre and Bloch's ideas to develop the history of mentalities. This generation of scholars − Robert Mandrou, Emmanuel Le Roy Ladurie, Jacques Le Goff and others − learned from criticisms levelled against Braudel's 'totalist' approach, which it was claimed could not be achieved on such a scale as the Mediterranean world. Consequently, historians such as Le Roy Ladurie focused their works on to what they called regional or local 'total history', or what Giovanni Levi later called microhistory. These histories were still all-encompassing, but the geographical scale has been pared down.

Braudel, despite his critics, was not completely lost to the later *Annalistes*. Some, for example Le Roy Ladurie, shared Braudel's ecological determinism − a belief in the centrality to human history of the natural world; that man's history was an unending history of toil against the elements. Le Roy Ladurie's interest in population and food supply, for instance, was central in his decision to develop quantitative techniques for sifting masses of data − which he did for *The Peasants of the Languedoc* (1961), although here (as we see more fully in Chapter 4), he owed much to Ernst Labrousse and Pierre Chaunu, who had applied Braudel's *longue durée* to quantitative economic history. Thus, the quantitative techniques and computer-aided methodologies employed by *Annalistes* like Le Roy Ladurie were not developed in isolation. In fact, this technological revolution in data-handling is one of the key features of 1960s historiography. While it was promoted by French historians it was harnessed more religiously by the Cliometric historians (also known as New Economic Historians or Econometricists). The term Cliometric, derived from Clio, the muse of history, sums up perfectly the grandiose aspirations of the statistical revolutionaries: they believed that with computers and economic models they would effectively take over the discipline; that their pioneering works would become the new orthodoxy for historians. Even Le Roy Ladurie, who was not a Cliometrician, argued in the 1960s that historians would become programmers or would be nothing at all. E. P. Thompson dismissed this 'Brave New World' attitude as overblown and overambitious.

The New Economic Historians operated on three levels. First, they concentrated on precision in methodology, description and analysis, and it was here that computer-aided history achieved its status. Secondly, they employed economic and statistical models. R. W. Fogel, the 1960s guru of this 'school', claimed that these models could be used to measure what might have existed but which no longer does. Thirdly, and most controversially, some New Economic Historians employed the so-called counter-factual technique. Fogel argued that the historian could not understand past events that happened without understanding the things that did not happen, but which might have done if certain things had changed. Fogel, for example, applied this idea to the importance of the North American railways which historians – including Fogel himself – had previously thought to be crucial in the economic development of the USA. The counter-factual approach at work in Fogel's *Railroads and Economic Growth* (1964) enabled him to argue that if the railways had not existed, alternative transport would have almost wholly accounted for that share of American gross national product which can be attributed to the impact of the railways. These New Economic Historians set themselves apart from the older generations of economic historians. However, most economics (and therefore economic history) is neo-classical, often marked by a greater interest in theory than fact. For all their methodological advancement, the New Economic Historians were extremely rigid in their interpretation of the economic past. Just like neo-classical economists, New Economic Historians from the 1960s subjected the past to 'utility-maximisation', by which is meant that they argued in favour of understanding the economic past as a totally observable environment. This approach, of course, made little or no allowance for independent mental and social factors in the search for causation.

Since the 1960s, the high point of Cliometrics, quantitative approaches have become less dogmatic. Le Roy Ladurie, for example, who became an enthusiast of large-scale quantification at the same time as Fogel, produced work which was never concerned with manipulating data to answer preconceived questions. Rather, he was concerned to determine the cycles, fluctuations, patterns, changes and repetitions of history; these questions, he argued, could only be answered over *la longue durée*. Moreover, Le Roy Ladurie's interests in the totalist perspective diminished in the 1970s, when his work became much more focused on mentalities and the structure of popular belief.

CULTURAL HISTORY

Therefore, despite the importance of quantitative techniques shown in *The Peasants of the Languedoc*, perhaps the greatest development of the third generation of the *Annales* School can be seen with the advent of 'l'histoire des mentalités' (the history of mentalities) – what we in England call cultural history. Febvre and Bloch, as we have argued, were keen on this approach. Febvre's desire to understand the mental frameworks of the past was born out of a hatred of anachronism. The worst kind of anachronism, he argued, was psychological anachronism – the false assumption that past people thought about things in the same way that we do. Febvre, then, blew the trumpet of 'historical psychology' and this inspired later generations. Robert Mandrou, for example, answered the call with his seminal study, *Introduction to Modern France: 1500–1640* (1961). In it, Mandrou examined the fears of early modern people who, living much closer to nature than we do, carried through their lives a fear of natural disaster and ailments which we would find hard to appreciate. These fears, Mandrou argued, were represented by morbid hypersensitivity, excessive grief, pity and cruelty. Theirs was a harsh world. In England, Keith Thomas's major study of belief, *Religion and the Decline of Magic* (1971), was heavily influenced by the *Annales* School. Writing of a similar period of English history to that examined in Mandrou's book on France, Thomas argues that 'one of the central features was a preoccupation with the explanation and relief of human misfortune'. In this respect, by painting an image of a people locked in fear of their world, Mandrou shared Braudel's social determinism – the idea that the world was shaped by forces extraneous to humankind. This tradition of understanding past states of mind was continued in the work of various *Annalistes*. These ranged from Jacques Le Goff's European survey, *Medieval Civilisation, 400–1500* (1964), to Le Roy Ladurie's *Montaillou* (1975) and *Carnival in Romans* (1980), incisive miniaturist studies of beliefs and ideas.

A DIFFUSION OF IDEAS? HISTORY TO THE PRESENT DAY

It would be trite, not to say erroneous, to argue that each country's historiographical tradition was an hermetically sealed entity, borrowing nothing from other nations, 'schools' or scholars. One of the key features of post-war history writing, along with a growing interdisciplinary focus, has been the internationalisation of perspectives. Improvements in communications naturally facilitate more broad-ranging dissemination of knowledge, but the breaking-down of frontiers also has something to do with the *esprit de corps* which brought the European Community into existence. Braudel, for example, was a committed European, although his works usually played up his beloved France and occasionally displayed nationalistic sentiments. This is noticeable in his *History of Civilisation* (1963), where he argues that America would have been a better place had the French and not the British been the major influence on its development from thirteen colonies to a republic.

Even in the time of Febvre and Bloch, the *Annales* attracted supporters in Europe, such as the Belgian Medievalist, Henri Pirenne. The Dutchman, Jan Huizinga's *The Waning of the Middle Ages* (1924) is in many respects an *Annales* book before the *Annales*. Braudel, too, had a number of followers and fellow-travellers, like the Pole, Withold Kula. Giulio Einaudi's huge *History of Italy* (1972) and Carlo Ginzburg's *The Cheese and the Worms* (1976) perhaps mark the high point of pro-*Annales* sympathies in Italy.

In America, the *Annales*, like Marxism, have been taken on board only slowly and patchily. This has been explained by American historians' liberal approach to the past, which mirrors the (Jeffersonian/Jacksonian) political culture of that country, and by an absence in America of the social chaos that has pierced European culture and self-confidence since 1914. In Germany, the *Annales* 'mentalities' approach did not take off till the 1970s, although even now the majority of German historians are understandably preoccupied with the modern period and the cataclysmic events of 1914–18 to 1945, the rise of Hitler and the spectre of genocide.

In Britain, the continued pre-eminence of traditional political history (especially in the 1950s and 1960s) is tellingly exposed by Peter Burke, in *The French Historical Revolution* (1990). Britain at this time, Burke says, was a good example 'of what Braudel used to call a "refusal to borrow"'. Despite the importance of the major works by *Annales* historians, they were met with an underwhelming response in Britain. When Braudel's *Mediterranean* was first published, the major journals, the *English Historical Review* and the *Economic History Review*, did not review it. Prior to the 1970s, the *Annales* works were only rarely translated. Moreover, Burke argues, the exception who proved the rule was Marc Bloch: 'One might say that Bloch's interest in English history and his penchant for understatement . . . allowed him to be regarded as a sort of honorary Englishman.'

Today, not even the British are unaware of the *Annales*; and they have ready access to the writings of the *Annalistes*, for all the great works of the *Annales* are available in English translation. Works of world history, for example, have British proponents. Simon Schama's massive *Land-*

scape and Memory (1995), which was accompanied by a BBC2 television programme introduced by the author, is a fine example of the global approach to emotion and belief. Schama argues that landscape takes on meaning from humans as a consequence of the interpretations that they bring to it, and that these interpretations are a function of memory. Like many huge and ambitious projects, Schama's thoughtful book is essentially a series of unconnected stories that illustrate the theme of landscape and memory, and that reveal, in particular, moments of recognition when the human appreciation of a place is directed by long-standing assessments and understandings of certain natural types – especially forests, mountains and rivers. Schama's book does not obey the familiar constraints of chronology, and weaves images together from far-flung places and different times to good effect.

New developments are not restricted to the West. In China there now appears to be a less overtly ideological approach to history. Perhaps Chinese historians will begin to re-learn the traditions of evidential selection and criticism displayed by Chinese scholars 200 years ago? Western historiography, which experienced an uplift in China during the 1920s and again in the early 1960s, also suffered reversals during the 'Cultural Revolution' (1966–68) and in the anti-democratic clamp-down which followed the Tianenmen Square massacre (1989). Most Chinese historians working in the West want to see China's political system overthrown, so that Western standards of academic freedom can allow historians to recover the lost history of ancient Chinese civilisations as well as the more contemporary history of life under Communism. This is not, of course, simply a division between East and West, but between autocracy and democracy. In East Germany, in the 1970s and earlier, historians were especially dogmatic, which for these scholars (as for the Chinese) meant writing Marxist histories.

One of the most important developments in history, following the political changes in the USSR in the later 1980s and early 1990s, has only just begun: the rewriting of the history of the former Soviet Union. The advent of Gorbachev's reforms, 'perestroika' and 'glasnost' (with their emphasis on greater freedoms and understanding), resulted in many new archive materials being available to scholars. With the disintegration of the Soviet empire in the 1990s, there has been a further loosening of the old bureaucracy, not only in Russia but also in the Baltic States and elsewhere. The acknowledged home, and testing-ground, of Communist revolution promises to promote much discussion and scholarly publication in this and the next generation. Important works include R. W. Davis's *Soviet History in the Gorbachev*

Revolution (1989) and D. J. Raleigh's edited collection, *Soviet Historians and Perestroika: The First Phase* (1989). Kevin McDermott, in his 'Re-thinking the Comintern: Soviet historiography' (*Labour History Review*, 1992), sounds a cautionary note on the first round of disclosures. He says even work produced in the early 1990s by Soviet historians of the Comintern tends to play down 'the contradictions and tensions' of, for example, the Leninist phase, preferring instead to see Comintern history as a single line broken only by the excesses of Stalinism. 'This is understandable, if regrettable', McDermott writes. 'It was not easy to renounce the views and beliefs of a lifetime. The more critical appraisals must have come hard to historians of the older generation. Nevertheless, more challenging conclusions are required.' McDermott's comment on this feature of 'new' Soviet historiography might stand as a broader statement about the problems faced by historians in a new era of academic freedom. At the same time, a more optimistic future is surely ahead as historians of all features of Russian, Ukrainian, Georgian or Estonian life come to terms with new ideas and new records. With the new generations of the future should come a 'new history' of the former Communist Bloc to match that familar in the West.

Meanwhile, the French continue to play a guiding role in key aspects of Western historiography. Disciples of 'new history' and *Annales*, since Keith Thomas and Peter Burke, and a wide range of Marxist, feminist and cultural historians, have led to British historiography moving into the mainstream of developments in the field. At the same time, British history has become the subject of *Annales*-type studies, one of the best of which is Ian McCalman's illuminating examination of English popular radicalism, *Radical Underworld: Prophets, Revolutionaries and Pornographers in London, 1795–1840* (1988). McCalman's own words, written in the preface to the 1993 paperback edition, sum up the new spirit which washes over the old terrain of historical scholarship: 'Perhaps the cultural history wave will suddenly peter out or dump me on the rocks, but like the protagonists of [my] book I will have enjoyed the ride.' In fact, it is extremely unlikely that cultural history will fade away.

CONCLUSIONS

Let us conclude this discussion by considering what is 'the New History'. Peter Burke, in his edited collection, *New Perspectives on Historical Writing* (1991), argues that 'Old' and 'New' history differ on seven key levels of interpretation of the discipline. While it might seem simplistic to reduce historiography to a series of bullet points, there is considerable insight in what Burke writes. Moreover, the following points provide a useful foundation for our later discussions:

1. History of the 'traditional paradigm' is concerned with politics; the new history, which 'has come to be concerned with virtually every area of human activity', is not.
2. Traditional historians 'think of history as essentially a narrative of events'; although new historians do not entirely dismiss the narrative form, greater weight is given to structures than was previously the case.
3. Traditional historians focus on 'a view from above ... concentrated on the great deeds of great men', whereas new historians favour 'history from below', the view of the common person.
4. Traditional history is shaped around documents (empiricism); new historians, however, approach history from the viewpoint that 'historians ... concerned with a greater variety of human activities ... must examine a greater variety of evidence'.
5. Traditional approaches fail to account for the variety of questions which historians must ask, whereas new history does not.
6. The tradition paradigm posits that history is objective, and focuses upon the all-powerful voice of the author (the historian) in articulating the past. New historians, however, are concerned less with objectivity, while the range of approaches and needs covered in the new history has resulted in a move from 'The Voice of History' to one of 'Heteroglossia', '"varied and opposing voices"'.
7. Traditional history is hermetically sealed as a distinct disciplinary unit, whereas the new history is inter/multi-disciplinary in approaches and attitudes.

The writing of history, we can see, is like history itself, the passage of time. Change is constant; new orthodoxies emerge; what were previously tablets of stone crumble to dust and become the subject of study and contextualisation by historians. Yet at the same time there are continuities, both in history and in its study. The purpose of this book is to introduce some of these changes and continuities, and to aid a keener understanding of them. In Part II we go on to examine something of the variety of approaches and methods utilised by historians, and to consider some of the main theories and constructs which frame our reference to the past. For here, too, historians and their practice can be wildly divergent.

PART II

4

Approaches to history: sources, methods and historians

INTRODUCTION

THE reasons why we study the past are innumerable; the range of sources available to historians is also immense. Today, all aspects of past human society are regarded as legitimate areas for historical inquiry. Despite multifarious changes in attitude and approaches over the past 100 years, however, historians are still source-based creatures; even those most 'modern' in outlook seek to re-read and reinterpret sources; none would claim to do without them, although the nature of sources has changed greatly over the last century.

The practice of history begins with evidence and with sources. The availability of sources is often the key determinant of what become most popular, for some areas, for example nineteenth-century France, benefit from a greater volume of documents than others, such as ancient Germany. Whereas historians of early modern and medieval popular culture face a constant battle to find material, or else to reassess extant records creatively, those concerned with modern political history face a veritable forest of official documents – more than any one person could marshal in a lifetime. It is vital, therefore, that students of history are aware of the scope of historical sources, and the methods which historians use to order them.

This chapter cannot hope to cover the entire scope of historians' sources or methodologies. Instead, it seeks to demonstrate something of the range of approaches to history by drawing examples from a number of important types of historical inquiry as well as from those branches of the discipline which received least treatment in the existing corpus of introductory texts. The central focus of this chapter is on the distinction between 'old', or 'traditional', forms of inquiry and the 'New History'. The chapter first offers a broad overview of the relation between historians and their sources. It then goes on to consider the nature of national and local history, for this is an area in which great changes have taken place; the division between the centre and the periphery also marks the traditional boundary between professional and amateur historians. In the nineteenth century, national history was the *sine qua non* of the profession, whereas local study was tainted by accusations of antiquarianism. Over the past century, however, local history – history by case-study or specific geographical area – has become regarded much more as a legitimate branch of inquiry. This spirit of democratisation, which has influenced history writing in all countries from India to Italy, is in keeping with developments like 'history from below'; local communities, regional and local identities, as well as non-national nuances in the historical scene are now part of the historian's remit and require consideration. This chapter then goes on to assess the enduring role of traditional history, and the resilience of traditional approaches and methods. Focusing on narrative and biographical forms, this section shows that although the role of the individual and the story of human action are usually associated with nineteenth-century historiography, such approaches are in fact still popular today. Traditional forms of history, such as biography, have always been popular with the public, and have been continually produced in academic circles. For these reasons, if no other, traditional types of history must command our attention.

The latter parts of the chapter turn to what can be called aspects of 'new' history. Here we intend to introduce readers to something of the variety of innovative methods, approaches and assumptions that have inspired historians over the past generation or two. It will be noticed that both continuity and change emerge throughout the chapter, as does the revelation that many of the 'new' methods and explanatory frameworks hail from the Continent and especially from the *Annales* tradition. Nevertheless, British scholarship is sometimes accused of an excessive reliance upon old-style history. Later sections of this chapter demonstrate that many features of British historiography are actually dynamic, taking on board the methodological and attitudinal developments advanced elsewhere. This chapter, then, is centrally concerned with the variety of historical methods, the different types of history and the varying ways of doing history.

HISTORIANS AND SOURCES

The fragmentation of history, noted in the previous chapter, is partly the product of the demise of national self-confidence, the break-up of the Victorians' self-professed hegemony of cultural advancement and the role of theory in taking the subject across new (mainly disciplinary) frontiers. The same trend has, however, been exacerbated by the increasing range of sources available to historians. Few historians today claim to master more than a relatively small aspect of history's true scope. All, it seems, are governed by the fact that for the period since the Middle Ages instances of the preserved written word are enormous. The closer to the present we get, the more this abundance is apparent. Between 1475 and 1640, 30 000 books at least were published in England alone. From 1641 to 1700 the figure reached 100 000; during the eighteenth century a further 350 000 appeared, and since then the number runs into many millions.

The scope of the historian's endeavours is also prescribed by attitudes. The broadening of the discipline and the increased number of participants, as well as the burgeoning of university-based scholarship since the 1960s, have led historians to concentrate on smaller and more fragmentary pieces of the past. Whereas Acton claimed to pursue 'ultimate' (meaning universal) history – a history requiring no subsequent revision on account of its perfectibility – the past has since become an arena for interpretation and reinterpretation. History today is demarcated by chronological divisions (medievalists, early modernists and modernists); by national distinctions (British historians, Germanists and Americanists); by thematic or subject-based identifications (social, economic, religious); by methodological differentiation (oral historians, family historians, quantitative historians); other aspects are distinguished by ideology, for example in the Marxist and Weberian interpretations of Weimar and Nazi Germany. Even social history, once a sub-discipline itself, has fractured into a myriad of distinct groups researching feminism, socialism, labour history and the world from 'below' – although many share the same source materials and aims. This break-up of the family of historians has led to (or is perhaps derived from) a much greater scope in terms of how the past is approached, the methodologies employed and how the sources are mined. Thus historians of trade unions might use local Labour Party records to detail trade affiliations of members, women's historians might investigate the gender characteristics of the party, while historians of migration might link the names of the membership with their census and parish records surveys to uncover its ethnic composition.

Part of the problem for historians is defining what is a source. Although primary sources are usually those closest, or indeed contemporary, to the period under observation, and secondary sources those works written subsequently, the distinction is actually quite blurred. Once we move away from simple cases (like politicians' diaries, or cabinet minutes) which are clearly primary, difficulties of assessment do arise. Take Benjamin Disraeli's novel of 1845, *Sybil; or, the Two Nations*. This is first and foremost a piece of fiction. It is read by literature students as part of the 'condition of England' genre, along with the novels of Charles Dickens, Elizabeth Gaskell or Charles Kingsley. For historians of Chartism or of elite attitudes, however, *Sybil* is something of a primary source: it typifies the milieu of the young Tory Radicals of the day (of whom Disraeli was one) and is a manifesto for the earliest form of 'one nation' Toryism.

Similar problems come from social commentaries, newspaper and periodical journalism, political tracts and other such works. Written with a contemporary audience in mind, often containing rich historical analogies, they are essentially secondary materials, incidental to the events of the time. However, for historians of attitudes or *mentalités*, these are primary materials.

A rigid definition of sources, or a reliance upon traditional materials, constricts historians and puts many aspects of the past beyond our knowledge. Even then, the dividing line between official and unofficial sources is also blurred, depending very much on the way in which they are used. For high-political historians, for example, the types of sources preferred have hardly changed since the time of Bolingbroke or of Acton. The lives of politicians and the machinations of statecraft require, as they have always done, a close reading of personal correspondence, memoirs and diaries. The copious volumes of the Gladstone diaries are a classic example. At the same time, our knowledge of other political figures might be flawed by the absence of such materials. Parnell, for example, kept no diaries, which adds to the mystique of the 'uncrowned King of Ireland', a man who, in the 1880s, strode the Westminster stage like a Colossus. Yet men such as Parnell never escape the historian's gaze: *Hansard*, the proceedings of the Houses of Parliament in Britain, contains every speech he made in the Commons and friends and enemies alike corresponded with him and about him.

'New', 'social' and 'non-traditional' historians rarely use these kinds of sources; or else, they use them for reasons other than to recover the lives of 'Great Men'. Marc Bloch once argued that official sources could occasionally illuminate the lives of ordinary people, so long as historians used 'the evidence of the witnesses in spite of themselves'. This was the case in Carlo Ginzburg's *The Cheese and the Worms* (1975), in which the records of a sixteenth-century papal inquisition were used to try to uncover all manner of things about the mentality of one man, a miller known as Mennochio, who was eventually tortured and executed for his Anabapist heresy. The book is a *tour de force* exposing the hopes and fears of this lowly miller, his preferred reading, and the way he made sense of his world, although his world is refracted through that of those hostile outsiders who compiled the source.

The early nineteenth century in Britain witnessed a massive growth in production of official documents and data. With the process of industrial modernisation, urbanisation and social problems, as well as the emergence of a huge state bureaucracy, government publications proliferated. Many of these are available in original form in the British Public Record Office (founded in 1838) at Kew. National archives in most European countries and America also date from the Victorian period. Many university libraries also hold microfiche copies, which makes them easily accessible to students and scholars. Political historians look on these mountainous collections with an avaricious delight which is matched only by a fear of being overwhelmed: hundreds of thousands of foolscap pages covering all manner of areas of government work, every report delivered to the House of Commons and the Lords; every word of all Select Committee inquiries; material on population (the decennial censuses), trade and empire, economic distress, trade unionism, disease and sanitation, urbanisation, poor relief, vagrancy and pauperism and Irish immigration in the 1830s. While this seems like the stuff of bureaucratic history, these materials actually have a greater range of uses. The attempts of successive governments to understand and ameliorate the pressing social problems of the 1830s and 1840s, for example, are captured in what historians dubbed the 'sociological blue books'. Each of these contains evidence from thousands of local dignitaries – employers, poor-law guardians and priests, etc. – which in turn provides historians with more than just evidence of government action or inaction. Instead they are fine examples of interaction between the 'national' and 'local' bureaucracy, the variable implementation of social policy at the local level, as well as providing crystallisation of contemporary attitudes, hopes, fears and anxieties. This demonstrates, then, the precariousness of separating records into one category or another.

LOCAL HISTORY

The seeming division between 'national' and 'local' history represents more than a difference of geography or of semantics. The rise of local/ regional history as an acceptable, indeed praiseworthy, area of study also marks something of a shift in emphasis, a downplaying of the national or centralist perspective.

What, though, does 'local' or 'regional' mean in this context? For ecologists and environmental geographers, the term 'local' is usually used as an opposite to the term 'global'. To historians, local/regional is preferred to differentiate subject matter from the national or international emphasis of other, often traditional, forms of history. Thus the emphasis is shifted from the singular nation to the plural region: from the uniformity of national language to the richness of a multitude of dialects: for example, Québecois French (rather than English Canadian), Breton (as opposed to French), Catalan (against Spanish), and the myriad of languages that are spoken in India. Local history, in terms of historians' aspirations, also carries something of the baggage of 'people's history': the idea that recognition of localism comes with the democratisation and decentralisation of the discipline, born of a belief that for every Louis XIV, Napoleon or de Gaulle there are millions of ordinary lives waiting to be uncovered. These lives – whether conceptualised individually (through oral testimony) or collectively (through family reconstitution or community history) – provide integral pieces of the loosely formed patchwork that constitutes the 'nation' or 'people'.

In all countries, local–regional perspectives are governed by the availability of materials. In this, they are partially prescribed in the same way as any other genre of historical writing. Researchers on early modern American legal history, for example, have always been drawn to the state of Virginia (and especially the Chesapeake area) because the sources are peculiarly plentiful. While this work clearly illuminates vital social relations in early American history – between landowners, indentured servants, slaves, indigenous people and the law – it cannot necessarily be taken as reflective of the entire United States experience. A similar picture emerges for early modern urban development in Massachusetts, which has attracted historians in disproportionate quantities because of available sources. The settlers in these towns were highly literate, and left many records, but are not typical of the wider colonial experience in America.

In the nineteenth century, the growth of new communities, through urbanisation and migration, and the demise of old settlements, due to structural population change, invested contemporaries with a desire to record their history at local and regional level. Thus from the 1860s history groups (such as the Cumberland and Westmorland Archaeological and Antiquarian Society) proliferated, dedicated as they were to promoting an understanding of their regions. The results, which can be seen in the published proceedings of these organisations, touch on many aspects of the past: from the history of local churches and parishes to reports on the discovery of flint axe-heads in previously unknown sites of archaeological importance. As this formalisation of local and regional identity marched in time with the professionalisation of the academic discipline in the late nineteenth century, such far-flung endeavours were dubbed 'antiquarianism', and the appellation is still used in certain circles today.

Many of these local societies still exist today. At the same time, one of the most vigorous areas of local history is that of genealogy and family history. The local groups dedicated to uncovering family trees are numerous. Recent times have also witnessed the emergence of community history of a different kind. Local history suggests there is a unity of purpose which underpins our idea of community, and the numbers of those writing their own local histories are immense, touching most ethnic and all social groups. With such endeavour grows a new history of life-style, consumption and attitudes, and a vital source-base of autobiographical materials and oral reminiscences.

Local perspectives unite a disparate army of researchers, from genealogists to community groups; from the pioneers of people's history to the *Annales* School. The classic study which set this genre in motion was Bjorn Hansen's *Österlen* (1952), while Le Roy Ladurie modelled his classic study, *Montaillou*, on 'community studies' of Andalusia, Provence and East Anglia.

Although in Britain the spirit of amateurism (this time used in a positive sense) still pervades local history, from the 1930s a different, professional strand began to emerge. In that decade, two concurrent trends changed the face and the reputation of local history. The first was encapsulated in A. H. Dodds's *Industrial Revolution in North Wales* (1933). Later, another key development was the appearance of an *Annales*-type historical geography, as represented by Hoskins's classic, *The Making of the English Landscape* (1955). While this book is a genuinely national study, it is also superbly nuanced with distinctly local and regional examples of the way modernisation or decay have altered the world in which we live. The first developments, leading from Dodds's book, were dominated by the perspectives of social and economic history, examining in particular the impact of the Industrial Revolution in a regional context. The best examples are W. H. Chaloner's *The Social and Economic Development of Crewe, 1780–1923* (1950) and J. D. Marshall's monumental *Furness and the Industrial Revolution* (1958). The jacket of Marshall's book carries biographical details which sum up the context of many local historians. J. D. Marshall, we learn, is of north-country stock. For this reason his intimate knowledge of the region he writes about is formed on residence, kinship and friendships, as well as academic considerations. Other aspects of Marshall's life are also revealing. He spent many years working as an amateur historian, and his *Furness and the Industrial Revolution* was researched and written as a thesis which he prepared without academic supervision. Despite working full-time while ploughing this lonely furrow, Marshall was awarded a doctorate by the University of London in 1956. Marshall's introduction captures his vision of local history. Declaring his contribution to knowledge modest, Marshall goes on to say: 'In order that it could be of any value at all, I had to sift and assemble the results of research into many aspects of Furness (and also English) history, to show their interconnections and significance.' There is a sense, then, in which works of local history are acknowledged by their authors to be a building-block from which some larger edifice is built, as it is with the *Annales* School. Marshall's and Chaloner's works are, of course, dated now – nevertheless, nothing has usurped their particular contributions to their own localities, and they are still required reading for students studying the Industrial Revolution in any depth. Marshall's footnotes are exhaustive, testament to his reading of all important secondary material, as well as his trawling of newspapers, personal correspondence, trade union records, etc. National records are also used to assess the broader context of local developments. As such the methodologies employed owe much to the pioneers of social and economic history, such as Postgate and Cole, and Clapham. These works on Crewe and Furness are in spirit 'total' local histories written in the age of Braudel.

While Marshall's and Chaloner's books predate the invention of microhistory, which occurred in the 1960s and 1970s, and was exemplified in the *Annales* work of Le Roy Ladurie, they nevertheless meet with Giovanni Levi's definition of this brand of 'new history'. Levi claims, in 'On microhistory' (in Peter Burke (ed.), *New Perspectives on Historical Enquiry*), that 'Microhistory as a practice is essentially based on the reduction of the scale of observation, on a microscopic analysis and an intensive study of the documentary material.' Thus, the pioneering local histories published in Britain in the 1950s were linked to the masterpieces of microhistory, like *Montaillou*. Marshall's and Chaloner's perception of local history suggests agreement with Levi's view that microhistory is not concerned simply with the uniqueness of 'different dimensions...in every social system', but with explanation of 'vast complex social structures without losing sight of the scale of each individual's social space and hence, of people and their situation in life'. Thus local/microhistory is not the natural result of the historian's emphasis on empirical detail. In France, for example, microhistory grew at least partly as an acknowledgement that Braudelian total history, with its grandiose schemes for long-run, often comparative history, flattened the contours of regional difference. For this reason, microhistory was viewed as the only dimension in which totality could actually be discovered. This is a compelling reason for the study of the local in history, although, as we now see, traditional forms remain popular.

TRADITIONAL HISTORY

Traditional history usually assumes the narrative form. Narrative, the sequential telling of a story, the history of events, and inevitably the history of those men who act them out, has for long been the subject of debate. Paul Lacombe (1839–1919), who influenced the later *Annales*, argued that the main problem with the historians of his time was their preoccupation with contingency and chance, with people and events. From its inception in 1929, the *Annales* dismissed narrative as simply the 'history of events', that which Braudel dubbed mere foam on the waves of history. And since that time, the historical community has been riven between those, usually political historians, who write biographies and narratives, and those social and economic historians who emphasise the importance of structures. More recently, Hayden White has argued that narrative is a kind of fictional device utilised by historians to impose an order and uniformity on dead people and past events.

Whatever the reservations among academic historians over the narrative tradition, the academic works that sell the best and are most accessible to the general reading public are those written in a traditional fashion. Biographies and narratives are at a premium, so that, for example, Simon Schama's largely narrative *Citizens* (1989) has and will sell far more copies than the more analytical *Oxford History of the French*

Revolution (1989) by another leading British scholar of the subject, William Doyle. Narrative history is especially popular. This can be seen in child, adolescent and adult reading patterns and there is an interesting parallel in literature, where the continued preference for stories, and a narrative approach, defies powerful academic literary fashions. The persistent popularity of the detective novel is especially noteworthy. This genre stresses the role of individuals and chance, has little directly to say about social background, and thrives on strong narrative structure. It offers exciting, often exemplary, stories, which are precisely what are sought by most readers of history. In combination, the Whig approach and narrative offer the most accessible means to produce a clear account of what is a highly complex subject: human history.

Left-wing and socialist historians, moreover, also accept the importance of narrative history, although they stress the way in which it changes like any other, written and rewritten by generation after generation. Raphael Samuel, in his essay 'Grand narratives' (*History Workshop Journal*, 1990), incisively comments: 'The contours of the national past are continually changing shape. Mountains turn out to have been molehills while conversely tumuli, as they appeared at the time, may seem, on a longer view, to be foothills of a mighty peak.' To illustrate his point, Samuel asks: 'Who now remembers Henry VIII's capture of Boulogne? Yet in the seventeenth-century almanacks . . . it was rated of equal importance to the Norman Conquest.' Thus, we might ask, are there events which we remember today which might mean little to our descendants in fifty or five hundred years? What will Britons make of our obsession with Dunkirk many years from now?

Historical imagination, national pride and personal prejudices dictate the events which flow from the historian's pen. What else makes narrative so interesting to historians? G. R. Elton, in *The Practice of History* (1967), argued that history comprises a series of unique and unrepeatable events and thus does not lend itself to theorisation. At the same time, although Elton was a critic of theoretical history, he also rejected biography as unhistorical and disconnected. Thus Elton undertook a narrative-type history: his Henry VIII or his Thomas Cromwell all had character; his stories had meaning; yet his creations were underpinned by theories of sort – the notion that there was a revolution in government under the Tudors. Elton was concerned to re-create, to reconstruct history in the tradition of the finest chroniclers. At the same time as Elton was writing, however, others like Christopher Hill, Rodney Hilton, Eric Hobsbawm and E. P. Thompson were producing a more theoretical history.

In the late 1970s, Lawrence Stone, in 'The Revival of Narrative' (*Past and Present*, 1979), claimed that narrative history was ascendant again; that the history of structures was in some way receding next to the story-teller's art. Moreover, in 1989 Simon Schama published to considerable attention an epic tome, *Citizens: A Chronicle of the French Revolution* (1989), in which he wrote the French Revolution as a connected and longitudinal story. Indeed, Schama himself claimed that his method was to return to the style of the nineteenth-century chroniclers. His justification for this approach constitutes a defence of narrative. This is what Schama says of the French Revolution: 'If, in fact, the French Revolution was a much more haphazard and chaotic event and much more the product of human agency than structural conditioning, chronology seems indispensable in making its complicated twists and turns intelligible.' This is why Schama returns to the style of the great historians of the nineteenth century, charting the ebbs and flows of history as they happened: year after year, month after month, day after day. Thus Schama adopts a survey format: to unfold history as it happened. To write chapters on 'economy', 'peasantry' and 'nobility', Schama says, 'privileges their explanatory force', and others agree with him. David Carr (*History and Theory*, 1986) argues that narrative is valuable because narrative histories are written in the way that historical actors themselves saw their world, while Schama, again, says: 'As artificial as written narratives might be, they often correspond to the ways in which historical actors themselves construct events.'

Narrative, of course, has the advantage of being readable. At the same time, narrative often overlooks causation, and there is always a risk that the narrative of events becomes the history of many biographies, and that colourful characters of little historical importance might obscure our overall view. For this reason narrative and biography are often one and the same thing; it is also because of this that both draw the same criticisms. Let us consider biography itself, for biography is in a sense both the zenith and nadir of the chronicler's art, of the literary narrative form.

Although biography has a long history, only relatively recently has there emerged a genuinely critical tradition in this area of historical writing. Thus some Victorian biographies, informative though they often were, degenerated into hagiography. Modern biographies attempt to place and understand the individual in his or her historical context. Today the lives of the great, colourful or important are usually 'warts and all' analyses, utilising *all* available and relevant materials. This genre of biography is, and always has been, hugely popular. Publishers sometimes offer substantial advances and other benefits: for example, Lord Skidelsky was allowed to stay in John Maynard Keynes's château to write his three-volume life of the great economist. This privileged position of the biographer is wholly derived from the market. In recent years, Charles Darwin, Robert Burns and Daniel O' Connell have each been the subject of huge studies. At the same time, François Mitterrand, Margaret Thatcher, Alan Clark – and even John Major's brother! – have made substantial sums from their reminiscences, memoirs or lives. Equally, the past decade or so has seen the penetration of tabloid journalism into every recess of political life, which has shifted public concern from discernment at the interplays of statecraft to prurience at the bedchamber farces of the actors' hidden lives. The thrust of the narrative has thus changed direction.

Biography has generated criticism. In the first place, biographers are accused of a sentimental attachment to the life they study. There is likely to be, in a sense there must be, an identification with the subject matter. In turn, it is argued, this necessarily provides for an interpretation which is biased, overly sympathetic, insufficiently detached or unobjective. Secondly, it can be argued that biographical approaches encourage a linear view of history – birth, life, death; one generation of the 'great and the good' to the next. Because of this, Maurice Cowling argues that 'Biography is always misleading.... Its refraction is partial and is relative to the [political] system. It *abstracts* a man whose public action should *not* be abstracted. It implies linear connections between one situation and the next. In fact, connections were not linear. The system was a *circular relationship*: a shift in one element changes the position of all others in relation to the next.'

What other deficiencies does biography as history have? Park Honan, in 'Some problems in biography' (*Victorian Studies*, 1973), suggests that, historically, it has *always* relied too heavily on intuitive method and *selective* use of source materials. A biographer, in other words, will obtain a 'feel' of what a character is like and then select evidence which proves or illustrates the biographer's perception. The notion that biographers are selective was formally acknowledged a long time ago in Lytton Strachey's debunking *Eminent Victorians* (1918). Here he argued that his generation (those living around the time of the First World War) could never properly write of the Victorian age because they knew it too well already. Strachey went on: 'ignorance is the first requisite of the historian – ignorance, which simplifies and clarifies, which selects and omits. The Victorian age had produced such a quantity of information that the industry of a Ranke would be sub-

merged by it, and the perspicacity of a Gibbon would quail before it.'
Brevity, for Strachey, was of the essence for the biographer: 'exclude
everything that is redundant and nothing that is significant', he argued.
But here we are back at the root of the problem – how do we select and
what do we select? Who decides?

On the other hand, a characteristic of *modern* biography is its inclu-
siveness. The huge and imperious 1000-page tome of today, the size of
which is meant to imply authority, is a real departure from Strachey's
appeals for brevity. Biographies today get fatter and fatter as authors
become more and more fearful of omitting stuff of relevance, and are
pressed to say more about the private as well as the public life of their
subject. This contemporary fixation with weightiness, what amounts to
the philosophy of modern biography, is encapsulated in the words of
James MacKay, the acknowledged expert on the great Scottish bard, in
Burns: a Life of Robert Burns (1992): 'My approach has been to examine
every so-called fact about the life of Robert Burns, and trace it right
back to its source as far as possible in order to establish its provenance.'
MacKay goes on to list the sources he used: parish registers of baptisms,
marriages and burials; Kirk Session books; masonic lodge minutes;
Sheriff Clerk Office and Commissary records; even, he adds, 'the
day-book of the surgeon who treated Burns in Irvine – as well as
contemporary newspapers, periodicals and directories'. Having used
all the sources he could find, MacKay declares, 'The results have
been nothing short of astonishing, for many of the discrepancies in
the Burns story have now been resolved', so that 'it is possible, for the
first time ever, to provide a definitive life of the poet'.

There is a certain positivism to these outpourings. Part of the explanation for the stodginess of biography is born from its source-base.
Political events, and individual roles in them, are particularly well
documented. This in itself might be a justification for biography; that
'Great Men' show up frequently in state papers – in *Hansard*, in cabinet
minutes – is taken to imply their right to be studied. Also, the presence
of political actors in the state papers of their day reduces the historian's
reliance on the subject's own conception of themselves, as witnessed
through diaries and memoirs. Past politicians might write their diaries
for posterity, but they cannot – theoretically at least – doctor their
official documents, although the reality can be very different.

Historians are much more accommodating towards historical biography, the contextualised life; the life as part of a wider sequence of
events and occurrences. Let us consider the arguments put forward by
Norman Gash, a noted political historian and biographer of Lord

Liverpool and Robert Peel, in his article 'A modest defence of biography' (*Pillars of Government*, 1986), and by Ben Pimlott, the left-wing political commentator and biographer of Harold Wilson, in his recent work 'Frustrate Their Knavish Tricks' (*Writings on Biography, History and Politics*, 1994).

Gash notes the clear paradox that while political biography has never been more popular, questions continue to be asked of its *legitimacy* as a branch of historical inquiry. Professional historians involved in the genre have been accused of being meretricious and of adopting biography as a soft, money-spinning option, or a chance to go public with the 'my favourite historical character' approach to writing history. As part of his case, Gash reminds us of two famous defences of biography. First, Thomas Carlyle's claim in his nineteenth-century study, *Heroes and Hero-Worship*, that 'universal History, the history of what men have accomplished in their works, is at bottom the history of the Great Men who have worked here'. Secondly, he remembers Disraeli's exhortation: 'Read no history, nothing but biography: for that is life without theory.' Here, then, we find ourselves at the core of the problem: that biography works bests in a nineteenth-century context when 'Great Men' wrote about each other when they had time to do so; for they had servants, but no telephones. For Victorian scholars history writing was seen as an ameliorative against the new social science; similarly, biography was seen to rescue men and men's actions from the reductionism of science.

Biography has come a long way since the nineteenth century and certainly does not have to be trivial or trivialised. After all, there is good and bad biography, just as there is good and bad history. At root, though, is the problem of who writes historical biographies. In many cases they *are* the products of amateurs – often amateurs without a sufficient sense of historical context – who flit, as Gash notes, 'like butterflies from flower to flower, from century to century, from country to country in their endless quest for rewarding subjects'. The important point has to be that without the historical context in which they should be embedded the subjects of these biographies, the actors themselves, can easily loom 'larger than life'. Amateur historians, therefore, almost by accident or omission, oversimplify and distort. In this way, the case might be made for historical biography rather than simply biography.

Much history is concerned with the analysis and interpretation of situations, events, policies, organisations, legislation, and so on. Biography poses different problems. It focuses, or it should focus, on temperament, character and personality; moreover, these are less precise and

more difficult things. Equally, historical biography is nothing but hagiography if the writer fails to understand and state those crucial
matters of context which dwarf even the giants of history like Hitler
and Stalin. Thus, it can be argued, historical biography is demanding
indeed. Gash's eloquent defence of the art form, which he would rather
were more scientific, is extremely persuasive. He refutes the charge that
biographies are easy to write. On the contrary, Gash argues, the
biographer must know the subject's society as well as his own, and
must convey the actor's character to the reader in a convincing fashion.
In addition to this, the task of the biographer is to balance 'private
motives and public issues': to encompass the many spheres of influence
of the central character. Not only this, but also 'to give physical
appearance, the voice, the gestures, the little human touches familiar
to contemporaries, to bring to bear on evidence a disciplined imagination without which the biography itself remains dead'.

   Gash then goes on to articulate three key and distinct justifications of
biography as a legitimate, worthy, but above all, scholarly branch of
historical inquiry. First, he says, it is 'philosophically legitimate' to study
men and their actions. Secondly, that it is 'professionally valuable' to do
so – that there is something to be learned, that the skills required *are*
those of the historian and not those of the hack or hagiographer.
Thirdly, that it is 'humanely important' to write lives, by which he
means that we cannot reduce all of our past to a science without
people.

   Defenders of traditional approaches argue that unless a deterministic
view of history is to be accepted, historians must be prepared to
recognise the existence of chance and accident in human events: the
idea (expressed by Elton) that history is a series of unrepeatable events;
that people are important in history; that a narrative of human events *is*
the stuff of true history. The actual question of determinism (the idea
that everything is determined by an unbreakable, in a sense unknow-
able, chain of causation – whether social, economic or, as the *Annales*
said, 'ecological') is one for theologians, philosophers and physicists; but
it is not clear to the layman that they are agreed on an answer. In fact,
it might be argued, in defence of biography, that there are few things
which are certain or inevitable in human history. But to accept this is
not to argue that all is chaotic chance; instead it is simply to say that
there is in human activity an *element* of chance – of will, choice, the
personal, the unpredictable, and the fortuitous. Surely, proponents of
biography would argue, the individual is a significant element in the
process and therefore a fit and proper subject of historical inquiry.

Marx, for example, never questioned the importance of individual actions in history. The introduction to H. C. G. Matthew's *Gladstone, 1809–1874* (1986) confirms this. Taking as his starting point Marx's dictum, 'Men make their own history, but not of their own free will; not under circumstances they themselves have chosen but given and inherited circumstances with which they are directly confronted', Matthew goes on to say: 'Of few can Marx's truism be truer than of William Ewart Gladstone. His epic public career – first in office in 1834, last in 1894 – confronted the prime of Britain as the first industrial nation.' Although Gladstone's lifetime was circumscribed by forces of change which were beyond his control, his 'interpretation, execution and explanation ... hold a central place'.

Thus, we might argue, biography might also been seen as a useful corrective to impersonal history, for the past with the people taken out might lead to generalisations and abstractions. Can we understand class, feudalism or revolution without some recourse to the people involved? Then again, that is not necessarily an appeal for or defence of biography, but an appeal for a humanistic approach to the past. Biography might also take the historian along paths which he/she might not have anticipated; or with which he/she is not familiar. With biography, more than any other form, the subject matter dictates the nooks and crannies of investigation. Perhaps the most persuasive defence of biography is the most simple of Gash's arguments: that it answers a profound human need. Gash notes the comment of the celebrated Dutch historian, Pieter Geyl, who wrote that what attracted him to history was that it seemed to be 'a key to life – in its richness, in its triumphs and in its tragedies'. And biography by definition offers a key to the understanding of life. Gash also notes that literary characters such as Hamlet or Don Quixote can often seem more real than historical characters such as Catherine the Great or Gladstone. But why is that the case?

In fiction the writer is God; omniscient and omnipotent; a giver and taker of life. He or she invents characters and takes hold of their lives; we are told of their every foible and skill and we share in the author's sense of destiny, the idea of the guiding hand. The historian, by contrast, cannot or should not fabricate; although many do speculate about aspects of their subject's ideas and actions. But the evidence for the historian is prescribed. The historian, the best sort of biographer, can only use the available evidence. But the historian is dealing with reality, not with the product of imagination. The truth, of course, can be stranger than fiction.

The literary connection in biography is pursued in Ben Pimlott's work. Citing Aneurin Bevan's dictum that 'biography is fiction', Pimlott suggests that biography's most important relationship is in fact with the novel. Looking at the history of biography writing, Pimlott argues that all biography has a constructional similarity – all biography begins with birth and ends with death; that it tells a story of a life, from beginning to end. Pimlott also argues that much biography is compartmentalised into public and private aspects – separate boxes, if you like. Yet if we take Churchill, for example, Pimlott argues that the private failings (such as at Harrow School) of the great wartime Prime Minister were central to explaining his political career. At the same time, he adopts a censorious tone in asking that future biographers should be driven by the need to 'understand' a public life, not to sink into the mire of 'kiss-and-tell' revelations, which are always the focus of tabloid serialisation. The short, contextualised life will necessarily avoid these things, glossing over more important biographical details to strike at the ideas and actions of individuals in the space allowed by publishers and editors. The Manchester University Press series, *Lives of the Left*, is a fine example of the 'bare-bones' approach. In the introduction to his short study of the American Socialist, *Daniel De Leon* (1990), Stephen Coleman writes: 'I must plead guilty to an absence of biographical interest in the deeper qualities or defects of De Leon's personality, nor would I expect others to evaluate the political ideas of a Marx, a Mill or a Morris on the basis of criteria which are best left to computer dating agencies.'

Historically, biographies have been written as propaganda; in admiration of their subject matter. They have drawn heavily on the correspondence of the subject and similar documentation generated by contemporaries: letters, diaries, memoirs, etc. Most of this material naturally deals with adult life, and the years of childhood and youth (when sources are often limited) – what psychologists would call 'formative' periods – are often given only a few pages – which in itself flies in the face of Pimlott's claim that private lives impinge on public ones; surely, then, schooling, as in the case of Churchill, should get more attention? Here we have another example of the subject's own material and emphasis driving biography in a particular direction. To criticise biographers and their subjects is to criticise a particularly Victorian *modus operandi*. Yet the 'Great Man' thesis is by no means dead and buried today. However, the interest in long-run, structural history has grown apace since the days when Disraeli pleaded for a history made up of people's lives.

COMPARATIVE HISTORY

The pursuit of comparison in history is dogged by methodological and source-related problems. Traditional historians might argue, for example, that any comparison of, say, politics in Germany, France and Britain should involve research in the national archives of all three. Therefore, this would require a working knowledge of three languages and massive resources of time and money; as the comparative framework grows, so too does the requirement for linguistic competence. For this reason, many of the great comparative works of this century are based predominantly on secondary reading. In the case of Braudel's *Civilisation and Capitalism* (1979), for example, that secondary reading is prodigiously wide. Originally intended to complement volumes by Febvre (who died before they could be written), *Civilisation and Capitalism* bears a striking structural resemblance to a Marxist conception of society. Its three volumes are principally concerned with modes and impacts of consumption, distribution and production in the old regime (1400–1800). The project constitutes a genuine attempt to write world history, for in it Braudel attempts systematically to unite, by comparison, the major civilisations of the Eastern and Western worlds – India, China, Japan and Indonesia; the Americas and Europe. In so doing, it combines the 'history of everyday life' with greater social and economic developments. Its central quest is to discover the material culture of the period. One of the best examples of genuinely wide-ranging comparative history, written in recent times, is Barrington Moore, Jun., *Social Origins of Dictatorship and Democracy* (1966), a monumental study of the landowner–peasant relations in a bewildering array of countries: England, France, America, China, Japan and India. Moore's aim was to show how varying material and cultural circumstances in different places gave rise to parliamentary democracy, Fascism or Communism. It is a breathtaking book when read as one complex whole; however, historians of different countries or different subjects tend to atomise such studies, so that while the *Origins of Dictatorship and Democracy* is seductive in general, its component parts are criticised. This reflects both the problems of comparative history as well as the tendencies of historians themselves. At the same time, comparison remains something that historians – especially those with a strong theoretical grounding (for this enables the ordering of complex materials) – try to achieve.

In the mid–1970s, when the journal *Social History* was first published it contained a kind of constitution for social history. In that constitution, the editors outlined the philosophy of their journal. Social history, they argued, should be about big ideas as well as small ones; about structural change as well as specific instances of what are broadly social factors in society. The same constitution also contained the words 'comparative history'. Comparativity, they stated, could add perspective to social history; comparativity could alleviate national prejudices or narrow-mindedness; comparativity was intellectually sound and was a defence mechanism against inward-looking attitudes. This was the age of growing union in Western Europe and the beginning of the Global Village (the idea that the modern world has been drawn together by communications), factors which clearly affected historical scholarship.

Comparative history premises the notion of extending knowledge, or of locating historical phenomena in comparative context, and this itself provides reason enough for students and scholars to come to grips with the implications of comparative approaches. But we also have equally pressing personal reasons for so doing. While professional historians usually specialise during research, they have to teach much broader aspects of history to be of any use to students. The latter are often faced with courses that are at least subconsciously comparative: for example, 'Anglo-American relations, 1945–1996', 'Medieval Europe, Islam and Christianity' or 'The Emergence of the Working Class, 1750–1950'. Each of these courses assumes some degree of comparative element. Thus to make the comparative element of such courses explicit is to understand specific and general historical occurrences.

Comparison allows us to understand both the *essential* and the *particular*. What is meant by these terms? The *essential* factors are those things which apply beyond rigid boundaries. *Essential* factors are what we might term *general* factors. These phenomena have some kernel of meaning across religious, cultural, national and historical boundaries: class, kinship, feudalism or democracy might be examples. Each should be sensitive in terms of national/local practice, but their core assumptions are applicable on a comparative level. For example, while the term 'working class' might mean something different in France and Scotland, scholars and students can use agreed indices of measurement in comparing this difference. We might talk about economic influences or cultural influences; we might chart different events in the history of class – but certain statements will provide the bedrock of the comparison.

On the other hand, *particular* factors are things with which comparative historians are less concerned. The *particular* is usually confined to surface occurrences: remember, for example, Braudel's comment, in his *Mediterranean*, that events are 'surface disturbances, crests of foam that the tides of history carry on their strong backs'. Thus a comparison of class in France and in Scotland is less concerned with particular events, or with the Trades Union Council (the leadership of British trade unions) or of individual unions, except to see how, for example, unionisation did or did not reflect socio-economic factors and instances of class-consciousness. On the other hand, class cohesion or antagonism would concern the comparative historians, because of the framework provided by Marx and because struggle or compliance serve as useful indices of historical development, although the Marxist analysis is limited in some regards when it comes to explaining long-run social change *and* more immediate political pressures. The events would merely provide support to a statement such as 'Class organisation in France and Scotland responded to basically similar economic impulses, but diverged wildly as a result of religious–cultural influences as represented by Catholicism, on the one hand, and Calvinism on the other.'

Comparative dimensions to historical inquiry also provide a crucial check on explanatory models, leading, for example, to the conclusion that explanation in case x may not be applicable in case y. For this reason comparison occupies a special place in social theory and was vital in the formative years of the development of sociology. The nineteenth-century French sociologist, Emile Durkheim (1858–1917), claimed that 'comparative sociology is not a special branch of sociology. It is sociology itself' (*Suicide*, 1895). Durkheim offers two principal areas of comparison. First, societies which were/are apparently similar: Greek and Roman; German and French; British and American. Secondly (and here we might use 'contrast'), those societies and civilisations which were different: for example, British and Indian, Chinese and European. Max Weber (1864–1920), the German social theorist, supported the principle of comparison as central to understanding the past. He wrote: 'We are absolutely in accord that history should establish what is specific, say, to the medieval city; but this is possible only if we first find what is missing in other cities' (G. Roth, 'History and sociology in the work of Max Weber', *British Journal of Sociology*, 27, 1976). By the latter he means ancient Chinese and Islamic cities. A classic example of comparative history on a grand scale is Weber's 'Social Psychology of the World Religions' (1915). This essay, the introduction to more detailed works, is a grand tour of five major beliefs – Confucianism, Hinduism, Buddhism, Christianity and Islam – in fifty pages of text. In this study, Weber identifies what he believes are the salient comparisons and contrasts between the various religions, in terms of their rise, leadership, support-base and charisma, etc. Weber's study effectively covers thousands of years and ranges across the Orient and Occident. It is not, however, a study primarily in the historian's mode, and is not based upon primary research. Instead it is an attempt to draw out comparative trends. It is based fundamentally upon Weber's conception of the social–pyschological role of religion which was, for him (as for Marx), underpinned by key factors which existed irrespective of time, location or denomination. This, it might be argued, is the key feature of comparison in social theory, although most historians would balk at claiming such work as 'history proper'.

Comparative history, of a modernist kind, was first promoted by the *Annales* School. Indeed, Marc Bloch's *The Royal Touch* (1924) is one of the classic examples of early comparative history. *The Royal Touch*, as we saw in the previous chapter, is a study of culture, superstition and belief in early modern France and Britain, where it was believed that the monarch's touch could cure the skin disease scrofula. Another of Bloch's works, *Feudal Society* (1940), is also classically comparative. This book is not confined to an examination of land tenure and social relations under feudalism, but looks at the whole of feudal society. Moreover, although Bloch's focus is primarily upon European feudalism, it also considers Japanese Samurai culture. While historians might question the utility of comparison, these are fine examples of the principle in action.

What, then, are the strengths of comparative history? The historian's perspective can be strengthened by syntheses which range broadly over space and time. In the case of communities we can begin to understand something of the dynamic of work-place, residential and life-chance experiences by the comparision of one or more communities, as this brings home the multi-textured, multi-layered nature of the historical past. At the same time, no society should be viewed in isolation, for none in practice exists in a vacuum, and our analysis cannot be advanced in isolation. Even in times before mass communication – say, the ancient or medieval periods – people knew about other countries and cultures, and often generally defined their own identity with reference to the perceived civilisation or barbarism of these other countries and cultures. Particularly, then, in the age before the modern nation–state, there were supra-national institutions and practices which transcended the nation or the locality. The internationalisation of Catholicism in the high Middle Ages is a good example. Rome was more than just the centre of the Papal States. The Pope was spiritual overlord of most Western European peoples. 'Eastern' religions, like

Islam and Buddhism, also expressed belief systems which went far beyond the domains of rulers or individual territories.

Similarly, perhaps, the Hanseatic trade organisation in northern Europe connected the medieval economies of The Netherlands, Germany and Scandinavia, and while its ships may have taken wines to England or Scotland, they transported ideas as well. People, even then, had a sense of the exotic, of what was going on elsewhere within diferent cultures. Pilgrimages and the Crusades expanded the imaginative worlds of Western Europe. Some Western Europeans knew about the Islamic cultures of Asia and Africa, just as they would come to know the Mongols in the thirteenth and fourteenth centuries. The Spanish were only too familiar with their Moorish neighbours, and during the later medieval period great southern cities like Granada, Seville and Cordoba housed the three religions of Christianity, Islam and Judaism.

Most historians naturally think of their material in an implicitly comparative way, even if only to elicit national or regional 'differences' and to make judgements in terms of, say, success, failure, aggression and prosperity. These notions only take on their real meaning in a comparative context.

Comparative approaches to history, and the methods which underpin them, have come under assault at various times. Certain criticisms are not without validity. Many early social theorists – such as Marx, Durkheim and Weber – employed comparison to measure the evolution of societies, presenting society as a kind of biological entity, evolving all the while. In this sense there is a positivism, an apparent inevitability, about social development; that, for the Victorians, Britain in 1850 was at a later (superior) stage of development to that of earlier British society or to the contemporary tribesmen in colonial Africa. Tied into this is an innate comparison of lesser and greater civilisations. Such approaches imply that society is inevitably progressing down a particular path. Nothing is allowed for the fact that African tribesmen lived in a completely different world from the Victorians. One of the key problems, then, is that certain comparisons – say of European modernism or African backwardness – are ethnocentrist, and do not allow for the plurality of interests and experiences which in fact make comparison so difficult. Moreover, such comparison implicitly suggests that the European world is the norm by which all others should be measured. Comparing feudalism in Europe and Asia can lead to superficial comparisons – or to comparisons which are, at heart, simply cultural contrasts or possibly racist. Thus we see a continual tension in approaches and applications of historical method.

'HISTORY FROM BELOW'

To move from comparative history to 'history from below' might seem a long journey, but it is in fact a perfect metaphor for the huge scale and range of historical inquiry. At this stage, readers will begin to see that history is an organic discipline – evolving, changing and responding to its environment. The emergence of 'history from below' is a classic example of this development. As a sub-area of historical inquiry, 'history from below' has elicited great interest among Indian and South American as well as European and North American scholars.

In the first sense, 'history from below' was reactive; it provided, as its name suggests, an alternative to 'top people's history', or the 'Great Man' view of history. In the sense that history has grown away from a lofty nineteenth-century vision of the great deeds of ruling elites, 'history from below' is perhaps the most obvious single expression of that growth. 'History from below' is an attempt to understand 'real' people. It also promoted the evaluation of those seemingly lost in the past: the lives and thoughts of pre-modern peasants; the development of the working class; the activities and actions of women and men whose lived experience was thought by scholars to be of no interest. History from 'below' rather than from 'above' thus called for new methods and sources, or else for the radical reinterpretation of traditional materials. 'History from below' is classically brought to life from fragments of the past: by reading the ballad, poster or the protest banner; by delving into working-class autobiography or oral reminiscences; by re-reading records of state surveillance of working-class movements, for here might be displayed some of the tensions between upper and lower society, governments and ordinary people. 'History from below' is the study of the hedgerow or the allotment; the poor-law record or the headstone. The search for sources for the view from below is fuelled by the idea that everything has a history and nothing is without a story to tell.

In different quarters, 'history from below' has different names. Terms like 'people's history', the 'history of everyday life' – while not always exactly 'history from below' – are parts of the same movement. Each reflects the democratisation of history, as is the case with local history, and the desire to give back to the people the right to study their own history, and to have their own history studied. Democratisation, then, means to take history back from elites and to give it to the people. True 'history from below' must be for the majority and about the majority, a history which above all is about the working class and its progenitors. The roots of 'history from below', therefore, lie in the reaction against elitism. During the early twentieth century, a number of groups began to compile 'people's history', drawing their inspiration from writers such as Thorold Rogers, the anti-Tory author of a huge seven-volume study, *History of Agriculture and Prices* (1864–1902), which was, effectively, a treatise on social and domestic economy. In the 1920s and 1930s, Marxist and Socialist self-educators in Britain, many published by the Left Book Club, produced cheap histories, and encouraged community history-writing, looking back to Rogers and his generation. 'History from below' also had exponents in the *Annales* School, although, as we shall see later, they usually went under the banner of the parallel movement 'cultural history', or the 'history of mentalities'. In the 1940s and 1950s, this development of British Marxist traditions continued under the umbrella of the Communist Party of Great Britain's Historians Group, where historians such as Eric Hobsbawm and E. P. Thompson began to build their powers of historical argument. It was this forum – a mixing together of European Communist thought, political activity and intellectual fertility – which also saw the birth of the journal *Past and Present* (1952) and, later, the Society for the Study of Labour History and its journal, *Labour History Review*.

'History from below' approaches encapsulated a growing desire to expand the frontiers of social history, and were driven by what Marx called the need to understand the 'masses'. An interest in 'history from below' developed rapidly as a sub-current of labour history, which began with the Webbs' bulky study of trade unionism. Yet many of these early labour histories were elitist and exclusionist, reflecting the tensions within the labour movement and its hierarchical make-up, as well as the nature of the sources used. Thus they concentrated on formal labour organisations, such as trade unions, and largely excluded the study of women and non-unionised labour, in favour of a triumphalist look at the growth of the TUC and the birth of the Labour Party. In short, this grass-roots history was not really grass-roots at all, and might be dubbed the 'Whig view of labour history'.

In 1985, Frederick Krantz pooled the writings of a number of historians to produce a volume of essays, *History From Below: Studies in Popular Protest and Popular Ideology*, in honour of George Rudé, a leading Marxist historian of France and Britain. Krantz, in his introduction, argues that Rudé's work – from his *The Crowd in the French Revolution* (1959) to his study of popular protest in France and England, 1730–1848, *The Crowd in History* (1964) – was all concerned with 'history from below'. He writes that Rudé's work has been concerned with ordinary urban and rural workers, 'participants through various forms of "popular action" in the great French and Industrial Revolutions which have shaped modernity', and not with dominant elites. Here, then, we have the literal interpretation of 'history from below' as 'people's history', the foundation of what Eric Hobsbawm calls 'grass-roots history'; the history of the *real* 'common people'. Rudé, Krantz argued, is emblematic of the 'history from below' school: expressing a concern with ordinary people and the crowds they formed – not only popular actions but more precisely with what made them tick; their ideas as well as their actions. Rudé himself, in *The Crowd in the French Revolution*, stated that his intention was to get inside the minds of those past groups and peoples that he studied: to understand the crowd: 'how it behaved, how it was composed, how it was drawn into its activities, what it set out to achieve and how far its aims were realised'.

We know, then, that since the late nineteenth century, there has been a reaction against 'top people's history'; however, it has been argued that not until the 1960s was 'history from below' formulated in cogent and clear fashion. It was Georges Lefebvre, the French historian of the French Revolution, writing in the 1930s, who first used the term 'history from below'. Yet Jim Sharpe, in 'History from below' (in Peter Burke (ed.), *New Perspectives on Historical Writing*), argues that the publication of E. P. Thompson's essay, 'History From Below', in the *Times Literary Supplement* (1966), was the real starting point, not only of the term, but of attempts to define it; to intellectualise about it and to give it a coherent agenda. 'Thereafter', Sharpe claims, 'the concept of history from below entered the common parlance of historians.' Thompson's essay was born directly out of his monumental study of class development, *The Making of the English Working Class* (1963). This classic work is in itself an exposition of the basic tenets of bottom-up approaches to history. In the preface, Thompson expounded a clear view of what history should be about; his words have become something of a totem for practitioners of 'history from below': 'I am seeking', Thompson states, 'to rescue the poor stockinger, the Luddite cropper, the "obsolete" hand-loom weaver, the "utopian" artisan, and even the deluded follower of Joanna Southcott [the early nineteenth-century prophetess and author of *The Strange Effects of Faith* (1801)], from the enormous condescension of posterity.' The 'enormous condescension' to which Thompson refers is a hangover from the nineteenth century, when most historians saw the working class as an incidental thing next to the history of politicians, kings and queens. Thompson, though, was also reacting against more enlightened studies of the Industrial Revolution which, nevertheless, ignored or dismissed Luddites and the handloom weavers as the inevitable victims of the process of historical change, as a tragic aside to the rise of the modern factory system and the progress of mature industrial capitalism.

The major criticisms of 'history from below' concern the ideological interests of its major protagonists. Many critics suggest 'history from below' is too Marxist in approach. It has been argued that because of its Marxist tradition, 'history from below' concentrated more on struggle than on acquiescence, and focused on 'heroic' or revolutionary phases in the development of the working class, for example, radicalism during the French Revolutionary period and after (Thompson) or the Chartist movement (John Saville). At the same time, criticisms were also levelled at the chronological leaning of the 'history from below' writers in Britain, saying that too much emphasis was given to the period after 1789 because of the preference for class and class-consciousness as explanatory devices. This tendency towards the modern period derives partly from the nature of sources, premised upon the idea that the further back the historian goes the harder it is to find evidence of the common life, but it is a valid criticism.

The chronological criticisms, nevertheless, have some foundation, although if 'history from below' is defined very broadly then the cultural history we examine later can be seen very clearly to be of the same school, and this, like the *Annales* generally, very much centres upon the early modern world. Moreover, cultural historians have succeeded in uncovering a wide range of disparate materials. Some British historians of the 'history from below' tradition, such as Rodney Hilton (the medieval period) and Christopher Hill (the seventeenth century), have focused on earlier periods, but they meet criticism on the grounds that they simply project modernist notions of class-consciousness backwards into a period before class existed. At the same time, however, we must remember that these are stock criticisms of the Marxist tradition, and do not relate to 'history from below' alone.

Within the *Annales* School the reception of Marxism has been at best ambiguous and 'history from below' approaches there have consequently received much less ideologically driven criticisms. One of the classic works of the genre is, in fact, Emmanuel Le Roy Ladurie's *Montaillou: Cathars and Catholics in a French Village, 1294–1324* (1975). As the title suggests, this micro-study is an evaluation of ideas and beliefs in a peasant community. As such it represents a double breakthrough. Not only does Le Roy Ladurie give us an interpretation of the lives and actions of real people, but he also offers insights into the grass-roots of the medieval period. In addition, Le Roy Ladurie's work presents us with something of a revolution in sources, using official church records to write 'history from below'. The development of these newer and more broad-ranging approaches to 'history from below' have led to an improvement in this new branch of history. Of course, 'history from below' is not a separate discipline. It does not exist in a vacuum, nor does it survive without reference to the 'history from above'. The wider social structure cannot be ignored, nor can the actions of elites.

CULTURAL HISTORY, OR THE HISTORY OF MENTALITIES

Cultural history, what the French call 'l'histoire des mentalités' ('history of mentalities'), is closely allied to 'history from below'. Although less reliant upon Marxism, it is arguably, nevertheless, part of the same family. In its most obvious sense, the 'history of mentalities' is the study of people's cultures; their individual and collective ideas. There are Marxist cultural historians, such as Michel Vovelle, but Burke, in *History and Social Theory*, says it is possible to argue that certain cultural historians or social anthropologists (Lévi-Strauss in particular) 'turned Marx on his head, in other words returned to Hegel, by suggesting that the really deep structures are not economic and social arrangements but mental categories'.

Cultural history and the 'history of mentalities' are used interchangeably here. The 'history of mentalities' emerged in the *Annales* School. It must be borne in mind, however, that some historians still use 'cultural history' in a narrowly defined way, to refer to the history of artistic artefacts. This is not what the French historians, nor the social anthropologists who inspired them, meant by 'cultural' history. We are thus writing about cultural history as the defining types of popular belief and emotion in the way the *Annales* conceived it.

Cultural history developed in the 1960s with Le Roy Ladurie, Robert Mandrou and Jacques Le Goff, who were critical of the 'religious pyschology' approach of earlier generations, particularly Febvre. Febvre, it was argued, looked at big ideas like religion over long periods, with the result that his work allowed little room for the impact of grass-roots notions of popular culture. At the same time, these scholars were also criticial of traditonal histories of ideas and faith which, they claimed, tended to be elitist. The 1960s generation of *Annalistes* moved towards a more populist conception of history, attempting to offer new insights into past worlds by suggesting that ordinary people were involved in the manufacture of their own ideas and cultures. This represented a clear move away from the perception that the lower orders or working class simply received ideas imposed from outside or above. This is the world similar to that manufactured by E. P. Thompson, where the working class was an active participant in its own making. The emphasis, then, is upon the independence of popular culture, often in a world of ribald, Rabelaisian indulgences; popular songs and ballads; 'rough music' and communal justice. Here traditions and ideas were created, not in the chapel or by the middle class, but by 'the people' themselves. This is not hegemony – the imposition of values from above on those below. Nor is it a trickling down of culture. It is robust and seemingly independent.

Peter Burke, in 'Strengths and weaknesses of the history of mentalities' (*History of European Ideas*, 1986), argued that there are three main features of the history of mentalities. First, he says, it stresses collective attitudes: what Durkheim once called 'representational collectives'. Secondly, it concerns unconscious assumptions and everyday thought; practical reason as seen by groups. Thirdly, it focuses on the structure of belief. The 'mentalités' approach thus resembles aspects of social anthropology and owes much to the work of Clifford Geertz, whose analysis of historical artefacts – texts and symbols – added a new dimension to social-anthropological historical inquiry. Geertz's 'Deep play: notes on the Balinese cockfight', in his *Myths, Symbols and Culture* (1971), argues that 'the culture of a people is an ensemble of texts, themselves ensembles, which the anthropologist strains to read over the shoulders of those to whom they properly belong'. Geertz's work employed what he called 'thick description, using intensive case-study material to interpret culture much more broadly'. Latterly, there have been calls, for example by Peter Burke, in *History and Social Theory*, for 'thick narratives', based on the Geertz model. Whereas Geertz's method focused on prominent individuals, Burke argues that 'thick narratives', or 'micro-narratives', 'include stories which present the same evidence from multiple points of view'. The emphasis here seems to be on charting change, rather than assessing ideas or assumptions frozen in time.

Cultural history is thus the history of popular ideas, and therefore different from the classical history of ideas (e.g. that of Hobbes and Locke), because it concentrates on the ideas which influence everyday actions, like riots, ceremonies and rituals, and so on. Cultural history of this type tries to evaluate the mentalities of the past by explaining what were once considered to be unconventional matters, for example, the history of lunacy, crime or magic. Peter Burke claims that the history of mentalities grew up to fill a conscious gap between narrow definitions of the history of ideas and social history. Its development prevents historians from having to make a choice between 'an intellectual history with the society left out and a social history with the thought left out'.

The 'history of mentalities' is more besides. As a leading and influential American practitioner, Robert Darnton, argued in his *The Great Cat Massacre and other Episodes in French Cultural History* (1984), it attempts to show 'how' people thought, not just 'what' they thought. It is concerned with people's construction of their world, 'how they invested it with meaning' and 'infused it with emotion'. Darnton calls mentalities 'anthropological'; history in the 'ethnographic grain'. This is the idea that 'the past is another country'; that we cannot understand the past if we impose our own values on it; that meanings and actions change over time; that the social and cultural pastimes of history do not necessarily equate with the present or have equivalents in our vocabularies. Darnton acknowedged a debt to Claude Lévi-Strauss, whose work on Amazonian totems and taboos in the 1960s was the kind of ethnohistory which might usefully be used to understand the dead world of European culture. Claude Lévi-Strauss, in his *The Raw and the Cooked: Introduction to a Science of Mythology* (1964), argued that myths are objectifications of thought. Building on such insights, Darnton argues that cultural history is not simply the history of 'high culture', in the tradition of Herodotus or Burkhardt, but instead concerns the 'cosmology' of past peoples, 'to show how they organised reality in their minds and expressed it in their behavior'. Cultural history, then, is a sub-species which questions the seemingly age-old dichotomy in history that scholars were either theorists or empiricists, while Ginzburg summarises this dichotomy in these terms: 'historians must adopt either a weak scientific standard so as to be able to gain significant results, or adopt a strong scientific standard to attain results of no great importance'. In other words, historians can crunch numbers by the million and reveal nothing sparkling; or they can make sweeping generalisations, with little data, that seem important, but which cannot be verified. Thus, cultural history represents a move away from quantification as well as from the ideas of 'Great Men'; it is another development to claim intellectual distance from the material and methodological treatments of traditional historians. The key point of methodology and source evaluation for cultural historians is relativism: an acceptance that, as Burke says in his *New Perspectives on Historical Enquiry*, 'reality is socially or culturally constituted'. This approach to history owes much to Michel Foucault (1926–84) and Jacques Derrida (1930–). Derrida, the poststructuralist

linguistic philosopher, and his disciples rejected representational theories of meaning. Instead – Burke, in his *History and Social Theory*, tells us
– they shared a 'concern for unravelling their [texts'] contradictions,
directing attention to their ambiguities, and reading them against
themselves and their authors'. This in turn questions the very essence
of what is central and what is peripheral to history. Thus Darnton
argues that all historians who have read documents should realise that
'other people are other', that historical actors do not think the way we
do. To capture the essence of the past, Darnton claims, is to capture
'otherness'. At the same time, this is not simply a 'familiar injunction
against anachronism'.

Darnton's point about anachronism is important. What is anachronism, this accusation which has plagued every historian, and every type
of history? Anachronism is the imposition of contemporary ideas and
agendas upon the past. Darnton often writes of seemingly simple things,
like habit and custom. He claims that books of proverbs are full of
things we cannot understand, quoting the example, 'He who is snotty,
let him blow his nose.' What does this mean, apart from the obvious?
Darnton argues that such puzzlement is important, for when we don't
get an eighteenth-century joke we are on to something.

Where 'history from below' has traditionally concerned itself with the
actions of political or economic groups – handloom weavers, bread
rioters, the English working class, trade unionists, etc. – cultural historians have written more about community; about ideas; about beliefs;
about reading; about lowly individuals whose brushes with authority
are recorded in documents which suddenly throw a shaft of brilliant
light over that which normally lies in historical darkness. Cultural
historians, however, are also historians of 'below' in that they are
anxious to bring back to life those seemingly unimportant events,
such as the ribald customs of the past and the ritual massacring of cats.

There are of course problems with this highly inventive and creative
historical form. Carlo Ginzburg, in *The Cheese and the Worms* (1975),
gives four principal areas of concern:

1. Is there coherence to the fragments of the past?
2. What is the relationship between the cultures of subordinate and dominant classes?
3. To what extent is lower-class culture actually subordinate?
4. To what extent is popular culture independent?

These four points provide an interconnected series of problems. No one
could doubt the desire of the historian of mentalities to separate upper-

or lower-class culture, or to emphasise the role of the latter, but, as point 1 suggests, the evidence is limited. A classic example is the primary material for Darnton's stirring essay, 'Workers Revolt: the Great Cat Massacre of Rue Saint-Severin' (1984). Darnton opens up a world we cannot easily comprehend, where starving apprentices took out their disillusionment with the master and mistress on all the cats they could find. In a ribald pageant of slaughter, the lads, soon accompanied by the journeymen, rounded up the cats and killed them in a variety of horrific ways. Some were put through mock trials, others were burned, still others were cut to pieces. Among the dead felines was the mistress's favourite grey. Darnton explains this episode on a number of levels: he exposes the economic hardship of the period; he discusses the social relations of production in eighteenth-century France; he considers the role of ritual in the lives of these people; and he also discusses the symbolic and diabolic undertones of this outburst of 'rough music'. Yet the initial source is in fact just a few hundred words of one witness's autobiographical ruminations written many years after the events, and questions have been raised about Darnton's methods. At the same time, Darnton's explanations illustrate the tension between mentalities and Marxist explanations of popular action: was this outburst really about the independent exercising of judgement, or were the apprentices simply responding to the social relations into which they reluctantly entered?

None of the potential criticisms are easy to answer with any confidence. Historians face real problems when they cannot find the kinds of sources that make them happiest, and are easiest to interpret in an agreed, or indeed any, fashion. Even today, little of what is popular culture gets written down; popular culture is – and always has been – oral. Thus cultural historians are faced with the task of reconstructing (or deconstructing the meaning of) past popular culture using archaeological sources and written documents. And if official-type documents are employed to resurrect the popular past, might not the historian simply reactivate the divisions and differences, the biases and the value-judgements, which he/she is supposed to eliminate? A real problem for cultural historians is the question: are your findings typical or are they eccentric? Do colourful examples of popular culture illuminate what was common practice: does the riotous massacre of cats by starving apprentices in eighteenth-century France tell us about French printers' lives; or does it tell us of the mad antics of one printer's shop in Paris? Indeed, the very fact that it is written down, or leads to government/police intervention, suggests that it is atypical.

What then of the cultural historian's amateur psychology? How can cultural historians know the things of popular mentality they claim to uncover? With its concentration on scraps of evidence, or its possibly eccentric subject matter, is cultural history a return to antiquarianism? Then there is the related question of what cultural history means for the learning experiences of students. Is it necessary that, in order to understand cultural history, Darnton asks, students should be introduced to rhetoric (arguing the indefensible); textual criticism (understanding the incomprehensible); semiotics (the study of human behaviour through communications); and anthropology? These are all valid questions raised by Darnton.

Many of the criticisms of cultural history are only those levelled at historians *per se*. Moreover, the criticism of, say, Darnton's primary sources might in fact be levelled at many of the sources with which we are more familiar. It is important, when we consider sources, to think about levels of usefulness. Is a newspaper report of a magistrates' court action necessarily worse than that transcribed by the clerk of the court? Is the journalist a better recorder than the clerk? It depends. If he is simply recording the proceedings, without comment; if he is a good journalist; if he is assiduous; if his shorthand is good, then yes. If, however, he litters his report with subjective references; with value-judgements, then perhaps no. Then again, we might ask, how possible is it to have non-subjective references? One of the classic examples of this was in the last century, when reporters made snide remarks about Irish drunkenness and brawling. References to 'Paddy' and his fondness for 'Bacchus' or 'John Barleycorn' might detract from the court report. On the other hand, however, if we are searching the archives for evidence of the 'language of anti-Irish hostility', then our prejudiced reporter tells us much. This kind of problem has been addressed by cultural historians. Finally, let us consider Carlo Ginzburg on such problems: 'The fact that a source is not objective does not mean that it is useless. A hostile chronicle can furnish precious testimony about a peasant community in revolt.'

QUANTITATIVE HISTORY

Cultural history or the 'history of mentalities' is far removed from the pursuits of quantitative historians. For the former history is about feeding off the scraps of the past: thin, elusive but often brilliantly illuminating snatches of past culture. In the case of the latter, historical research is often concerned with processing vast quantities of material and applying the methods of economists to interrogate data concerning past society and past economic performance.

Quantitative history is perhaps the most widespread element of the many new directions in historical inquiry. It can be used in all spheres, from geography to political science. Statistics have been used by all manner of social scientists and historians. Collective family and manorial records have been used to chart the fortunes of the aristocracy and gentry by major historians such as Tawney, Stone and Trevor-Roper. Data have even been used to assess historical changes in metereological conditions. Today we are used to being reminded that 'this is the coldest winter since 1710', or 'the driest summer on record'. Such statements are rooted in the fact that data has been collected for centuries. While almost all areas of historical interest have been touched by the utility of quantitative techniques, they are pervasive in the areas of social and economic history. Historical demography, for example, is unthinkable without quantitative sources. Other spheres with abundant materials include trade output, exports and imports, trade union affiliation, agricultural outputs and levels of urbanisation. Despite the obvious uses of quantitative techniques in certain types of history, very few types of research are unable to benefit from the innovation in techniques and methods implied by quantitative analysis. Most practitioners of history are at least aware of the uses of computers in pursuit of their discipline; whether students using word-processing and simple spreadsheet packages, or scholars sifting thousands of rows of structured data (from, for example, medieval rolls or nineteenth-century census returns), the implications of new technology have been considerable. Thus wherever quantitative methods have been developed, the computer has usually been the engine powering innovation. We have already seen (Chapter 3, pp. 76–7) how the technological revolution of the 1960s (personified by F. W. Fogel of the Cliometrics School), what E. P. Thomspon tartly described as 'positivism with computers', threatened to dominate the discipline. This section is, however, more concerned with the methodological implications of quantification than with some protagonists' claims that a new science beckons us.

Quantitative history is another sub-disciplinary area where historians and others interested in the past have pushed the emphasis of history from the study of individuals to that of the masses. Unlike with Marxism, however, this is not just a case of moving from 'Great Men' to the working class, but, instead, means the interrogation of large amounts of long-run data to uncover patterns and trends over time. The *Annales* call this approach *histoire sérielle* (serial history), and it could just as easily account for studies of trade or agricultural output as of the standards of life.

Since the age of J. H. Clapham, British historiography has been represented by a core strand of quantitative economic history. Clapham, and later T. S. Ashton and Max Hartwell, turned the original standard of living controversy around by attempting to show, through the use of numerous indices of prices and wages, that there was a discernible increase in these standards in the first half of the nineteenth century. However, the 'pessimist' case (being the opposite of Clapham's 'optimist' stance) was reinvigorated in the 1950s by Eric Hobsbawm's devastating criticism of the limitations of the same indices. The 'standard of living' debate is one of the longest and mostly fiercely fought wars in social and economic history. The key point is, however, that ever since the controversy over wage–price indices was thoroughly worked over, the debate has primarily been one of sources and methodologies. In the 1920s, Clapham had questioned the hermeneutical naivety of the Webbs and the Hammonds, and their use of biased qualitative sources, but since that time the debate over approaches has become much more scientific, reaching a peak in the models and tests of econometric historians. A corollary of this debate has been increased creativity in the discovery and interrogation of quantitative sources. The controversy over wages and prices seems very limited next to more recent works on the economic value of people and on historical heights. The latter development, which sees height as a sensitive indicator of nutritional status and thus of standard of living, is best represented in R. Floud, K. W. Wachter and A. Gregory, *Height, Health and History: Nutritional Status in the United Kingdom, 1750–1980* (1990), based upon a massive data set of members of the armed forces, for whom such vital statistics as height have long been meticulously recorded. These authors demonstrate that although the average height of recruits has increased over the past 200 years, there was a noticeable downturn in the second quarter of the last century. A parallel work is John Komlos, *Nutrition and Economic Development in the Eighteenth-Century Habsburg Monarchy: An Anthropometric History* (1989). Other similar researches have been undertaken on transported convicts; and work is now emerging which looks at children's heights in this way.

The 'standard of living' debate is a microcosm, a case-study of the historian's evocation of statistical methods, quantitative analysis and computer-aided interrogation. Since the 1950s, though, and especially from the 1960s, quantification with computers has been firmly placed on the agenda – even though machines were then large, slow and inaccessible to most people, lacking the convenient processing power of standard desktop PCs used in the 1990s. Although it is wrong to see quantification and computers as entirely inseparable, because they have simply grown together in the past twenty years as the technology has become available to assist in the handling of large amounts of data, yet the fact is that today the two are very closely linked, and few would attempt large-scale quantification without computing. What, though, are the implications of quantitative history?

Quantitative history by definition requires quantities of data. Historians, of course, use sampling techniques, but many of the larger, funded projects currently under way seek to use long runs of data in their entirety. The emphasis upon quantities rests largely upon the kinds of questions historians wish to consider. Way back in the 1920s, Clapham was exhorting historians to use their 'statistical sense' and to ask questions like 'how much' and how often', rather than vaguely stating 'many' or 'sometimes'. Thus while all historians work with some definite quantities – '1717' or 'seven millions of population' – quantitative historians are anxious to eliminate bold but meaningless statements such as: 'in 1841, a considerable proportion of the population of Manchester died before the age of twenty-one'.

One of the central questions for quantitative analysis is the concern over the reliability of data. For this reason, the majority of quantitative history in, for example, Britain is associated with the period from 1801, because the publication of the first national population census in that year began what was to be something of a flood of officially generated materials. This is not to say that other periods cannot be approached with quantitative methods in mind, but there are problems with data in the largely pre-statistical age. The first Danish census was taken in 1769, whereas the first in Spain was taken a year earlier, and recorded individuals, not families. Nevertheless, in Britain, poor-law records for many parishes date back to the early seventeenth century, and these can be used to uncover complex patterns of population, migration, poverty and pauperism, as well as the variable nature of charitable action. Some parishes even contain complete runs of such material. Similarly, the study of crime in England can be taken back to the early modern period by the use of quarter-sessions and assize records. Medieval documents – the Domesday Book and Hundred Rolls, etc. – are also available for those wishing to quantify the various features of English medieval society.

Members of the first and second generation *Annales* School (from Febvre to Braudel's time) were among the first to apply rigorous quantitative techniques to earlier periods. A key practictioner was the Marxist Ernest Labrousse, who led the field from the 1930s till the 1960s, when later generations, such as Le Roy Ladurie, developed quantitative history still further. Labrousse's most important works were *Sketch of the Movement of Prices and Revenues in the Eighteenth-Century French Economy* (1933) and *The Crisis of the French Economy* (1944), of which the latter is a classic study of the economic precursors of the Revolution of 1789. Ten years later perhaps the most impressive – and certainly the largest – study in French quantitative history began to be published. Pierre and Huguette Chaunu's *Séville et l'Atlantique (Seville and the Atlantic)* (1955–60) is an immense serial history of Spanish trade, using Braudel's philosophy and quantitative techniques. It runs to twelve volumes. As if to prove that history is a shifting terrain, Chaunu statistics were challenged in the 1980s by M. Morineau, who argued that Chaunu had undervalued late seventeenth-century silver flow in part because he treated under-recording, for example smuggling, as a constant. Thus even the most massive projects elicit problems.

The principle which underpins quantification is that which takes historians away from the 'particular' to the 'general', in much the same way as comparative history is meant to do. Although quantitative history is highly technical, there is a level upon which it is accessible to us all. No real degree of specialism is needed to understand its basic tenets, nor to appreciate its value. At root, quantitative history simply employs techniques which make the job easier, and it is here that the role of the computer is crucial. Nor are new techniques and methodologies restricted to economic historians. Social historians who use census material (itself structured and organised into households, streets, parishes, towns, etc.) in an unstructured and disorganised fashion risk reducing its usefulness. In fact, it really is important to get away from the notion that computing and quantification only apply to the most dry, complex and mathematical types of history; nor is quantification a sort of super-empiricism employing economic theory, although most of what practitioners produce is problem-orientated history. Moreover, things like databases are used by historians for some of the most mundane purposes, for example, organising bibliographies, card indexes, research notes, student essay marks, etc. The great advantage of databases for research, however, is that they allow historians to give structure to previously unstructured data. It is possible, taking but one example, to use them to compile prosopography – collective biographies. That is, to collect material from a disparate array of sources – registers of births, marriages and deaths, newspapers, obituaries, etc. – to build complex pictures of individual lives, and to seek trends and connections in such lives. This type of methodology might be particularly useful to elicit the milieu of, say, members of a particular political party, trade union or club. Such methods are especially useful in the case of working-class lives, for which data is far-flung. The same approach might also be taken to company or family histories. The database method will allow a large amount of unrelated material to be cross-referenced and stored in one place.

In all, the implications of quantificative history are perhaps broader than for any other field of the new history. While the imperialist tendencies of the 1960s, as exemplified by Cliometrics, alienated large sections of the historical community, the more modest claims of the current generations of quantifiers can only make the discipline stronger. It is not just the techniques of quantification which offer the historical community a new lease of life, but also their tools. The use of computers makes data management (something historians have always done) easier. As Evan Mawdsley and Thomas Munck, in *Computing for Historians* (1990), argue: 'The revolution in Information technology (IT) applies as much to historical information as to any other type.' Those unaware of this fact are missing out, for, as the same authors argue, professional historians who do not use computers are denying themselves a useful tool. More importantly, however, 'Students of history who are not exposed to some form of computer work are being deprived of an important part of their historical education; they are also not benefiting from one of the ways history can prepare students for a range of professions in the modern world.' If nothing else, the emphasis of the computer in history teaching and learning is upon the transferability of skills.

CONCLUSIONS

This chapter has indicated the scope of historical approaches and methodologies. History, we have seen, is an active and vibrant discipline and it has produced many sub-areas. Today even the sub-disciplines have sub-disciplines, and none of them are entirely distinct from the others. Most of the sub-disciplinary divisions are well defined by practitioners, and almost all are represented by societies of members and periodical publications. One of the most important developments in British academic history of the past ten years, for instance, was the founding in 1987 of the British Association for History and Computing, a testament to the importance of methodological aspects of quantitative history. Perhaps the salient theme of this chapter has been the emergence of a more self-conscious philosophy of history. History is a subject whose practitioners now, more than ever, commit themselves to questioning rigorously and relentlessly the way they conceptualise the subject matter of the past.

Throughout this discussion, reference has been made to theories and concepts, like class and gender, which historians use to frame their research. The development of history as an increasingly conceptual discipline owes to other disciplines from the social sciences, including economics, geography and anthropology. Above all others, however, history owes much to its discourse with sociology. Dennis Smith, in an article published in *Sociological Review* (1982), once described social history and sociology as 'more than just good friends'. The next chapter demonstrates why.

5

Theories and concepts

INTRODUCTION

Historians seldom explore the philosophic foundations of their subject, and when faced with conceptual difficulties instinctively reach for the facts. They are suspicious of orthodoxy, dislike abstractions, and rather than waste time on what many would regard as metaphysical speculations, prefer to get on with the job.

Editorial, 'History and theory', in *History Workshop Journal*, 6 (1978).

DESPITE this somewhat gloomy assessment, historians today increasingly recognise the importance for their discipline of theoretical developments and conceptual innovations in the social sciences. The practice of history has come a long way from Acton's exhortation for historians not to submit past human life to 'the crucible of induction'. There are, of course, traditional historians who, like Elton, would have supported Acton's emphasis upon people and story-telling in the grand narrative tradition; most, however, accept the utility of applying some organising principle to history. This does not mean that empiricist sentiments are dead: far from it. The typical historian still searches out facts and records in an effort to paint a likeness of the past; history has not become pure theory, nor has it returned to the vast speculative philosophies which typified eighteenth-century social theory. The collapse of the grand intellectual enterprise of Marxism has hit theoretical accounts, especially in formerly Communist states, although the tradition lives on in China. Even before the Berlin Wall came down, and the positivism of Marxism was brought fully into question, E. P. Thompson, perhaps the foremost Marxist historian in British history, described himself as a Marxist empiricist. Thompson also worked extensively on archival material. History has become in recent times a conceptually stronger, although still source-based, discipline.

At root, the student of history must know some of the substance of this transformation, for the coming together of history and sociology has had enormous repercussions. This chapter frames some of the most important of these developments. It examines the relationship with sociology and explains how history can learn from the social sciences. The chapter then goes on to consider the relationship between theory and history, focusing particularly on the works of Karl Marx, for his ideas have been more influential than any other. Finally a number of key concepts used by historians are considered. One of the achievements of more sociological history has been to make historians think about the terms they use with impunity and which they once took for granted. The list of concepts covered – among them class, gender, community, ethnicity – is not intended to be exhaustive; instead it gives the reader a taste of what are the controversies and purposes of conceptual thinking. The key point is to apply the same critical approach to any concept that your reading uncovers. Do not simply accept terms like 'Industrial Revolution', 'nationalism' or 'imperialism': ask 'what do they mean'? Development of the critical faculty is the historian's first task. Understanding the past then becomes more difficult, but findings tend to have more meaning.

HISTORY AND SOCIOLOGY

The disciplines of history and sociology have always been close in terms of their shared interest in aspects of society. While the majority of sociologists concern themselves with the present or recent past, this has not always been the case. Early sociologists, who aimed to understand the science of society, were often fundamentally or solely concerned with the past. Auguste Comte and T. H. Buckle, two leading nineteenth-century sociologists, for example, looked to the history of society to elicit the rules that governed social change. Indeed, it was the connection that such sociologists presented between past, present, and, in some cases, future, that saw positivism worked out to its fullest extent. In this respect, much of Marx's and Engels's work could be called sociology, in that they too searched for the rules by which social change occurred, claiming the answer lay in historical materialism and class struggle, concepts we will examine later. The relationship between sociology and history today is not closer because of some return to the positivistic tendencies of the nineteenth century, although critics like Elton may have argued that such was the case. The link between the two disciplines is today mediated by the utility of each discipline to the other, though principally by what sociology can offer history. Just as economic historians have been known to interpret the data of the past using contemporary economists' models, so too some social historians approach their task from the perspective of using contemporary sociological findings and models to frame the past. This approach may have been questioned, but the spread of sociology into areas of social history has been considerable. The influential American sociologist and historian, Charles Tilly, in his 'Sociological historians and historical sociologists' (*Current Perspectives in Social Theory*, 1980), argued that three main areas of history had become popular with sociologists:

1. The structure of cities and other communities.
2. The structure of population: processes, families, marriage, etc.
3. The structure of elites: stratification, social mobility, etc.

These areas remain popular today, for sociologists clearly identify with the parts of the past which are most obviously sociological. The family in history, for example, has benefited massively from the work of sociologists, like Michael Anderson, with the result that many of the myths of family structure – such as the once common belief that past European society was organised around extended families – have been exploded beyond repair. Historians in these fields readily identify with the work of sociologists – in fact many of them are called historical sociologists or historical demographers – and use models and concepts from the modern world. Equally, many new areas have come under the sociologist's scrutiny and certain aspects of the past, for instance gender and lunacy, are inconceivable without initiatives from the social sciences. Others, like crime, would be denuded of much explanatory force without sociological insights. Even the traditional world of biography and 'Great Men' has been opened up to conceptual analysis by the use of psychoanalytical approaches, famously introduced in the 1920s by Lewis Namier. In the USA this approach is very popular, especially when applied to the past minds of tyrants like Hitler, and has a journal, *Psychohistory*, dedicated to such work. Early *Annales* writings, like Febvre's study of Martin Luther, focused on the psychohistorical dimension.

This partial and often uneven merger between history and social science not only results from a natural or subconscious modernising spirit. It is mainly informed by new social historians breaking free of the dynastic stranglehold of empiricism, accompanied by the demise of the historian's once unbreakable belief in what has been termed 'naive realism'. Few historians today would claim that they reconstruct a perfect story of what happened in the past. Critics have long argued that unless history took on board the intellectual and theoretical rigour of the social sciences, it would be relegated to the creative arts, placed next to novel-writing. Today, many historians would agree with the claim made by Gareth Stedman Jones, in 'From historical sociology to theoretical history' (*British Journal of Sociology*, 1976), that 'history, like any other "social science", is an entirely intellectual operation which takes place in the present and in the head'. At the same time comes an acknowledgement that historians, whether consciously or unconsciously, construct their histories around preconceived ideas. Historians, in short, have always used ordering devices. Whether driven by a belief in the immutability of the facts, the role of contingency, or by the forces of progress, historians apply an overriding reason to historical reconstruction which amounts to theorising. Thus, Stedman Jones argues, 'the distinction is not between theory and non-theory [in history], but between the adequacy and inadequacy of the theory brought to bear'. The same author ascribes the traditionally weak link between history and theory to 'the persistence of positivistic working assumptions about causality', which have dogged every kind of history since the Victorian age.

While history and sociology are no longer strangers or enemies, it is difficult to define precisely where they meet and to say what the product of their relationship should be called. Most historians might settle for calling history, with a pinch of sociological theory, social history. However, this probably is not enough. In its broadest sense, social history is history concerned with the 'social'. Beyond this, many historians do not go; consequently social history is shapeless. For German scholars, social history is often mooted as 'the history of society'. But what does that mean? A 'totalist' or 'total-ish' history, broadly sketching the way society in one age is different from that in another? R. S. Neale, in *Class in English Society* (1981), expresses concern as to the loose and catch-all definitions applied to social history. He states: 'social history which does not as a matter of concern seek to unravel the connection between... [the changes in ideas and perceptions about the nature and potential of men and women]... can never warrant the name history of society'. This is an appeal for a dynamic approach to history. Material conditions, economic systems, capitalism, mercantilism and feudalism – each stress the two points Neale raises about 'ideas' and 'the nature and potential of men and women'. True social history, then, is to elicit the structural, mental and social changes which impact upon people and their ideas and distinguish one age from another.

This question 'what is society?' is central if we are to define the role of theory in history. Without a definition, that includes past and present, the historical dimension becomes hermetically sealed; something from which no lessons can be learned; an entity without relation to the world of the scholars researching it. In an influential article, 'From social history to the history of society' (*Daedalus*, 1971), Hobsbawm argued that social history *is* societal history. Things like social movements, working-class organisations, neighbourhoods, and the role of the state might all be social history, but they are too-finite in their conception of the 'social'. Case studies of 'this' or that 'social' phenomenon give preference to the *particular*, not the *essential*, features of the social world. Societal history is not finite, and concentrates upon the wider trend rather than the narrower focus.

The task of theoretically-inspired social history is to locate underlying and key trends. The essence, whether Marxist or otherwise, is to find the dynamic which makes the process of history ('change', 'development', 'progress', etc.) happen. As Keith Wrightson, in *English Society, 1580–1680* (1982), has written, 'society is a process. It is never static. Even its most apparently stable structures are the expression of an equilibrium between dynamic forces.' The social historian's job, Wrightson says, is 'that of recapturing that process'. Wrightson's emphasis is upon dynamics. At the same time, social history, in this conception, must be about the structures of history (whether material, social, political or cultural), the dynamic that determines their interrelationship (class struggle, in the Marxist case) and the way the whole interwoven texture creates a society as we look back on it at any given time. Understanding the material, social and mental conditions of people is quite a task; counterpointing structures which change with structures that remain intact is not easy; then interweaving them with examples from politics, life-style, religion, culture and everyday life makes the task more difficult. But this is what Wrightson does so well. The history of society, written in this way, is almost impossible without the guidance of some framework, theory or idea. Nineteenth-century historians managed to delineate change (in their case progress) because they had an uncomplicated sense of where history was going. Their Whiggish project had the marvellous effect of implying simplicity – the grand national story – without neccessarily being accurate.

History is in fact very complex, and theory can play a part in ordering those complexities and uncovering trends and the long-term shape of historical change. Works such as Roger Chartier's *Cultural History* (1988) and Christopher Lloyd's *The Structures of History* (1993), for example, share the laudable aim of trying to uncover those patterns and structures which underpin the social process in its historical dimension. These writers aim, as all social historians should aim, to uncover the dynamic of history – that which gives it motion. The only way to do this is to frame the past at the structural level (economy, regions, communities, politics, identity), over a Braudelian medium term (decades and centuries) in which the ebbs and flows can be observed, where momentum gathers pace. Thus societal history concerns matters which define society at a given time. A good example of this is R. I. Moore's *Annales*-style *The Formation of Persecuting Society* (1988), which examines the emergence of a centralised, bureaucratic and dominant Catholic Church. The powers of this church, Moore shows, had great effects on later society by defining the nature of insider and outsider, and formed something of the foundation-stone of later manifestations of persecution, legitimising the notion of persecution itself. Moore cuts to the core of Catholic hegemony in Europe in the central Middle Ages. Therefore, his book, by uncovering the socio-cultural dynamic of religious dominance, can truly be called 'societal'.

THE HISTORICAL PROCESS

The list of philosophers, social theorists, historians and others who have tried to explain the process of historical change over the long term is immense. It is impossible to do justice to all of them in the space we have here. From Vico and Hegel, to Weber and Durkheim, the engagement of history and social theory, philosophy and ideas, has been impressive. Medieval scholars, guided by the notion of Providence, tried to explain the emergence and passage of civilisation in terms of God's will, although they saw that this could be worked out via human agency; others, in the Age of Reason, believed the course of human society was determined by the ideas and rationality of humankind itself. In the nineteenth century, the idealist conception of history was replaced by a materialist conception, in which economic circumstances rather than ideas were perceived as the root of human history. As Sidney Pollard, in *The Idea of Progress* (1968), trenchantly observed, the Age of Innocence came to an end with the death of Condorcet (1743–

93), the French mathematician, philosopher and politician. Thus, although after the French Revolution there remained those who believed miraculous change might come through the application of 'such metaphysical concepts as "Justice" or "Natural rights" ', most thinkers came to accept that 'Society was more complex than had been thought, and a new foundation had to be laid for a credible system of social laws.' These were the ideas, and the realities, that served as background to the emerging socialist agenda of the early nineteenth century in Europe, personified by writers like Saint-Simon. From this tradition sprang Karl Marx and Friedrich Engels, two of the most important nineteenth-century philosophers of history.

MARXISM

Karl Marx takes the credit for developing a philosophical system which was partly the work of his lifelong collaborator, Friedrich Engels, and which was much influenced by strands of German idealist philosophy of the Enlightenment. When Marx and Engels emerged on the intellectual scene in the early 1840s, they claimed to have read and understood all of the basic strands of European thought: German idealist philosophy (Hegel, Herder, Kant); the ideas of French socialists, like Saint-Simon; as well as the writings of British political economists, such as Adam Smith and David Ricardo.

Marx's first contribution to the understanding of historical processes was the development of *dialectical materialism* (dialectic meaning 'contradiction'), developed in criticism of Hegel's ideas-based dialectic, in which relations were made up of opposite forces (thesis and antithesis), while the motor of change was class struggle between these poles which eventually led to a new mode of production and new epoch (synthesis). The practical application of Marx's dialectic can be summarised as follows:

$$\frac{\text{THESIS}}{\text{ANTITHESIS}} \rightarrow \text{conflict} \rightarrow \text{SYNTHESIS}$$

Which for Marx's own epoch, would appear like this:

$$\frac{\text{BOURGEOISIE}}{\text{PROLETARIAT}} \rightarrow \text{class conflict} \rightarrow \text{SOCIALISM}$$

Marx developed dialectical materialism in criticism of Hegel's dialectic and Feuerbach's crude materialism. At the centre of Marx's dialectical materialism (also known as historical materialism) was the notion that humans are social animals, forming societies and maintaining relations with other men. The key factor in this relationship between men, Marx argued, was the material requirement of Man: clothing, food, shelter. Social organisation provided for these needs and thus shaped human society. As material factors changed, so history seemed to move on through different stages, each one distinguished by the conditions of material life. Marx explained this position in the preface to his *Contribution to the Critique of Political Economy* (1859). Of the material facts in life, he wrote:

> In the social production of their existence, men inevitably enter into definite relationships, which are independent of their will, namely relations of production. The totality of the relations of production constitutes the economic structure of society, the real foundation, on which arises a legal and political susperstructure and to which correspond definite forms of social consciousness. The mode of production of material life conditions the process of social, political and intellectual life. It is not the consciousness of men that determines their existence but their social existence that determines their consciousness.

Using this as the starting point, Marx and Engels periodised history according to the material circumstances of any given time. For them, history was essentially divided into three epochs: the Ancient (Greek and Roman), the Feudal and the Bourgeois, the latter defined by the capitalist relations of the modern world of Marx's own time. Each of these epochs grew from the chaos of the last (remember the dialectic), and each was characterised, in material terms, as more modern than the last. The epochal approach of Marx was similar to that of previous writers, like Vico and Hegel, except that Marx saw the rise and fall of each stage progressing in linear, rather than circular, fashion. The idea of modernisation and the development of increasingly antagonist relations with successive epochs, was central to Marx's conception of historical change. Perhaps the best overview of Marx's theory of history is to be found in Steve Rigby's *Marxism and History* (1987).

Each of Marx's stages was different, but each was characterised by the fact that the nature of the economic base – the mode of production – determined the 'superstructure' of society: that is, ideas, institutions, politics and government. Marx argued that in each epoch the nature of the 'base' threw up class antagonisms via the relations of production: that is, the way in which different groups were positioned in relation to the 'mode of production'. Thus these conflicts were hinged along the lines of owner and slave; lord and serf; landowner and peasant; employer and worker. Marx argued that each system was marked by conflicts which developed between old modes of production and the new. The consequence of these class antagonisms was, he argued, social revolution. This, then, was Marx's material conception of history, his dialectical materialism, which seemingly offered little hope for the existing owners of the means of production, that is, manufacturers and factory owners. Marx, moreover, added a particularly bleak coda to the Bourgeois epoch. He said that, whereas in the Feudal system there had been a considerable gradation of class – lords, knights, vassals, peasants, serfs, bondsmen and others – in the Bourgeois era there were only two classes: those who owned and those who did not.

Many critics have argued that Marx put too much emphasis on materialism – that he was an economic determinist – that is, that everything was explained in terms of the economic system at any given time. This economic determinism came to be known as the 'base–superstructure' model – the idea that the base (the economic system) directly influenced the nature of the superstructure (institutions, politics, ideology, social and cultural life, and so on). Marx and Engels, however, never intended a unilinear and monocausal conception of history to be their epitaph. Their conception of the forces of production, for example, included much more than just the economic system or that produced by the sweat of workers. Science, technology and other aspects of creative output were also included. In 1890 Engels defended himself and Marx in a letter to Ernst Bloch:

> Marx and I are ourselves partly to blame for the fact that the younger writers sometimes lay more stress on the economic side than is due to it. We had to emphasise this main principle in opposition to our adversaries, who denied it, and we had not always the time, the place or the opportunity to allow the other elements involved in the interaction to come into their rights.

Their philosophy was in fact much more complicated, as Engels went on to tell Bloch:

> According to the materialist conception of history the determining element in history is *ultimately* the production and reproduction in real life. More than that neither Marx nor I have ever asserted.... The economic situation is the basis, but the various elements of the superstructure – political forms of class struggle and its consequences, consitututions established by the victorious class after a successful battle, etc. – forms of law – and then even the reflexes of all these acutal struggles in the brains of the combatants: political, legal philsophical theories, religious ideas ... also exercise

their influence upon the course of the historical struggles and in many cases preponderate in determining their *form*. There is an interaction of all these elements in which, amid all the endless *hosts* of accidents (that is of all things and events whose inner connection is so remote or impossible to prove that we regard it as absent and can neglect it), the economic movement finally asserts itself as necessary....We make our history, but in the first place under very definite presuppositions and conditions. Among these the economic ones are finally decisive.

While the notion of base–superstructure and the emphasis upon economic determinism clearly had a utility for Marx and Engels, they also argued that no economic system was completely without the vestiges of the previous one. How else could the hugely powerful aristocractic landowning class – still the premier political force in Europe, including industrialising Britain in 1850 – be reconciled with the emergent, powerful but ultimately immature bourgeoisie? In other words, Marx and Engels were accepting the notion of historical change at different paces. Marx saw economic structures as placing limitations upon the superstructure rather than simply defining it without possible variation.

Furthermore, both men wrote works which allowed for variations within his notion of the materialist conception of history. Marx's essay 'Eighteenth Brumaire of Louis Napoleon' is a classic example of the role of opportunism and individual action in shaping the course of history. However, the intrigues of the Bonaparte dynasty did not stop France developing class antagonisms, nor could these individual actions shape the material conditions of French life over, say, a century. The point is that Marx accepted short-run, and divergent, change within the overall framework. At the same time, however, Marx's identification with Britain's vanguard proletariat meant he was surprised when revolution happened in France or Germany in 1848, and not in Britain. Consequently all the real history that Marx and Engels wrote (except Engels's *Origins of the Family*) centred upon revolutions. In *Class Struggle in France* and *Germany: Revolution and Counter-Revolution* (both dealt with the 1848 revolutions), Marx and Engels showed a great understanding of the forces which make it hard to confine history to models. They understood the linkage between objective forces – the vast, impersonal social and economic changes, and subjective factors, such as the actions of men and groups of people, and the implications of social change for people.

Other critics have said that Marx's dialectical materialism (like Hegel's dialectic before) was based purely in the abstract realm of ideas, saying that because it could not be disproved, it could not be proved either. This is, however, unfair. Marx tried to understand real change. He was different from Hegel in that he used the dialectical approach and applied it to try to understand the process of historical change. It is true, of course, that Marx was not an empiricist. He dealt in theories of explanation, not in facts. However, he did have similarities with Comte, the sociologist: both were rightly viewed as positivists. Marx saw the job of the historian as understanding the past and elucidating causes of change. Both Comte and Marx believed they had found the natural laws that governed historical change, and argued that their system of ideas could be used to determine the future development of human society. It is important to remember that most social theorists of the first half of the nineteenth century addressed themselves to grand ideas about history, on a vast scale, as a process of progress.

Marx and Engels fundamentally did not believe (as most before had done) that ideas existed independently, nor that ideas were the motor of change. The statement in the *Contribution to the Critique of Political Economy* – 'It is not the consciousness of men that determines their existence but their social existence that determines their consciousness' – neatly sums up their move away from idealist conceptions of history. Idealist philosophy, then, proposed that the ideas of humans changed society; that human progress was within the bounds of humankind's rationality, reason and understanding; that their consciousness could determine their social existence. This was the opposite of Marx's notion that the material conditions of life governed the nature of society at any given time and fuelled historical change.

Marx's ideas shared with Enlightenment thinkers the belief that above all history was about the idea of progress. The transfer to dominant mercantile or capitalist modes may have focused class antagonisms, and driven down the conditions of life for the working class, but for Marx, such social realities, with their roots, he alleged, in grievous exploitation, were necessary preconditions for violent change – social revolution.

Marx and Engels, like Saint-Simon, accepted the idea that some phases of development were stable while others were not. For Marx and Engels, though, the bourgeois (capitalist) epoch was altogether new, primarily because of the immensely increased productive powers of modern economic organisation. This was essentially an observation on the instability generated by the dichotomy of increased consumption and growing inequality. This conception of historical development was rooted in contemporary observation. Those trying to understand the role of Marxism in history need to consider the context of Marx and

Engels themselves. Both lived in Britain (often in exile) and based their works on what they believed were faithful observations of the development of the British working class. The revolution did not come, but there are many explanations for this. Later Marxists have indeed spent no little time directly or indirectly, explicitly or implicitly, addressing this very problem. Thanks to Marx and Engels the question of class has become central to our understanding of nineteenth-century history.

CLASS, STRUCTURE AND AGENCY

What is class? Class is both controversial and fraught with methodological and ideological difficulties. Can we take it for granted as some finite category of socio-economic status or as an objective measurement of the social relations of production? The term 'class', in its modernist sense, was a creation of the nineteenth century and of Marx and Engels. It also means far more than a simple socio-economic descriptor. What do we mean when we apply such terms as 'social class' or 'class-consciousness'? There is disagreement, even among Marxists, as to what Marx and Engels meant by class. For some historians, class is considered to be the relationship between groups in society, objectively defined by those groups' relations to the means of production – that is, their position in the productive system (e.g. workers or owners), and their share of the wealth created. Thus, class might be seen here as a structural thing; a condition born out of material circumstance, shared among individuals, making them into a class of common interest, resulting in shared values, outlooks and objectives. To other historians – for example, E. P. Thompson – class is a creation of 'agency' not of 'structure'; an '*historical* phenomenon'; 'something which in fact happens (and can be shown to have happened) in human relations'. At the same time, the same writer also acknowledges, in *The Making of the English Working Class* (1963), how difficult it is to define examples of class: 'The finest-meshed sociological net cannot give us a pure specimen of class, any more than it can give us one of deference or of love.'

Thompson's analysis has been enormously influential in left-wing circles. Moreover, as his stance was deliberately anti-theoretical, and his methods of research were rigorous and intensive, Thompson provides a useful, accessible and relatively non-dogmatic introduction to Marxism and history. His work is also eminently readable. In all, a good starting point for young scholars.

At the same time, however, we must acknowledge other viewpoints on the role of class in history. Recently, for example, historians of what John Belchem has dubbed 'the linguistic turn' – those who emphasise the rooted and historical nature of language itself – have stressed the paradoxes inherent within usages of the very word 'class'. Gareth Stedman Jones, in *Languages of Class* (1983), argued that because the term 'class' is a word 'embedded in the language' it should be considered in that 'linguistic context'. Jones then pointed out that because there were different 'languages of class', the term cannot be employed as an 'elementary counter of official social description'. Whether concerned with productive relations, 'culturally significant practices', or political and ideological 'self-definition', class, Jones argues, is locked into 'an anterior social reality'.

Of all the philosophical concepts raised in the writings of Marx and Engels, class has been welcomed as one of the most important and, conversely, criticised by many historians as one of the most controversial. In the eighteenth century, the term class was not used to represent an homogenous social group of shared experiences and outlooks as it came to be used in the following century. In its Marxist connotation, in fact, class was not used at all. Social relations in the early modern world were framed in terms of 'sorts', 'orders' or perhaps 'classes', in the plural sense. These categories were, moreover, closely allied to both relative wealth and status; they were not necessarily ideological in the ways that social class was from the 1830s. In a semantic sense, 'class' – like 'industrial', bourgeois', 'liberal' or 'conservative', and a host of other terms – developed in response to the rise of a language of analysis, underpinned by the rapid modernisation and changing social circumstances of the period beyond the French Revolution.

No one can date precisely when social 'order', for example, became social 'class'; instead historians console themselves with charting incidents, or conceptualising social and cultural change, whether in terms of older or modernist notions of group relations. In 1709, Daniel Defoe, the British journalist and novelist, observed a society divided on these terms, into seven broad social groups:

1. The great, who live profusely;
2. The rich, who live plentifully;
3. The middle sort, who live well;
4. The working trades, who labour hard, but feel no want;
5. The country people, farmers &c., who fare indifferently;
6. The poor, who fare hard;
7. The miserable, that really pinch and want.

By the 1840s Marx believed this graded division of society had become increasingly more sharply defined, in terms of the relations of production. Marx's laboratory for working out his ideas of class was Britain, where, according to his formulation, the Industrial Revolution was in the throes of creating the world's first authentic proletariat, defined by mechanised, factory and, above all, waged labour; by starker contrasts between owners and producers than had existed before; by social discord; and by deep-seated antagonism across class lines. This was the age of political agitation and socio-economic unrest; of Chartism and the years of revolutions (1830 and 1848). Marx was not alone in believing this age was a chaotic one: writers on the right, such as Thomas Carlyle, shared Marx's observations, if not his resulting theories or panaceas. Equally, Marx was not alone in underestimating the innate and deep-seated stability of British society.

The earliest statements of Marxist positions on class are found in *The German Ideology* (1846), which followed Engels's sociological polemic, *The Condition of the Working Class in England* (1845). Where the first is, as the title suggests, an ideological statement, the second is a closely researched study of everyday life in early industrial Britain, written in a strident and appealing manner. The opening words of Engels's study of the working class neatly summarise the role allotted to Britain in his and Marx's conception of the proletariat and, thus, of class:

> The history of the proletariat in England begins with the second half of the last century, with the invention of the steam-engine and of machinery for working cotton. These inventions gave rise, as is well known, to an industrial revolution, a revolution which altered the whole of civil society; one the historical importance of which is only now beginning to be recognized. England is the classic soil of this transformation, which was all the mightier, the more silently it proceeded; and England is, therefore, the classic land of its chief product also, the proletariat. Only in England can the proletariat be studied in all its relations and from all sides.

While class and Marxism are indistinguishable, Marx's greatest work, *Das Kapital* (1867), says little about class, whereas the most straightforward statement of Marx and Engels's position on class is contained in a short and polemical pamphlet, *The Communist Party Manifesto* (1848), which was intended for a popular audience. Some of Marx's most detailed writings can be found in the *Grundrisse*, written in 1857–58, but first published after his death. This volume contains many developments on earlier ideas and is wide-ranging in the themes it tackles. The *Manifesto* is by comparison a relatively easy and accessible statement of popular Marxist ideology, in which is contained the most famous phrase in the language of Marxism: 'the history of all hitherto existing society is the history of class struggle'.

One of the most important features of the *Manifesto* is the contrast it establishes between capital and labour. Marx and Engels believed that while the social relations of production in previous epochs (for example, under feudalism) had been marked by lesser levels of distinction between classes, under the capitalist mode of production, divisions were starkly set between just two classes: bourgeoisie (capital) and proletariat (labour). This model has the conceptual advantage of simplicity but, more importantly, ensured clear distinctions between those who 'owned' and those who 'made', with the result that the final struggle would be more violent and more decisive. Thus antagonisms were bitterest under capitalism (witness Engels, in *The Condition of the Working Class in England*), and revolutionary change was inevitable. Antagonistic social relations, and abject hardship and despair, were necessary prerequisites for the transformation of the bourgeois epoch into the socialist one. Critics, of course, point out that revolution never occurred in England; and that events like the revolutions of 1848 passed England by. Equally, Marx thought Germany a more likely venue for revolutionary change, and thus Communism, than Russia.

While Marx fails as prophet, however, it is important not to dismiss out of hand the Marxist contribution to historical knowledge. At the same time, class − as an historical reality rather than as a theoretical concept − has taken on different meanings in different times, circumstances and in different countries. While class is difficult enough as a theoretical control, varying national historical experiences further cloud the issue: in Germany, France or America, class does not mean the same things as it does in, say, Britain. Thus, problems of definition clearly exist. Also observable historical phenomena, such as the failure of Chartism, or the emergence of an essentially reformist British labour movement, further complicate the Marxist analysis.

Much discussion as to the usefulness of class as an historical tool has centred upon semantics. Subsequent Marxists, who have developed and refined the original idea, are still concerned to explain the emergence of what they see as a genuine case of class-consciousness. While critics to this day habitually repeat that Marx was an economic determinist, Thompson, along with other members of the British Marxist School, as well as American sympathisers, like Eugene Genovese and Herbert Gutman, have honed the idea that class is an agency, a social and cultural factor 'which cannot be defined in abstraction; that class only has meaning when it is seen in terms of relationships between classes'.

As Thompson has remarked, 'class is conflict ... class is not a thing, it is a happening'. This analysis gave rise to significant divisions between Marxists as to whether class is a structural or cultural creation. Thus the British Marxist School has gained the label 'culturalist' or 'socialist–humanist'. This division was most obvious during a heated debate in Oxford in 1978 between Richard Johnson – an Althusserian structuralist–Marxist sociologist – and Thompson. The debate simmered on for several years and a number of important essays on the subject were published in the *History Workshop Journal*. Thompson's damning attack on the structuralist approach can be found in 'The poverty of theory', which works out more fully material contained in the short preface to *The Making of the English Working Class*. Yet as early as 1965, Thompson had launched this stinging critique of structuralist interpretations of class, and upon systemic accounts, in his essay 'The peculiarities of the English'. He lambasted sociologists who claim that, after stopping 'the time machine' and going down to the engine room, they cannot find an example of class, but only various people with different jobs, status and incomes. With a typically trenchant metaphor, Thompson continued: 'Of course they are right, since class is not this or that part of the machine, but *the way the machine works* once it is set in motion – not this interest and that interest, but the *friction* of interests – the movement itself, the heat, the thundering noise.'

In a faithful reading of early Marx – one which emphasises the idea that 'social existence' determines 'consciousness' – class, like all other superstructural manifestations (politics, art, society in general), is created by the nature of the base (economic system). This is the basic structuralist argument – that class is a structure, determined by economic life, just like any other structure. For Thompson, this is only partly true. He argued: 'The class experience is largely determined by the productive relations into which men are born – or enter involuntarily.' This is pure Marx. The following statement, however, is not; at any rate, not in its materialist conception. Thompson continues: 'Class-consciousness is the way in which these experiences are handled in cultural terms: embodied in traditions, value-systems, ideas and institutional forms.'

Thompson's work is important because it lacks rigidity and allows for variety within class-consciousness. This is a theory for those who feel class is a useful term, even if Marx's prediction of social revolution in Britain proved to be wrong. Thompson's thesis also implictly promotes Marx and Engels's idea that elements of each epoch were stable, and others unstable, and that there were features of what broadly might be called the superstructure which did not conform to the rigid base–superstructure model. He accepts that cultural edifices are constructed by humans which defy the base–structure 'logic'. At the same time, Thompson's shared inheritance with other British Marxists – such as Christopher Hill, Eric Hobsbawm and Rodney Hilton – passed back through Maurice Dobb and Dona Torr (two earlier Marxists) to Karl Marx himself. Collectively, the British Marxist School has sought to uncover a wide variety of subject matter – from medieval and early modern history; feudalism, the English revolution and the crisis of the seventeenth century; peasant studies, world labour history, class formation, British social history – with one thing uniting their work: the centrality of class struggle. Their aim is to look at the real lives of real people; and to emancipate the voiceless who are lost in time – men and women – using the fragments of history they left behind. In applying his cultural model to 'history from below', Thompson developed an interest in what has been dubbed 'the structure of feeling', which has many connections with the mentalities approach of the *Annales* School, although the latter, as we'll see in a later section, is generally less reliant upon Marx.

GENDER

There is a common language shared by class and gender which frames our reference to the past, although gender offers a different conception of the nature of historical relations and social change. Gender history is, like that of class, premised upon the notion of elite–popular relations, social stratification, exploitation, domination and struggle. Class and gender seem to couple quite neatly; problems arise, however, when one is awarded primacy at the expense of the other. We will need to think about this presently.

The initial impetus for feminist history was political, as it was clearly an offshoot of the radical movement of the 1960s. The desire to uncover a female past, and to 'gender' history, went hand in hand with the struggle for knowledge, power and equality in other spheres of life. Even so, today, though much less so than in the 1960s, academic history (like the universities at large) is a male-dominated preserve. Although female-to-male ratios have significantly improved, they are yet to reach a level that reflects the gender balance of the wider population. This demographic factor has clearly affected the quest to study this aspect of our past. Some traditionally-minded males tend to be deeply sceptical about women's history, as John Vincent, in *An Intelligent Person's Guide to History* (1995), shows: 'things are as they are, and not as we (or modern feminists) would have them be; it is a bit late to set about re-modelling the past in accordance with modern standards'. It is little wonder, perhaps, that feminist scholars have a reputation for radicalism: while many come from leftist perspectives, and have been marginalised because of it, the reception of their ideas in some establishment circles has undoubtedly exacerbated and exaggerated radicalising trends in the sub-disciplinary area.

The development of feminist historiography has occasionally been halted by semantic debates or by attempts to introduce weight, power and importance into past situations where none can be seen to exist. This does not, of course, apply only to feminist history, but has been at times especially obvious in this sphere. The idea of recapturing 'her-story', rather than the traditional 'his-story', is one example. This is not just a ridiculous word-play; it is in fact a serious point. It attempts to convey the idea that for too long history has been a male preserve telling stories of men for men. This is correct, for history has unquestionably been biased towards males since Herodotus wrote his *Histories*. The problem is not with the diagnosis but with the prescription: can we turn history around to ameliorate the bias of past generations? We can, of course, study women, but can we give them a retrospective political importance which suits the political agenda but distorts the historical picture? The real quest of the historian should be 'their-story'; although feminist historians might counter (with some justification) that the imbalance between 'his-' and 'her-story' must be resolved before 'their-story' can be told. In addition to which, the separation of 'his' and 'her' in this context is possibly arguably the same one which purists use to distinguish the objective and the subjective in knowledge. Objectivity was once the clarion call of historians, whereas few today cling to the idea that they can be truly objective. From this position, subjective history becomes much less forbidding and 'her-story' becomes stronger. We can also see from this problem that gender history is as much about masculinity and the role of men as about women; it concerns dominance as much as emancipation.

Gender history, like that centred on class, concerns history in its totality. Its essence is to reformulate our understanding of the past on gender lines. Gender historians attempt to bring their theoretical conceptualisation of gender roles, and the relations between the sexes, to bear upon all aspects of past society. Gender history is totalist in perspective, trying to offer a different way of understanding the historical process itself. Its central premise is that gender is socially and culturally constituted and this leads to the idea that what we perceive as natural differences between masculinity and femininity are actually social constructs. Much of the most important work of Michel Foucault (1926–84), the French linguistic philosopher, is dedicated to the artifical nature of our modern social categories.

While gender and class meet in the attempt to understand social hierarchies, communities, conflict and subordination, they do ultimately conflict over the 'totalisation' of history. Here class and gender compete to explain the dynamic of history: the pace, scale and nature of social change. Many historians refer to both class and gender in the titles of their books – often as a sop to one or the other – but problems of competition continue to exist. Take, for example, the role of women in social movements. Historians of food riots have long noted the important role played by women in exerting what Thompson termed the 'moral economy of the crowd', pressing merchants and middlemen to set morally acceptable prices in times of shortage. How do we reconcile class and gender in this case? Do these female participants express class concern, or are they extending their control of important private (domestic) practices – in this case the consumption of foodstuffs – into the public domain? We can see how historians of both class and gender might claim this as proof of their case. Similarly, women's participation in the Chartist movement of the 1830s and 1840s is also laden with problems of conceptual interpretation. While there were women's groups involved, some of which demanded womanhood suffrage, by far the largest female role was played alongside family and friends, as 'faces in the crowd', supporting the movement's quest for, among other things, manhood suffrage. Thus we can see problems of explanation along the class/gender dichotomy.

The relationship between gender history and women historians is also rather puzzling. Militants might argue that gender history is something that only women can understand; yet many men are becoming involved in the quest to deconstruct masculine norms and thus to gender the past; and we do not say that only those born in the eighteenth century can understand it. At the same time, not all female historians are historians of gender, although women are not usually so overtly hostile to gender studies as are some men. Some of the most eminent historians today are women, yet they occupy ambiguous positions in relation to gender perspectives on the past. Linda Colley is one example. Her *Britons: Forging the Nation, 1707–1837* (1992) is seen as an important analysis of the factors accounting for the emergence of a

British identity. Yet it contains one chapter on 'womenpower', which is in some ways the most strained aspect of an otherwise flowing text. This 'single chapter' approach is common – particularly with men – and has been seen as paying lip-service to something important. It also undermines the integrated nature of women and society. Malcolm Smith, in *British Politics, Society and the State Since the Late Nineteenth Century* (1990), sums up this problem when he argues that although there are major theoretical difficulties with treating women separately, 'it is an insurmountable historiographical problem that unless one treats women separately, they may not be treated at all'.

At its worst, gender history is ahistorical, ideological and hectoring. Such history uncovers what is not there, or confers importance on that which is of limited value. At best, however, gender history is creative, stimulating, rigorous and historical. In other words, good gender history is just like other good history. Studies of domesticity strongly emphasise women's roles in both a positive and enlightened way: there were no women MPs in the early nineteenth century, for example, so why look for them? In fact, the shift from public to private spheres is bound to bear fruit. In the realms where women did exercise influence and roles, gender has a crucial role to play; where they did not, questions of masculinity and control need attention. In a very broad sense, then, women's history can add significantly to our knowledge and conceptualisation of the past. Gender approaches have made historians think about things they previously took for granted or ignored. Histories that were written without women in mind – in terms of subject matter, periodisation, social, economic and political roles, etc. – are constantly being reassessed.

COMMUNITY AND IDENTITY

These terms have taken on greater relevance in the field of historical inquiry in recent times. Once they were used uncritically; now they are much more closely appraised. Identity is an oft-used concept, one which has a multitude of textures. It is generally seen as broader in scope than community, and has been the subject of much critical examination, particularly when used in conjunction with 'national'. In its broadest conception, identity refers to a sense of belonging, rooted in notions of what people feel an affinity for: group, class, locality, town, region, nation, etc. By contrast, community is a term used by historians with impunity but rather less critically assessed. In fact, Raymond

Williams, in *Keywords* (1976), states that 'unlike all other terms of social organisation, it seems never to be used unfavourably'. This is less so today, perhaps, although its general woolliness persists.

Sociologists have been developing more conceptually challenging forms of social organisation since the later nineteenth century. Tönnies in 1887, for example, coined the terms *gemeinschaft* and *gessellschaft*, to distinguish between the idyllic (often rustic and romantic) notion of community and the individualistic traits of modern civic society. Still greater conceptual rigour is required as the term 'community' is at once useful and problematic. Communities tend to be seen as things of solidarity and social stability, creations of mutuality, compromise and equality. Yet this is far from always the case. Rather than being passive creations of subconsciously aligned individuals, communities can just as easily be divided or conflictual entities. Where is the 'community' in Ulster or Belfast? What does 'community' mean in other ethnic–sectarian hotspots like the former Yugoslavia? The media talk about Belfast as a divided community, but is not that city really made up of two communities (one Catholic, the other Protestant), each one partially defined in negative terms as 'against' the other? A community is not necessarily homogenous. Class, gender, age, culture, ethnicity and other such affinities each make a play for individuals' support in a way which is against the notion of community.

Senses of identity are more atavistic, amorphous and changeable than the secular positivism implied by any stress on constitutions and laws might suggest. Identity is neither exclusive nor constant: a sense of collective self-awareness can include a number of levels or aspects of identification. These often develop or are expressed in opposition to other groups and their real or imagined aims and attributes, and these groups are frequently ones with which relations are close: for example, England and France, Canada and America, Australia and Japan. The role of the imagination is the subject of Benedict Anderson's challenging book, *Imagined Communities: Reflection on the Origins and Spread of Nationalism* (2nd edn, 1991), in which the author argues that nations and national identities are what people imagine them to be. Imagination has a broader utility than simply to the nation; it impinges upon all of our affinities and associations. Indeed, the reality of overlapping senses of collective self-awareness can be very difficult to grasp. Identities are a collection of feelings. As such, different elements of that collection come to the fore according to circumstances.

Thus community, like class or gender, is value-loaded, meaning different things to different people. Even in less starkly contrasting examples than Belfast, community implies competition as well as co-operation. In the rapidly urbanising world of Victorian England, community was premised upon the idea of middle-class 'supervision' and 'influence': that ordered and established civic hierarchies, and socialisation into certain notions of identity and pride, were prerequisites for the healthy and functioning community. Community in this context implied the universe of local power elites. Such a hierarchical, structural perception of community has the advantage of imposed uniformity, but is descriptive rather than explanatory. Of course there were local elites, enforcing civic responsibility and pride – they were, after all, supported by the emerging networks of local 'democracy' and decision-making powers introduced by a flurry of statutes, such as the Municipal Corporations Act of 1835. At the same time, these political developments imply an element of social control, as James Vernon shows in his *Politics and the People: A Study of English Political Culture, c.1815–1867* (1993). The central thesis of Vernon's book is that, despite the liberal–democratic legislation passed between 1832 and 1867, 'English politics became progressively less democratic during this period as political subjectivities and the public political sphere were defined in increasingly restrictive and exclusive fashions.' Thus the political communities of nineteenth-century England were becoming more tightly defined by the middle class.

The spatial–geographical notion of community is perhaps rather different. The idea that, for example, nineteenth-century Manchester might have been defined by a network of local government officials, bureaucrats and the enfranchised middle class, rather flattens the texture of our notion of community. Such a formulation gives no consideration to the independent, working-class communities that existed within the city. The web of connections implied by these mechanical notions of community crumbles when we consider the real social geography of the new urban centres. It was precisely because communities were breaking up that the middle classes tried to re-create artificially those social organisms – communities – which had previously been natural. The Manchester described by the social reformer, J. P. Kay, in his *Moral and Physical Condition of the Working Classes Employed in the Cotton Manufacture in Manchester* (1832), is far from homogenous:

> The township of Manchester chiefly consists of dense masses of houses, inhabited by the population engaged in the great manufactories of the cotton trade. Some of the central divisions are occupied by warehouses and shops, and a few streets by the dwellings of some of the more wealthy inhabitants; but the opulent merchants chiefly reside in the country, and

even the superior servants of their establishments, inhabit the suburban townships. Manchester, properly so called, is chiefly inhabited by shop-keepers and the labouring classes. These districts where the poor dwell are of very recent origin.

In Manchester there were (and are) dozens of communities: Scots, Welsh, Jewish, Italian and later West Indian, African and Asian. This spatial division of communities/cities, moreover, can be seen replicated many times over, from nineteenth-century Québec or Paris to present-day New York or Melbourne. In these cities some communities were working-class, others were based upon culture, religion or ethnicity, still others were not. Thus class and ethnicity offer different ways to categorise, and pointers to complex, overlapping tensions. Even in the last century, the term 'community' was hazily applied to a fuzzy range of local/regional identities.

'Community' has a huge range of meanings. Today, in the context of global ecology, for example, community might mean 'British' or European as opposed to the globe itself. For ordinary people, however, the crispest and most meaningful application of community is just as likely to be at street level. Some writers, as Rob Colls, in 'Save our pits and communities' (*Labour History Review*, 1995), reminds us, have seen community as most important at the very lowest level of personal/group interaction. Trevor Lummis (Colls tells us) argues 'that the greater part of what is subsumed under the heading "community" is simply the class experience of women'. At this level, community becomes a living and breathing entity; a series of relationships between people sharing space, surroundings and experiences. It is also a subjective relationship. Colls, in a deeply personal testimony, writes of a time when, as a sixteen-year-old, he looked out of his bedroom window and thought, perhaps for the first time, about the nature of community. It was 1965 and Colls had been reading Richard Hoggart's *The Uses of Literacy*. 'Looking down... on a street of Tyneside flats', Colls remembers thinking that this *was* a community 'as rich as anybody else's': 'By "anybody else's" I suppose I meant any other class's.... This street of families which earned its living in the shipyards, coal mines, and small workshops and factories of the town, lived coherently and, so it seemed, pleasurably.'

In recent years, Colls's community of South Shields, like those of so many other places in the North, has been challenged by the closure of most of its heavy industries. Coal is gone, ships have gone, the small workshops have gone, replaced by Nissan, Samsung, McDonalds, or else by nothing. Unemployment is high, although not compared to that experienced in, say, Calcutta or even Spain. Yet in the Tyneside town, the community living 'pleasurably' (which itself is partly mythical) has been replaced with a community more obviously strained by crime and decay, despair and hardship. The working-class communities that were seemingly unaffected by the ravages of time from the 1860s to the 'swinging 60s' have suddenly taken on a new meaning. Thus it seems that in working-class history the term 'community', as a conceptual tool of historical analysis, only comes to life (in a critical fashion) when the community itself is under threat. The argument about communities being built and rebuilt, heterogeneous as well as homogenous, becomes especially relevant in a case like South Shields.

Historians tend to see the term 'community' as a wholly positive concept: this is erroneous. In fact, many of the instances of 'community' detailed by historians are negative. Community values are usually very unforgiving if individuals or small groups do not conform to wider notions of acceptable behaviour. In both official and unofficial terms, communities tend to be dominated by oligarchs of often unelected individuals, whether paid bureaucrats or self-styled 'community leaders'.

The key to understanding community as a concept for historical inquiry lies in drawing a line between its descriptive and analytical dimensions. Too many historians say 'class' when they mean 'occupational status', and community has been similarly misapplied. Community is about sentiments, values and a sense of belonging; it is a series of dynamic relationships between people who share certain experiences, or who seek to create links by finding or emphasising such experiences. Used in this way, community opens up a new notion of identity which can include or subsume many other concepts – class, gender and ethnicity; family, neighbourhood and workplace – in a model which competes with and is more responsive than that of nation or country. Community, like nation or class, is a term with special applications at grass-roots level; it is as much about the street or housing estate as it is about the town or village. It suggests particular class affinities and shared workplace and neighbourhood experiences. However, it certainly is not wholly positive or constructive and should not be used as a blanket term without reference to its dynamism and variability.

ETHNICITY

American scholarship has always reflected the special, indeed central, part played by immigrants in the history of the United States. Since the first encounter between Amerindians (American Indian peoples) and the Spanish conquistadores, in the southern part of the continent (during the late fifteenth century), to the large-scale white settlement, the slave trade and massive population movements of the eighteenth, and particularly the nineteenth, centuries, American culture and ethnicity have been drawn from the four corners of the globe. The opening lines of Oscar Handlin's classic work, *The Uprooted: The Epic History of the Great Migrations that Made the American People* (1977 edn), sum up the importance of this dimension of the history of the USA: 'Once I thought to write a history of the immigrants in America. Then I discovered that the immigrants *were* American history.'

The identity of most countries, like that of Britain, has always allowed room for the regional and local dimension of national life. At the same time, Europe's regions, small nations and languages look to the European Union to protect and advance their precious cultural inheritance, or what can be defined thus. Support for the small ethnic groups of Europe, from the Scottish Highlands, to Wales, to Catalonia, has resulted in increased funding opportunities for cultural activities, including native-tongue radio and television broadcasting and historical research.

The history of Britain over the past century or so has encouraged the study of ethnicity. Why? The primary reason is mass immigration. Since the 1840s, when Irish settlement in Britain reached major proportions due to the Great Famine (1845–52), the scale, pace and diversity of immigration have been considerable. In the later nineteenth century, Irish settlers were matched by the arrival of Jews from eastern Europe, including those fleeing the Tsarist pogroms of the 1890s. At the same time, major migrations from Germany, Italy and Poland were also gathering pace. In the twentieth century, these predominantly white movements have been surpassed by what was dubbed 'New Commonwealth' immigration: settlers originating in Africa, the Indian subcontinent and the West Indies. Yet it would be false to see this as a purely modern development. Britain has always been a collection of ethnically composite countries, and in the early eighteenth century Defoe described England as a 'Mongrel Nation'. Recent history requires that scholars and students alike come to terms with the variety of our cultural and ethnic heritage. The idea of one history for one people (implicitly a white history for white people) has gone. Ethnicity, as much as class or nation, must be a part of the historian's project.

Britain, of course, is not a country almost entirely made up of immigrants (unlike the USA or the former dominions of the British

Empire) – not, that is, unless we go back to the last millennium and try to quantify the tribal movements across the Channel and the North and Irish Seas, which dominate the demographic and thus cultural history of the period between the fall of Rome and the Battle of Hastings. At the same time, study of our clearly ethnically-mixed recent history has been limited next to the American example. In fact, more words have probably been written on any one ethnic group in the USA – say Italian or Irish – than has been given over to all settlers in Britain since the 1840s.

The term 'ethnicity' questions dominant and received wisdoms. To talk of ethnic diversity in the United Kingdom, where ruling elites pride themselves on a unitary vision of one people, raises fear and excitement. The idea of a multicultural national curriculum is the subject of intense debate. So what is ethnicity? In a recent study, *German Immigrants in Nineteenth Century Britain* (1995), Panikos Panayi trenchantly describes ethnicity as 'the way in which members of a national, racial or religious grouping maintain an identity with people of the same community in a variety of official and unofficial ways', while Dale T. Knobel, in *Paddy and the Republic: Ethnicity and Nationality in Antebellum America* (1986), writes of ethnicity as 'socio-psychological rather than anthropological', taking ethnicity to be subjective and ascribed rather than objective and ideal. There are tensions in defining ethnicity. For example, as Knobel implies, there is a dimension of the term which is anthropological. As Elizabeth Tonkin *et al.*, in *History and Ethnicity* (1989), have stated, 'Ethnicity, and ethnic group, like so many less scholarly terms of human identification, occupy one side of a duality, tacit or otherwise, of familiarity and strangeness.' At the same time as ethnicity is a positive concept, concerned with the mutualistic identification of, say, migrant groups, it is also negative, because as much as being the creation of the ethnic group, it is also manufactured from without. In the case of, say, Jewish settlers in Britain, this means ethnicity is both the identity conferred by the group and the stereotypes imposed by the British or by wider European or Christian ideas of race and history.

Nineteenth-century mapping techniques reflect very clearly European notions of ethnic difference. In their conception of the peoples of the world, cartographers displayed an interest in geopolitics that reflected wider assumptions about social anthropology. Ethnic distributions were seen as important, and ethnographic maps depicted where European 'nations' lived in relation to other historical peoples. Thus ethnic factors were seen to be as natural, in terms of boundary-making, as climate, geography and geology, and this enforced the idea that there were natural laws to humankind's spatial development and cultural evolution. Thus different ethnic groups came to be represented by different colours on maps, changing patterns of which charted the progress, or otherwise, of individual peoples. As Edward Gower, in his *Historic Geographical Atlas of the Middle and Modern Ages* (1853), stated:

> To render the work easy of reference, special attention has been given to tinting and colouring maps, by which the tribes of particular races, as the Germanic, the Hunnish, the Mongols, and the Turkish are represented by distinctive colours. This method of colouring will be found of great utility, especially in tracing from map to map the onward or retrogressive course of such tribes, from their former localities to their present possessions, through the various changes and revolutions which have passed over the states, kingdoms and empires founded by them.

Ethnicity was thus both a means to interrogate the past and an important aspect of contemporary tensions in the nineteenth century. It was used to define separate communities and peoples. As with maps of state territory, there was no sense of a blurring at the margins, or of an overlap or mixture; multi-ethnicity or multiple sovereignty were also played down. Ethnographic maps can thus be seen as an aspect of the division of Europe and the world, past and present, into different and opposed units. The attitudes which underpin this idea of the landscape of ethnicity, of course, have a much broader application in terms of the lived experiences of peoples who in practice were far from being separate colours on a map.

At various times, the USA has been called the 'melting-pot' (a nineteenth-century idea, whereby immigrants were supposed to blend into a new race of people) and the 'salad bowl' (in which individual identities added richness, texture, variety and colour to the republic's ethnic complexion). The question of what constitutes American-ness has been much considered by social scientists and politicians. In the old world, however, there has been far less debate about what constitutes, say, French, German or British identity. In Britain, the dominant belief in social homogeneity means that studies of ethnic groups usually focus on the immediate settler generation – the group that was identifiably Irish, Polish or German, by accent, costume, culture or religion. At the same time, historiography in this country (especially labour history) is dominated by notions of class, which preclude divisions based on other than socio-economic or political lines. For this reason, historians have traditionally preferred an integrationist or assimilationist model of ethnic adaptation, wherein the first generation of settlers are obviously 'ethnic' and later generations become increasingly more class-aligned. The case of the Irish falls clearly into this class/ethnicity dichotomy. The same tension between national/ethnic and class allegiances might also be applied to many other settler groups around the world, from the Ukrainians in Canada to the Greeks in Australia.

The existence of ethnic enclaves, especially ones which persist over the generations, are seen as an embarrassment to the idea of progress and to the notions of Britain's uniquely tolerant liberal traditions. In terms of dominant ideologies, the idea of the United Kingdom has never meant a patchwork of peoples or identities. The idea that an ethnic group, by self-determination or by enforced difference, might maintain itself much beyond the initial period of 'settling in' is, in short, an affront to the homogenous and unitary conception of history which is at the heart of the Whig view. Thus labour historians have argued that Irishness was most obvious in the 1850s and 1860s (when anti-Irish violence was near-endemic) because, first, large-scale settlement in the Famine years was bound to throw 'differences' to the fore; and secondly, because the demise of Chartism broke the class-orientated affinities of English and Irish workers, centred on the campaigns of the Irishman Feargus O'Connor. The important role of Irishmen in the 'New Unionism' of the 1880s is, by contrast, seen as a measure of the assimiliation of Irish people into the wider working class. Thus ethnicity is seen in British labour history circles to be a lower form of consciousness than class – a starting point on some imaginary and linear scale of evolution for groups such as the Irish. At best ethnicity is seen as quaint (different food, clothes and customs); at worst, a spanner in the works of some greater project, as measured by strike-breaking or low levels of unionisation. Alternatively, in the case of the Irish, ethnicity is seen as of relatively little importance: the Irish, after all, were (and are) a white settler group. As John Rex, in 'Immigrants and British labour' (in K. Lunn, *Hosts, Immigrants and Minorities* 1980), has argued, 'The closeness of Irish and British culture has made the incorporation of the Irish into the working class relatively easy. Usually within three generations Irish families were able to move into core working-class positions and beyond them.'

There are two ways of looking at this. On the one hand, it might be argued that three generations is a long assimilation process for a culture allegedly so close to that of the receiver nation. On the other hand, it is possible to say that Rex's point supports the idea that class and ethnicity overlap and are not hermetically sealed from each other. This second point has been developed, in a trenchant critique of labour-history approaches, by Steve Fielding, in *Class and Ethnicity: Irish Catholics in England, 1880–1939* (1993). Fielding contends that the English working class was far from homogenous and that identities other than class have delineated the lived experiences of members of that class. These include gender, age, region and occupation; among the Irish, ethnic associations have also been crucial. For this reason, Fielding argues, the traditional working class has 'suffered death by a thousand qualifications'.

This argument has an applicability which stretches beyond the English or Irish working class. It might just as easily fit the experiences of the Japanese in America or the Indians in South Africa. The notion of a rich and diverse culture, in which ethnic as well as class traits are emphasised, promises to bear intellectual fruit for those studying a variety of immigration, minority and cultural groups. People of all regions, religions and ethnic origins carry with them bundles of beliefs, none of which are necessarily separate from the others. Thus endogamy (the notion of marrying exclusively within a tribe of people) is crucial and varies by society. In nineteenth-century Britain, for example, Irish Roman Catholics were much more likely to marry within their own religion than were indigenous groups. This brief introduction to the concept of ethnicity is meant to elicit thought among readers about their own roots and the roots of others. Conceptual clarity requires a broad mind as well as a focused one; difference is not always bad; uniformity is perhaps an illusion.

IDEOLOGY AND MENTALITY

These concepts are often used by historians; neither is without some controversy attached to it. Ideologies and mentalities are in some respects two sides of the same coin, being an attempt to understand the function of ideas at grass-roots level. Traditionally, the two have been conceptualised as the Marxist and non-Marxist approaches to popular ideas, what we might call 'the history of ideas from below'. We noted in the previous chapter, in our discussion of cultural history, that the division between the two was classically formulated around Marxist (social and economic functions) and Hegelian (where ideas are central) notions of beliefs and actions (see pp. 111–16). The dichotomy between the Marxist and non-Marxist in the French *Annales* tradition was never rigid – either epistemologically or ideologically – and is certainly much less so now.

Ideology is, in Althusser's famous definition, 'the imaginary relationship of individuals to their real conditions of existence'. Developing this idea, the influential French Marxist, Michel Vovelle, in his *Ideologies and Mentalities* (1990), argued that ideology is 'a collection of representatives, but also a collection of practices and forms of behaviour, whether conscious or unconscious'. Ideology also implies control and thus hegemony, being the diffusion of dominant ideas (say middle-class values) among the subordinate group (for example, the working class). There is a negative connotation to the term 'ideology': the idea that one person has 'beliefs' while another has 'ideology', a pejorative application which hinges on a twofold division of ideology discussed by Karl Mannheim in *Ideology and Utopia* (1936). The first is a total conception of ideology in which there is believed to be some connection between a set of beliefs and a particular group: for example, the working class, sharing common sense and consciousness. The second relates to the control aspect, whereby ideology is the imposition of a set of ideas to bolster a particular political order. Stalinist pressures in the USSR, with constant demands for the reworking of history and Communism, is a good example of the latter, but Western democratic governments have also promoted, through education and propaganda, particular sets of values and beliefs.

The mentalities approach, as we have seen in previous chapters, is encapsulated in the desire to know how past peoples thought. It drew initial inspiration from the ideas of nineteenth-century social scientists, particularly Durkheim's *représentations collectives*. Since Durkheim, the French *Annalistes* have picked up the baton of the study of mentalities, as is shown through great works like Lefebvre's *Great Fear*, Bloch's *Royal Touch* and Febvre's *The Problems of Unbelief in the Sixteenth Century*. Elsewhere, Huizinga's *Waning of the Middle Ages* is a classic of the genre. Each of these works attempts to understand past ideas and states of mind: mental structures, beliefs, superstitions and values. In more recent times, the mantle has passed to historians like Le Goff, Duby and Mandrou, whose *Introduction to Modern France, 1500–1640* (1961) is a good example of the mentalities approach, enlivened by a close reading of texts to elicit what they tell us about behaviour and ideas. The history of mentalities is history with an anthropological bent. The opening section of one chapter of Jacques Le Goff's *Medieval Civilisation* (1964) provides a trenchant summary of what mentalities are. For Le Goff, 'The mentalities and sensibilities of medieval men were dominated by a sense of insecurity which determined the basis of their attitudes.' Thus the Church was able to foster group solidarity, with religion at its centre, by constantly reminding people of their possible fate. Fearfulness in the medieval world was shaped not just by the harshness of life – the risk of death or disease – but by the prospect of what was to come in the after-life. The prospect of meeting the Devil and damnation was thought to be high; no amount of good work and conduct could guarantee a place at God's side. Salvation was an almost forlorn hope in the minds of medieval humans. In fact, Le Goff tells us: 'The Franciscan preacher Berthold of Regensburg in the thirteenth century gave the chances of salvation as 100,000 to 1, and the usual image for calculating the proportion of the chosen and the damned was that of the little group of Noah and his companions as opposed to the great number of mankind wiped out by the Flood.' This viewpoint, commonly held as it was, naturally strengthened the position of the Church and shaped the fears upon which orthodox religion could prey. In sum, mentalities, beliefs and human sensibilities were formulated primarily by the craving for identity and reassurance.

This is what Mandrou meant by 'visions of the world', and Bloch dubbed 'collective illusion'. The approach of the mentalities historians stresses collective attitudes rather than individual ones, which on one level is also true of ideology. Mentalities emphasise the unspoken rather than the explicit, the unconscious rather than the conscious, and seemingly natural belief systems. Ideology shares this ground, but is also expressly about the application of theory and is clear on where the ideas come from – that is, from above, by imposition. Whereas the history of mentalities allows for the seemingly independent generation of belief systems, hegemony (that is, ideas enforced from above), are seen not to be independent of the receiver group.

Mentalities and ideologies traditionally differ over what is termed the 'social' and the 'mental', between Marxist and anti-Marxist (or non-Marxist) traditions. Broadly speaking, argument exists about the rootedness of each approach: for Marxists, mentalities are mystifying and often seen as distinct from the social process, at the root of which is historical materialism. Thus historians of mentalities, so the argument goes, are good at explaining ideas as they exist at any point in time, but less convincing at saying how they got there in the first place; nor do they satisfactorily explain how ideas change over time. Mentalities have thus been accused of being static. In contrast, for Marxists, ideologies are an essential part of class struggle; they are superstructural creations used to maintain false consciousness among the working class – they are in the interests of the ruling elite. For example, Le Goff's *Medieval Civilisation* explanation of medival mentality could simply be evidence of the Catholic Church's hegemony, for the Church had a vested interest in making ordinary people feel that way.

For historians of mentalities their term is much broader than pure ideology; mentalities *are* sometimes meaningless, and are all the more important because they seem so meaningless to us. At the same time, whereas priests would be seen by Marxists as agents of social control (thus purveyors of ideology), Vovelle, who is both a Marxist and a mentalities historian, tells us that in late seventeenth-century Savoy there were 'a great many priests who were only too well integrated into the local rural community, sharing its vices and superstitions before the advent of the generation of "good priests" in the eighteenth century'. Similarly, observations can be made concerning priests working with the Irish population of Britain in the age of the Great Famine. These men were supposed to whip Irish Catholics into strict liturgical practices, to break their habit of heavy drinking and to discourage them from aligning with emerging terrorist groups, like the Fenians. English priests usually did these things; Irish priests, who were much more respected within Irish communities, sometimes followed the Church's lead, but often did not. Thus the tension between mentalities and ideologies is clear.

Whether historians choose ideologies or mentalities in approaching the past, there is much to applaud in inquiring into the order of thought in the past. The concern to tap past consciousness is exciting and dynamic; to understand what made people believe in the healing powers of the monarchs, or in witches, demons and the diabolic properties of black cats, is surely important. Mentalities and ideologies approaches differ only in method, not in subject matter, for both are essentially interested in real people and their ideas; both are forms of 'history from below'. The important things for students of history to appreciate is that we cannot simply say past people were different, or that past religious belief is the same as it is today; this is not a strong epistemological position (epistemology is the philosophy of knowledge). Since the 1920s, with Namier's psychoanalysis of eighteenth-century politicians, or Bloch's and Febvre's work, historians have been applying themselves very specifically to the riddles of past mental frameworks. Even before, and habitually since, historians loosely develop rough ideas as to how past actors thought: ideologies and mentalities offer a number of possibilities for ordering this process of empathy and understanding. The concept of 'history of ideas from below' gives us the chance to formalise the processes which all historians go through, to make conscious in our methodology what is already occurring subconsciously. Thus ordering ideas is perhaps the greatest conceptual leap of them all.

CONCLUSIONS

If we are to search for a philosophical reason for the emergence of theoretical or conceptual history, then it lies in the historian's perception of facts. The postmodern era has brought under scrutiny the once unquestionable belief that historians were realists and that the facts they uncover were real. Texts, it has been argued, do not reflect reality, but are instead cultural productions in themselves. Even if we avoid the philosophy of conceptual history, step back from interpretations of the epistemology of history, and concentrate upon the job in hand, there are still positive things to be gleaned from theoretical applications. Concepts help us to order and clarify. They help historians to distinguish between essential and particular features of history. Concepts can also simplify historical problems, or at least our view of them. There are, of course, pitfalls. History is not easy, and there is rarely one answer to a problem (as the propensity of historians to 'debates' suggests). Nor are concepts – created in the modern world and not used by the actors themselves – necessarily responsive to nuance. At the same time, historians inevitably *do* simplify; not even Lord Acton reported back on all of the past in its entirety: selection, ordering and choice are all in the historian's vocabulary; but definitions imply simplification. A better term is 'clarifying'. Theory need not be jargon, and it can be enlightening. Historians should be open-minded about new ideas, for they may improve our insights into the past. To test ideas in the light of theoretical developments is to show humility and insight: this is the sign of a good historian.

The essence of Part II of this study has been to consider the varying and developing nature of historical inquiry in terms of the methods, approaches and theories which historians have employed. Thus, Chapters 4 and 5 have focused upon the tools which historians bring to bear on their presentation of the past. We are left with the conclusion that history is diverse; that methods and theories, while central to the task of historical study, are neither uniform nor unchanging. It remains for us to consider how students can develop the themes presented in past chapters and apply them to their own work. Part III, therefore, presents ways of approaching this next logical step.

PART III

6

Studying history

INTRODUCTION

HISTORY is a demanding subject. Some of the most important features of this evolving and vibrant area of human knowledge have been discussed in previous chapters. A knowledge of what history is, how it evolved and its major currents and themes is, of course, vital to provide a context for your learning. At this juncture, however, our emphasis changes, for we must turn to the question of you – the students – as historians in your own right. Read as a whole, this book is noticeably about two constituencies: historians and students of history. The two are not entirely separate. The best students and the best historians are usually the ones who know the other's needs, aspirations and intentions. From here, therefore, we are concerned to try to give you guidance for your own personal development as historians. Not all students pursue historical studies to become historians; that much is clear. At the same time, however, it is obviously important that all students studying A level or reading for a degree should get the most from it.

The task ahead is thus to encourage you to develop efficiency, accuracy and understanding in the pursuit of historical inquiry. The achievement of good history grades is a demonstration of your ability to read and write, précis and debate. Studying history also tests coherence, originality and thought. To obtain a good degree you must show clarity, knowledge and depth of understanding and analysis. No historian can communicate effectively without basic written and oral skills. A love of history is the first requirement of the budding historian, but is rarely enough on its own. There is no guarantee that the qualifications attained will match the candidate's enthusiasm. Certain skills must be honed to maximise pontential. Harness your energy and read broadly;

159

try to take on board the advice offered over the coming chapters. Work on your methods of learning as well as the history itself.

Once your skills as a historian are honed, they will be of use in all manner of employment situations, irrespective of trade or profession. Talk to your careers guidance advisers: history degrees do not make historians alone, any more than literature degrees only make teachers. Computing, management, administration, sales, marketing, journalism: the list of work available to history graduates is seemingly endless.

The third part of *Studying History* (Chapters 6–9) focuses on the basic skills that your chosen subject of history will require. Too few students – even good ones obtaining consistently high marks – pay as much attention to form (writing style and presentation) as they do to content. A good starting point is to think about the clarity and consistency of your work; check it over with greater diligence; measure your output against the tips we give here. Every essay can be improved, each presentation sharpened up. Finally, remember, although we are writing about studying history, the majority of what we say could easily apply to other subjects. Also note that there are a number of dedicated, specialist texts available which address specifically the question of study skills. These include P. Dunleavy, *Studying for a Degree* (1986), which is a perennial favourite, and G. J. Fairbairn and C. Winch's more up-to-date, although at times more scientific, *Reading, Writing and Reasoning* (1995). Books like these will be available in your library and should be read in conjunction with what we say here, if you are really going to get to grips with developing a wide range of study skills, from basic research to well organised written work and documentary analysis. Before we explain approaches to these elements of study, this chapter considers the importance of the most fundamental of all the historian's skills: a structured approach to reading. Much of what is written here will be of use to students of history, whatever the level of study.

READING

The term 'reading for a degree' is not hollow or redundant. It means that if you want to do well in history you must read widely and deeply to keep abreast of the subject. In addition, history is one of the most book-based disciplines of all. The Internet and computers, etc., might be useful aids to study, but they are not substitutes for books. To achieve the best results in history courses, reading must be in evidence in *all* your written and oral work.

The job of history begins in the head. It develops through reading, further thought, and finally appears in the written or spoken word. In this respect, professional historians are no different from students. Even then, when good students, in the process of writing a good dissertation, get their teeth into previously unused records, they soon surpass their lecturer's/teacher's knowledge of that particular topic. When students move on to research degrees (as some do), their move into the darkness or the unknown becomes more noticeable. Students *can* make their own contribution to knowledge. Like professional historians, they are also entitled to their opinions. However, there can be problems with expressing views on the past without supporting evidence. It is here that reading and study are so important.

There is a hierarchy of knowledge, although some educationalists seem to have spent the past generation or so denying this. Some teachers emphasise that students' opinions are just as valid as those of the historians they read. This is, in fact, only partially true. In classroom discussions, there is absolutely nothing wrong with expressing an opinion. In essays, however, teachers will require evidence to support opinions. All the best essays sparkle with original concluding ideas; however, the main body of any essay requires an emphasis upon the balancing of others' opinions, and the judicious interpretation of secondary and/or primary material. Unsupported statements in essays will not draw a favourable response from markers. Equally, you cannot be expected to know as much about Daniel O'Connell or General Franco as Oliver MacDonagh or Paul Preston, who have written huge and acclaimed biographies of these historical figures.

If historical understanding begins with thought and reading, let us consider how to balance the two. This chapter focuses upon the variety of reading which lecturers and teachers expect their students to engage with. It is vital, therefore, that you are well organised. One of the keys to success in study is to do things when they need doing. Planning is crucial. At the same time, when you feel pressed, with deadlines looming, efficient working methods will help you immensely.

NOTE-TAKING

This section discusses the art of note-taking in general. What follows might be adapted to suit any situation in which you have to read and write quickly (and possibly simultaneously).

It is worth trying to develop a style of notation which suits your needs as early as possible in your school career. Think in terms of developing a system of shorthand. Do not rely on peers' notes because often you will not understand their particular notation style. In fact, this is one of the best arguments for you to maintain a good attendance record. Certain terms recur time and again in history. Begin by shortening them. For example, why write 'nineteenth century' in full when 'C19' is a common abbreviation which all historians use. Similarly, proper nouns: 'Victoria', 'Franklin', 'Pompidou' can surely be shortened; you might even write the first instance in full and write the elided version in brackets: e.g. 'Victoria (Vic)'. Look at the footnotes of journals (for example, *History*, the journal of the Historical Association [of Britain]). Notice that in many instances, the cumbersome full titles of journals, articles, books or records are elided thus: 'B. R. Mitchell, *Abstract of British Historical Statistics* (Cambridge, 1962) [hereafter Mitchell, *Abstract of BHS*]'. The key point is to develop a system of abbreviation you understand. Students, for example, often miss out words like 'and' and 'the' when making notes, and replace oft-used words or phrases – like 'historical change' – with some form of symbol. Whatever form of notation you use, make sure it is comprehensible *to you*. It might also be valuable to spend an afternoon compiling a glossary of the specifically historical words (nationalism, monarchy, Europe, First World War, etc.) which you use and decide a form of representation once and for all. The keenest among you might even think about doing a shorthand course. Journalists are still trained in this art, and students wanting to work in newspapers could do worse than pick up this useful skill in advance. However, do remember that shorthand notes *must* be transcribed in full at the first available opportunity, preferably on the same day as, say, the lecture was given. After all, this is when things are still fresh in the memory.

Once you are confident of your notation system, you should be able to take down the contents of an entire **lecture** or classroom discussion. You should never go into class with that intention, but it is good to know that, if you need more notes, you have the capacity to jot them down. More importantly, a well-developed and logical system of notation will allow you to write down the key points of a lecture or classroom session more quickly than many of your peers, and this will leave you free to listen more attentively. This then opens the door for effective lecture-room learning. Do not underestimate the importance of notes; by the end of degree-level studies you will be left with mountains of notes, book chapters, journal articles, handouts, past exam papers, essay questions and course/module guides. How else, but through effective notation and organisation, can you expect to glean all you can from this collection? Of course, you won't be able to use your notation system in essays or exams, but it will help you prepare for these logically and clearly.

THE KINDS OF WORKS YOU READ

Part of your studies programme will be to engage with a variety of historical sources. The sources available to historians are wide-ranging. As well as books, articles, and printed or written primary material, historians also examine the landscape, architecture, archaeological artefacts, and a host of other 'things' to elicit an understanding of past times. In local history you might look at churches, engravings and wrought-iron gates, as well as newspapers, local government papers and autobiographies. Your knowledge of non-written, non-textual sources will grow as time goes on; here, though, we are concentrating upon the evaluation of written documents. Even these are broad in scope.

The monograph.   The books that change the way we think about the world are often (though by no means exclusively) monographs. Your reading lists will teem with monographic texts. Reading monographs can be tedious: after all, they are often very specialised case-studies of detailed aspects of focused questions of historical importance. Others, of course, are much more memorable. For example, most of the works of the *Annales* historians, whom we have mentioned many times before, are monographs. Monographs are based on new primary research: this, at least, is their key determinant. Many are born out of Ph.D. (higher degree, doctoral) theses, rewritten, broadened out and published because they offer a new argument or a fresh look at old problems. Monographs are not usually published in great number (often fewer than 1000 copies), and, though some reach a wider audience, the majority do not. Monographs can be distinguished by their often huge bibliographies and copious footnotes referring to reams of primary material. Monographs are often technical and can be written in very dry, precise language. Nevertheless, many of them are important to students and they will provide perhaps your most testing secondary reading at undergraduate level.

The textbook.   What is general history? What is popular history? Certain historians view writing textbooks virtually as a crime, and would argue that writing a textbook is not the sort of task for which academics should be awarded study leave. Other historians write many textbooks, and/or excellent general studies, and do not view them with disdain. Indeed, textbooks serve a student constituency and also break into a general market. They make history accessible, both in monetary and intellectual terms: they are pitched more broadly and are produced much more cheaply than monographs. The best textbooks synthesise debates and controversies in history, as well as providing new ideas for the reader to consider. They effectively overview and condense drier works and can thus be seen as 'many monographs made comprehensible and accessible'. Textbooks will always be your starting point. When used properly, the textbook is a springboard to launch further reading and research. Textbooks are written to inform and clarify. All such works contain good bibliographies or sections on further reading in which authors often evaluate the literature in order to help readers who are unfamilar with a topic. In this sense, textbooks are invaluable.

The article.   The journal article is usually the most specialised of all. Most articles fit one of three definitions: (i) they are drawn from monographic research; (ii) they are contributions to key debates; (iii) they are side-products of monographic research which are too detailed or specialised even for a monograph. Journal articles appear more quickly than book-length studies and so are required reading for those who wish to stay up to the pace on given topics (it is necessary to qualify this by noting some journals, for example the *English Historical Review*, can take very much longer to publish work). It is important, therefore, to select the most relevant examples for essays; whereas for dissertations, the net can be cast wider.

The primary source.   It is almost trite to have one category labelled 'primary source' because many materials can fall under this heading. Primary sources are the raw materials − the sand, water and cement − of history. They include unpublished manuscript materials (like diaries), published materials (like journals or government department minutes, etc.) and the records − published, or otherwise; manuscript or not − of any historical organisation or individual. These are essential for original work and can be intrinsic to the best student dissertations.

Intermediate sources.   Newspapers, contemporary historical books and articles, etc., are more difficult to classify. Newspapers, for example, do not record what happened, but what journalists thought/ were told had happened. This might well apply to all manner of sources, but the criticism is especially levelled at the likes of newspapers.

Novels that date from your period of study are also intermediate in the sense that they are neither primary nor secondary. These sources are, of course very valuable to historians. Most history courses – whether at A level, degree level or their equivalent – will include analysis of primary and intermediate records.

EFFECTIVE READING

It is all very well having a logical system of notation, but if it encourages you to write down everything your teacher says, or to write down 70 pages of notes on a 200-page book, then the system is actually making work rather than encouraging efficiency or enabling more work to be done in a given time. The commonest errors students of history make during note-taking is (i) writing everything down, without discrimination; or (ii) simply taking quotations from a book. The first error shows a lack of selectivity and reasoning. If you write it all down, can you discern what is most important? The second suggests that as you simply mine a few juicy quotations you are not able to capture the essence of a historian's argument in your own words. Let us consider an example. This is a quotation from J. A. Sharpe, *Early Modern England: A Social History, 1550–1760* (1987), concerning the changing personal relationships within families in early modern England: 'The most important of these [changes] was a shift away from a situation where human relations were based on distance, deference and patriarchy to one in which they were constructed around "affective individualism"' (pp. 57–8). Is this true to Sharpe's argument? Is this even Sharpe's own argument at all? The inverted commas around 'affective individualism' give us a clue that, in both cases, it is not. In fact, Sharpe is actually pointing out another historian's (in this case, Lawrence Stone's) argument in a chapter entitled 'The early modern family: the debate'. Sharpe is providing his reader with a précis of the historiography of this subject and goes on to point out a number of criticisms which other historians have levelled at Stone's book, *The Family, Sex and Marriage in England, 1500–1800* (1977). Therefore, you must be careful when taking down quotations that you can be sure that (i) the phrase corresponds to the argument of the historian in question; and (ii) that it suits the needs of your writing and the shape of your essay work.

We can begin to see, then, that there is a deeper aspect to note-taking; a level of penetration which students must develop. This in turn takes us into the philosophy of reading. What, then, is good reading about? Can we make our reading more scientific? Do you remember in previous chapters (especially Chapter 2) we talked about 'hermeneutics' (the science of correctly understanding texts) and the great emphasis placed upon reading, research and interrogation by Ranke, Acton and the great European scholars of the nineteenth century? Historians, whether postmodern linguists, social theorists, or old-fashioned 'fact grubbers', all set great store by writing history which accurately reflects the meaning (however defined) of the texts they have chosen to analyse.

Reading any historical work or document is concerned with discerning meaning. Gavin Fairbairn and Christopher Winch, in their excellent introductory text, *Reading, Writing and Reasoning: A Guide for Students* (1991), state that there are three main levels of meaning to reading: the **literal**, the **inferential** and the **evaluative**. What do these mean in a history context?

Literal meaning is what you see at face value. 'In 1814 Napoleon was sent into exile on the island of Elba.' You know who Napoleon is; you could find out (if you did not already know) that Elba is small island off the west coast of Italy which the Allies gave to Napoleon as an independent state. Meanwhile, the rest of the words are common knowledge, both to you, the student of history, and to everyone else. Citing this sentence in an essay would gain you few marks. If you wrote it down and moved on, the tutor would write in the margin: 'what is the significance of this?' If, however, you engaged in further reading, you would discover that Napoleon's exile on Elba was brief, and that he escaped to launch his 'Hundred Days Campaign', which ended with the Battle of Waterloo (1815). If you went on to discuss how this led to his permanent exile on the much more distant British possession, St Helena, then you really would be making inroads into understanding: the fact that St Helena is in the middle of the Atlantic, 1200 miles west of Africa, would tell you something about the fear/retribution of the powers allied against the Emperor. By connecting the otherwise un-connected sentence about Napoleon's first exile to his briefly glorious, but finally ignominious, role in a series of important European events, your appreciation of history would suddenly burst into life. You would then be in the realms of explanation and evaluation; you would have moved on from simple statements to complex events.

History is full of seemingly simple words that have more than one meaning. If you study medieval European society but do not get to grips with fundamental phrases like 'land tenure', 'fealty' and 'feudal-ism', the chances are you will end up describing rather than evaluating history. If you write simple phrases (like the one above on Napoleon) without examination, the chances are you will display knowledge (in this case, an ability to render correct facts) without any understanding (was Napoleon's first exile important? How is it connected to his 'Hundred Days Campaign'?).

At the same time, reading the 'literal' aspects of history must be done correctly. While explanation and understanding are central to historical inquiry, there is no point in getting literal transcriptions wrong. How many times can your essay contain errors like this – 'Britain and France went to war in 1940' (whereas it was actually Britain and Germany in 1939) – without marks being deducted?

Inferential reading occurs on two levels. First, you have to infer meaning when writers use metaphors, for example: 'the storm clouds gathered over Europe in 1914'. The **literal** aspect of this phrase does not work very well. All the words are familiar, but when they are read together, they have two meanings: one literal, the other metaphorical. Imagine reading an essay on 'Working-class radicalism, 1870–1914' which ended with this sentence: 'The future of Europe's many militant working-class movements was to be uncertain as the storm clouds gathered over Europe in 1914.' Does this mean that trade unions in France, Germany and Britain were sent fleeing for shelter because of a downpour of rain in 1914? Of course it does not. What our imaginary writer is saying is that the outbreak of the First World War affected the labour movements of the world. So you have managed to infer from the text that war had an impact in this sphere. You have worked this out because you understood the metaphor: you were not bamboozled by the idea of torrential rain at a union meeting, and you already knew that the First World War broke out in 1914.

The next step is to allow the inference you have drawn to lead to the next block of reading. You have analysed the imaginary article, you understood it (even the metaphor at the end); now it is time to find out about its context. You then go to other works on the labour movement during the war and after to see how that war actually affected the labour movement of your chosen country of study (or else in comparative perspective). You are now making your way into the realm of peacetime versus wartime industrialism. Your reading may then uncover something of the varying fate of world labour, in different countries, during the economic depression of the 1920s and 1930s, or due to the rise of Communism and Fascism.

Evaluation, therefore, is crucial to your reading. Words like 'analyse', 'evaluate' and 'critically assess' are often used in history essay/exam questions. Although we will deal with them in the next chapter, their important application to reading is where you must first come to understand them. Evaluating a text implies more than was done above in our example of inferential reading. Inference really means to understand the meaning of a particular metaphor, clause, sentence or paragraph. Evaluation is a much broader term: evaluation is the assignment of importance to a particular text. Is one article better than another? Do you agree with the Marxist or the liberal interpretation? Which article do you think best explains the cause of the First World War? Evaluation is, therefore, about judgement: *your judgement*, and the adjudication over the judgements of others. Do you feel the author presents a strong case; what is the evidential basis of the author's assertions? This is a key criterion of evaluation.

Clearly, evaluation becomes easier as your knowledge of history and historians grows and your familiarity with a topic is developed through study. There is, of course, a scale of learning. For example, there is nothing wrong with beginning your reading on a specific topic – say, the social consequences of New-Deal policy in 1930s America – with a textbook: in this case, perhaps, Maldwyn A. Jones's *The Limits of Liberty: American History, 1607–1980* (1983). However, to bring your knowledge up to scratch, you will need to address up-to-date and specialist works.

In the case of specific texts, it is important to try to glean as much as you can. Do not simply dismiss something because it is not your cup of tea; give due consideration to all materials on your reading list. You might not like political history, but this is hardly an acceptable excuse for not addressing the 'political' dimension of something 'social' or 'economic'. When studying a particular period or theme it is worth finding out who are the main historians in that arena. You might enjoy reading Eugene Genovese's works on American slavery, but the effectiveness of your reading, and solidity of your conclusions, will be limited if you do not realise that he is a Marxist of the 'socialist–humanist' school.

THE STRUCTURE OF READING HISTORY

Reading is not a simple process. While it comes naturally – even subconsciously – to you, it does, nevertheless, require thought and reflection. If you can make salient the process by which you read, your ability to evaluate the methods involved will be enhanced. The first battle, therefore, is to allocate enough time to reading, and then to read broadly and deeply enough to allow for logical, informed or learned judgements.

You must also learn to read in different ways. If you tried to read every book on the French Revolution, you would not have time to read anything for the other fifteen or twenty modules your degree in history requires.

Begin by **selecting the text**. Obviously your module reading list is the starting point here. If your teacher says Simon Schama's book on the French Revolution is central to the course, then read it. Try also to read a little every day; do not cram, as this rarely works. Select appropriate articles for reading – articles which are central to the themes of your lectures, seminars and essays (again, guidance will be given). In addition, try to look for material of your own. Does your library contain Lafayette's letters, or the writings of some other prominent Frenchmen of the late eighteenth century? These might not be on your reading list, but might just add colour to your essays. However, do not force the issue: do not quote an irrelevant letter of Napoleon (Emperor till 1815) if you are writing on Louis Philippe (who reigned from 1830 to 1848) just because you think quoting printed primary material will gain you marks. Marks are awarded for the good or innovative use of **relevant** material.

Now for your choice of texts. If you have a book in mind, the jacket or inside cover may give some indication of the scope and range of the work. Also check the contents page and be sure to make use of the index. Then you must look at the preface/introduction, for these should indicate what the author is trying to say about what. For example, it is common for writers to 'puff' their books. A work might have a grand title – say, *A History of the French Working Class in the Nineteenth Century* – whereas it is really about dockers in Marseilles. At the same time, the presentation of a case-study under a grand title might be the result of the book's far-reaching importance, methodological advancement or path-breaking central argument. You must decide on a book's relevance to your interests, module and assignment. Scanning its structure, as well as the bibliography and sources, will help you to do this. Remember, keeping abreast of book reviews in journals will let you know whether or not new works are worth tracking down. There will always be journals dedicated to the particular topic that you are studying. Also with journals, note that some have a system whereby articles are abstracted at the beginning, or else carry key words (e.g. 'social revolution', 'anarchism', 'Bakunin', 'Communist', 'Russia'), which will help you to decide if the article in question is relevant to you.

Let us now consider some of these rules in relation to the specific types of texts (outlined above) which students of history must read.

USING THE SOURCES YOU READ

Books and articles. It is important that you develop a system to help you to maximise the material from your reading which you can internalise and understand. It is really a case of balancing depth with breadth: studying for a degree requires you to do a lot of reading but also to retain knowledge and develop understanding from it. When you start to read, always note the particulars of the book or article in question. List author and title; place and year of publication; and publisher. You might find it useful also to make a note of the place in which you found the book/article – was it in your school/university/college library; did a friend lend it to you (if so, who)? Making a note of these details will enable you to provide full references for your essay bibliographies. This will make revision easier, and will enable you to retrieve the book should you need to consult it again. As you begin to take notes, write down the page number in the margin. This will enable you to make precise reference to facts, figures or ideas which you subsequently quote in essays, etc. These are vital examples of good practice. Lecturers and teachers will require page references. These good practices aside, how else can you make your reading and note-taking more efficient? There are in fact a variety of ways of reading. When you pick up a book or article you have three basic options:

(i) **to read it in full** and make copious notes from every part of it, from the introduction to the conclusion. You might even decide to photocopy the most important chapter (your institution will provide guidance about the legal position on copyright for student purposes) because it is so central to your work.

(ii) **to skim read**, gaining only a general impression of the contents, perhaps making a few notes which encapsulate its position and which are most important for your particular essays or exam, etc.

(iii) **to dip into** the book or article, searching only for very specific material. For example, you might feel you need only to read one chapter on 'culture and consumption' from a textbook called *A Social History of Modern Germany*.

Each of these is a viable way of approaching your reading of history. The secret is not to use only one method all the time. It is also important to recognise that each of these approaches is related and can be used in conjunction with the others. At the same time, the second two methods actually speed up your ability to read books and must be seen as a preliminary exercise to help you decide 'what next?' for your reading.

Skimming is very important. It gives you freedom to consult many texts, and this can only broaden your historical perspective. For example, you can probably skim read more than five books in the time it would take to read one book in its entirety, and make notes on it. Most history teachers will advise their students to skim read all books and articles before deciding whether they deserve deeper treatment. Skimming will enable you to get the gist of what an author is trying to say; successful skim reading will leave you with a clear idea of the main thrust of a work. Remember, in this sense skimming is preparatory; only after deducing the general trends of a book can you then go on to register what is and what is not central to the text. It is possible to leave a book after skimming it; you might even feel that the material you glean could be used; but, as a rule, skimming should only be used to plot a future course through your texts. Use skimming to decide whether to read on in depth. Do not think that skimming alone can get you through; you will inevitably miss nuances, or sophisticated points if you only skim.

There are no set rules on how to skim. No two people will skim in the same way. Some readers just miss out large chunks (which is also known as **skipping**); others glance at pages (vertically, horizontally and/or diagonally), waiting for key words to leap out (this is also called **scanning**). Skimming must include examination of the introduction, conclusion and the beginning and end of individual chapters.

Dipping is something which historians do all the time. For example, you may sometimes discover that no more than one or two chapters from most textbooks are of use to you. Monographs are more difficult to dip read because this approach means you will then be breaking across the thesis (the central argument). Articles usually need to be either skimmed or read in full. Dipping is not really practicable for shorter works, where the argument will not appear until the whole has been read. Thus, skim first to see if a full reading is required. If you locate a book which has one or two relevant chapters, it is advisable that you should also read the introduction and conclusion to see (i) what the author is trying to say; and (ii) whether the chapters which concern you are consistent with the author's professed intentions.

Skimming and dipping are best done in conjunction with the table of contents and/or index.

In general, the notes you make from reading should distinguish between facts, hypotheses and conjecture. Always be critical of what the writer is asking you to believe. As you build up a corpus of notes, drawn against different sources, you will find that historians interpret facts in different ways. Concentrate your reading on learning which arguments and interpretations underpin the writers' positions. Your notes should also reflect this questioning position. When writing notes from reading, always use your own words; students sometimes quote passages that are not worth quoting. As a rule, you should ask yourself three things: (i) 'is that quotation definitive?'; (ii) 'does it contain a striking image or metaphor?'; and (iii) 'is it written in such a way that I could not match it for style and pith?' If the answer to any of these questions is no, then your chosen quotation would be better expressed in your own words. This also means avoiding close paraphrasing, because paraphrasing will inevitably result in the retention of key features of the author's original words (for example, a metaphor). If you avoid over-use of quotations, and use your own words (rather than simply paraphrasing), the risk of plagiarism will be reduced (plagiarism is discussed in the next chapter).

Is it possible to summarise the reading techniques that we have outlined here? Fairbairn and Winch suggest that students should use the five-stage **SQ3R** model: 'survey', 'question', 'read', 'recite' and 'review'. Each of these stages represents your reading and learning at a given point. It can be applied to any reading situation. The basic points, expanded into stages of learning, look like this:

1. **Survey** This is where you skim to find out whether the text is of any use. By the end of this stage you know broadly what the book/article is about.
2. **Question** This is the thought process which follows stage 1. At this point you are asking: is the text useful? If it is, you then ask, what does it contain and where can it be used? Your skimming has led to a conclusion as to whether you now go on to read in full, whether you dip in further, or whether you put the book down. Your questioning thus expresses a level of understanding about the text.
3. **Read** This involves detailed reading and note-taking. The decision to **read** has been made from conclusions drawn in stages 1 and 2.
4. **Recite** This is the final part of reading a particular text. Here you sit down and think about what the text has taught you. This section is about answers to questions.

5. **Review** This is a logical progression from the previous stage. At this point the context of your reading is explored. Where do I go from here? What other texts need to be consulted? What questons remain unanswered? This section is about questions arising from both previous questions and answers.

Primary sources. Reading primary sources is different from reading books in several important respects. First, the author has not usually written the primary source to argue a case (although this can happen). The primary text does not speak to the historian; unlike a book, it is not trying to convince anyone of an argument. The questions of authorship and context are thus absolutely vital in the analysis of primary material. If you imagine looking at a letter, a court report or a newspaper article, it is important to ask a series of questions about the text in front of you:

(i)   who wrote the document?
(ii) why (for what purpose) did they write the document?
(iii) what is the document's historical context (e.g. wartime or peacetime, Republican or Democrat administration, Jacobin or Girondin, etc.)?
(iv) what was the document's function?
(v)   who/what was the document's intended audience?

The health reports of a nineteenth-century doctor are less than useful if you do not know who the doctor was, if he had an axe to grind, and who he was working for. It is important with primary research that you give considerable time to questioning the document's very nature. Do not simply mine primary sources for quotations. Show that you have worked on the context. If names are mentioned, see if you can locate them; if dates or events are mentioned, see if they are significant; if, for example, your document is a letter, find who is the 'Dear John' to whom it is addressed. The context of primary materials is vital to give them a sense of time and meaning – a rootedness that connects them to the wider history of the times you are studying.

This is why at A level document questions are often broken down into a series of questions which not only probe the student's knowledge but also act as a template for treating most documents. In nineteenth-century British history, examiners have often used poetry, as an interesting, interdisciplinary and socially relevant art form, to frame document questions. Shelley's *The Masque of Anarchy* (1819) is commonly used. Here are a few stanzas from that poem:

As I lay asleep in Italy
There came a voice from over the
Sea,
And with great force it forth led
me
To walk in the visions of Poesy.

I met Murder on the way -
He had a mask like Castlereagh -
Very smooth he looked, yet grim;
Seven blood-hounds followed him;

All were fat; and well they might
Be in admirable plight,
For one by one, and two by two,
He tossed them human hearts to
chew
Which from his wide cloak he
drew.

Next came Fraud and he had on,
Like Eldon, an ermined gown;
His big tears, for he wept well,
Turned to mill-stones as they fell.
And the little children, who
Round his feet played to and fro,
Thinking every tear a gem,
Had their brains knocked out by
Them.

Clothed with the Bible, as with
light,
And the shadows of the night,
Like Sidmouth, next, Hypocrisy
On a crocodile went by.

What questions can we ask of these lines? As historians, our interests might be different from those of the scholar of literature. At the same time, we still want to know something about this young poet, Shelley, otherwise our understanding will be abstracted somewhat from the author's purpose. If we point out that *The Masque of Anarchy* was written in 1819, the context becomes much clearer, but we must know why the year was significant. Shelley wrote this long and vitriolic attack in Italy after hearing of the Peterloo Massacre, which occurred in August of that year. Any analysis of these lines must answer questions about the particular socio-political context: the radical upheaval of the era; the deaths that occurred as the Salford crowd gathered at St Peter's Fields to hear Henry 'Orator' Hunt; the apparent brutality of Lord Liverpool's administration, and the interplay between the government and the courts. It would also have to understand the significance of the timing: that the 'Peterloo Massacre' (the term itself was a skit on the great victory of Waterloo four years earlier) was perhaps the apogee of working-class radical discontent in the post-war years, 1815–19. The ruling elite feared revolution, and the legislation passed in this period (including the suspension of *habeas corpus* and acts to 'gag' radicals and seditioners) was, by modern liberal standards, brutal and punitive. Knowing who Castlereagh, Eldon and Sidmouth were is also crucial: what were their roles in Lord Liverpool's government? These questions – and answers to them – would also be central to any analysis of *The Mask of Anarchy* as an historical document. Equally, Shelley's atheism shines through in his attack: this too would provide valuable and necessary context. At the same time, the same model of evaluation should be applicable to any document or series of sources which you consult. Begin by reading the text to see if it is relevant for you. Once you have ascertained that it is, then begin to consider questions of context, authorship, timing and purpose.

Consider a further example. This extract comes from W. G. Todd, 'The Irish in England' (*Dublin Review*, Vol. 41, 1856):

> One of the most favoured objects of attack in the daily controversies between Protestant and Catholic is the priest. He bears in his person the reproach of Christ. Every eye is directed towards him with an unfriendly or an inquisitive glance, as he passes along the streets, and every tongue is filled with reproach. In England, more than in any other part of the civilised world, the Catholic priest has reason to feel the force and the consolation of our Saviour's words, 'If the world hate you, ye know that it hateth Me before you.' Now there is nothing which more readily excites the fiery zeal and anger of the Catholic poor, (and at the best of times they are very 'near their passion') than this incessant, never ending abuse of the priest. The Irish retain the most profound veneration for the Sacerdotal office and character.

This extract concerns native hostility and the relationship between the Irish Catholics and their priests. It is a piece of sentimental propaganda, but there is more than a grain of truth in it. What do you need to know to discuss this document? Here are some suggestions:

(i)   Who was Todd?
(ii)   Why do Protestants 'attack' Catholic priests?
(iii) What is the religious character of the Irish in England?
(iv)   What does 'sacerdotal' mean?

The key to this extract, as with all others, is context. Why did Todd write his piece; what is its audience? Why is it dated 1856? What does it tell us about the history of the Irish abroad and of the relationship between Protestants and Catholics? Did the Irish really love their priests like this? If so, why? If these questions were answered, drawing on secondary reading and evaluating key phrases in this text, you would produce a good discussion. Try this type of exercise with documents of your own choice.

CONCLUSIONS

Reading is very much concerned with evaluation. You must learn to read, question and reason as part of the same connected process. Some texts are more difficult than others to atomise, although it is possible to be scientific in your approach to all texts. Try to distinguish between primary (documents) and secondary (books and articles) sources. Your pattern and range of reading are good indicators of how well your studies are progressing. If you are not using articles, if you only ever read very general texts (useful as they often are), then you probably will not gain a sufficiently deep understanding of your subject.

Now that we have considered reading, the next task is to write. As we shall see in the next chapter, there are many different kinds of writing which teachers and lecturers ask of their students. However, all written work, like all reading, should be underscored by certain values and standards.

7

Writing history (i):
the essay

INTRODUCTION

HAVING considered, in the last chapter, how to make the most of the
learning environment and to improve your own study skills, we now
move on to the next stage: writing history. In general terms, most
historians, even the seasoned old pros, find writing a tortuous and
draining affair. While research and reading can be relaxing and fulfilling,
as well as enlightening, putting the latest review, article or book into the
right words can be frustrating and time-consuming. Most historians say
that research is the 'fun' bit and that writing is a struggle. It stands to
reason, therefore, that we all – professional historians and students alike
– must take care with what we write and how we write it. As a rule,
however, teachers find that students spend too little time thinking about,
planning, drafting and redrafting essays; most students' assignments
would benefit from a second draft. This is a common failing and does
not just apply to weaker students or those who do not try. Academics will
tell you that it is not uncommon for their writings to undergo five or ten
drafts before the final copy is ready for publication. While you do not
have time for ten drafts of your essay, there is a salutary lesson here:
writing takes time. History essays are an art form, but they also benefit
from an underpinning of scientific method: that is, they benefit from
your development of a logical and reasoned approach to writing, construction and organisation. These issues will be discussed in this chapter.

WRITING: SOME GENERAL POINTS

Style. How you write is as important as what you write. Badly constructed sentences, errant puncutation and poor spelling will prevent the

177

award of high marks. In these days of word-processors and spell-check-ers, there is no excuse for poor spelling. Packages like WordPerfect and Word for Windows (the commonest today) also have grammar-checkers that will point out, for example, where you are writing in **passive** language. The **active** voice is almost always best because, as it uses fewer words, it is clearer and leaves less room for double meaning. Here are two examples, the first passive, the second active:

Caesar was stabbed by Brutus.
Brutus stabbed Caesar.

A simple example, but the extra words of the passive voice can become crucial as sentences become longer. At the same time, however, the passive is necessary if the explanation is unclear: thus, historians will often write 'It can be argued that . . '.

No matter how well you perform in seminars, or with the spoken word, you must present written arguments in clear, uncluttered and intelligible style. Why spend hours and hours writing an essay only to see it awarded a low mark because it was not spell-checked and proof-read? Always read through your history assignments, checking for problems of form, style and content.

Language.   The language you use in history essays is very impor-tant. Try to use the correct language, but not the slang, of everyday speech. Do not try to be clever with your writing style just for the sake of it. At the same time, *do* build up your vocabulary. When you come across a new word in your reading, make a note of it and look it up in the dictionary. Only use that word when you are sure of its meaning and context. Never deliberately use long words as substitutes for short ones. Never use words that are surplus to requirements. That means checking sentences and asking 'are all those words necessary?' Do not use foreign phrases or scientific words where simple English versions are available. Try to avoid jargon. Napoleon was an excellent general, but historians would not describe him as 'cool'. Avoid using too many metaphors, try not to run metaphor after metaphor. When you use them, watch out for mixed metaphors. Do not use hackneyed meta-phors that you have seen in print many times before.

Language can enhance or diminish. Do not say things that are offensive or obnoxious, unless there is some important reason for so doing (e.g. if you are quoting Hitler for an essay on Nazi Germany). It is worth bearing in mind the nostrums of political correctness when you are writing. Ask yourself: is there any gender, ethnic or class group which would be offended by my essay? However, *mankind, man* and *woman* can be used in context. It is, however, perfectly proper to use the language of the historical actors themselves. More generally, the cult of political correctness can be so limiting and tedious that a more robust style of terminology may be preferred. Do not be pompous or pretentious in your stylistic construction. For example, don't use *persons* for *people*. Watch out for archaic words like *heretofore*. Beware of words that do not mean what you think they mean: *extant* does not mean *existing* (or at least not until the third or fourth definition in the *Oxford English Dictionary*); *disinterested* does not mean *uninterested*; *decimate* means 'to reduce by one-tenth'; criminals are *hanged*, pictures are *hung*; *imply* and *infer* are not the same. The written word is meant to convey meaning to the reader. Tendentiousness, hectoring and arrogance will raise the readers' ire; poor-quality writing will simply send them mad.

Construction. Keep sentences short and compact. If you have not made your point in, say, fifteen or twenty words, you probably have not said it as crisply as you might, although qualifying clauses are often a sign of maturity. If you don't know what a semi-colon is, for example, find out by reading a text like Fowler's *Dictionary of Modern English Usage* (1926). Remember, it should be possible to remove a clause (words that occur in parenthesis: between commas, dashes or brackets) from a sentence without losing its integrity and meaning. Thus:

Hitler, that cruel and merciless tyrant, came to power, in Germany, in January 1933.

If we remove the clauses (between the commas) we still have

Hitler came to power in January 1933.

Both sentences make sense.

Paragraphs are important. They are not simply breaks you make periodically. A paragraph does not begin with a full cup of coffee and end when the doorbell rings. Paragraphs are meant to be unified wholes: they encompass, in logical progression, a particular point, argument or event. As Fowler says, 'The paragraph is essentially a unit of thought, not of length; it must be homogenous in subject matters and sequential in treatment.' Therefore, avoid jumping around from point to point as the paragraph progresses; treat it as a little essay unto itself. Begin with an opening statement, proceed with the body of evidence and argument and conclude with something that ties the thread together and which might hint at the next paragraph's content. Avoid using too many single-sentence paragraphs.

Above all, when you are writing bear in mind the questions posed by
George Orwell in 'Politics and the English language' (1946):

What am I trying to say?
What words will express it?
Is the image fresh enough to have an effect?
Could I put it more shortly?
Have I said anything that is avoidably ugly?

Footnotes and references.   It is part of the professional practice
of historians (and of other social scientists) that essays, articles, books,
etc., should carry footnotes or endnotes. These are denoted by a super-
script (raised) numeral at the end of a sentence, like this[1] or with a
bracketed reference, e.g. '(Davis, 1991: 95)'. Historians prefer the former convention, although some might accept the second (known as the
Harvard system), which must correspond to the list of authors and titles
in your bibliography. Check with your teachers and lecturers which
system is preferred.

Footnotes are a matter of courtesy to those whose *facts, figures* or *ideas*
you have used to write a particular sentence or paragraph. Footnotes
also prevent the text from being cluttered with book titles and page
numbers, etc. They also protect students against charges of plagiarism –
if you do not cite your sources, you are effectively passing off someone
else's work as your own. This is forbidden in academic circles and can
be punished with a mark of zero. Persistent offenders may find themselves thrown off a course, so it is vital – for reasons of fairness,
academic professionalism and personal development – that you learn
the art of footnoting. Here is a sample of text with footnotes:

Population movement is such a central feature of human life that historians
have not given it much thought until relatively recently.[1] (general *idea*) Yet
since the middle of the sixteenth century, 100 million people left Europe
for an alternative life in the New World; while between 1820 and the 1980s
perhaps 5 million of these migrants travelled to the United States from Ireland alone.[2] (*fact/figure*) The Irish headed for all manner of places during
the nineteenth century, when migration from Ireland reached a peak.
Although a large majority went to North America, Britain, Australia and
New Zealand, there were other notable migrations, for example, to Argentina, where 30 000 had settled by 1864.[3] (*fact/figure*)

1. This is the argument of Philip Curtin, 'Migration in the tropical world', in Virginia Yans-
    McLaughlin, *Immigration Reconsidered: History, Sociology and Politics* (New York
    and Oxford, 1990), p. 21.

2. Yans-McLaughlin, introduction, in *Immigration Reconsidered*, p. 3.
3. Patrick McKenna, 'Irish migration to Argentina', in P. O'Sullivan (ed.), *The Irish World Wide: History, Heritage, Identity* (5 vols, Leicester, 1992–96), I: *Patterns of Migration*, pp. 63–83.

In general, you might follow a system like this (again, your department will have preferred styles):

For books:

C. Lloyd, *Explanations in Social History* (1988), p. 4.

P. Burke, *The French Historical Tradition: the Annales School, 1929–89* (1990), pp. 20–35, 110–12.

Repeat references should be denoted by short titles. For example,

Lloyd, *Social History*, p. 7; Burke, *Annales*, pp. 78–82.

Use 'Ibid.' if the reference is the same as the previous footnote.

For journal articles and books, titles appear in inverted commas, while the journal or main book should appear underlined, thus:

E. J. Hobsbawm, 'From social history to the history of society', <u>Daedalus</u>, 100, Winter 1971, pp. 20–45.

E. J. Hobsbawm, 'From social history to the history of society', in M. W. Flinn and T. C. Smout (eds), <u>Essays in Social History</u> (1974), pp. 1–22.

For repeats:

Hobsbawm, 'Social history', p. 24.

These styles are to be used in both foot/endnotes and bibliographies. You *must* be consistent; use the same style throughout. (It doesn't really matter whether you <u>underline</u> or *italicise* your titles, just as long as they are properly distinguished from page numbers, names and dates.)

WRITING AN ESSAY

The matters of form and style mentioned thus far are clearly important. They will improve your confidence and your marks. Ultimately, however, the essay itself is crucial to your development as an historian. You will be worried about it, you will want to achieve good marks. At the same time, try to see the essay as a learning tool, not simply a unit of assessment. Treat it as a creation, but improve it by clarity, coherence, organisation and argument. The aim of the essay is to show that you have understood an historical issue. As we go on to discuss essay writing, do remember that the advice we offer is applicable to *any* history writing you do.

No two history essays are the same. Different lecturers prefer different types of phrases and constructions. Your task is to tailor your basic skills to the job in hand. Thus, you must answer the question on the page, rather than the one you wished to see. Thereafter, you need to use your powers of organisation and exposition to answer the question as well as you can.

It is a common misapprehension that history simply tests your knowledge of facts. This is wrong. Historians like facts, but they are well aware of their selective and problematic character and are more concerned with (i) historical problems and controversies; (ii) the interpretation of the evidence; and (iii) historiography. Your job is not simply to recite facts. This approach will gain very few marks, a bare pass at the most. Facts are simply used to support arguments.

The question.   Do bear in mind that the answer you give will *only* be assessed in relation to the *exact* question which has been set. This means that if you do not answer the right question, it does not matter how good is your answer. If you are ever in any doubt about a question, ask your teacher to clarify matters.

The first thing that confronts you is the question itself. Once you have read the question, the key thing is for you to understand what it is trying to get at. Unlike in, say, science, there is usually no single answer in history. It is not so much a case of getting the answer *right* or *wrong* as making the best case, marshalling the evidence and arguments, and making strong conclusions. Was there an 'Industrial Revolution'? Some historians say 'no', whereas others maintain that economic change throughout the later eighteenth and nineteenth centuries was sufficiently wide-ranging and violent to merit the term 'revolution'. 'Was the French Revolution a bourgeois revolution?' This was a common exam question in the 1970s, when Marxist explanations were popular; now the view has been challenged. Thus, in answering these questions, your task would be to balance the differing opinions and to add your insights in conclusion. You might agree or disagree with either statement and get a first-class mark: after all, the examiner is looking for your powers of exposition, argument and analysis, not the answer 'yes' or 'no'.

Like literature essays, history essays are usually framed in quite gentle language. You might be asked to 'state the causes of the Second World

War', but it is much more likely that you will be asked: 'discuss', 'evaluate' or 'do you agree'. How, then, do we analyse questions?

The questions you have to answer will be drawn from the course/ module you have studied. As you grow in confidence, however, you will begin to realise that such courses cross historical themes. If you are considering a question on 'gender' it stands to reason that this concept has an application to almost every period, place or event. By all means allow yourself to see history across periods and countries (in fact, this is a sign of your growing maturity and confidence), but, at the same time, do not stray too far from the topic in hand. Be judicious, and organise your material with a question: 'is this relevant?' Also, watch out for dates, and other indicators of specificity. If you are asked to comment on American politics before 1850, it is crucial that you register *before* and *1850* prior to organising your answer. Your conclusion will probably make some mention of how earlier political forms in America (say the role of anti-Catholicism) influenced later political life − this will make a positive impression − but the question is about the pre-1850 period, so place emphasis on that.

Let us consider a straightforward question:

Why did so many Europeans leave Europe during the nineteenth century?

The first task is to make sure you understand the question. What is it about? Clearly, it addresses the topic of emigration. Having established that, now decide what the scope of the topic is. This is your *primary* task. First, it concerns Europe; secondly, it asks about the nineteenth century. Most importantly, it is asking *why* Europeans emigrated. These are the central themes you must address. What else is contained in the question? These will be your *secondary* considerations. Is there a contrast between different regions/countries of Europe? How does emigration relate to wider socio-economic conditions in Europe? Begin to think further about what is implied as opposed to what is actually stated in the question. Issues will be raised which are neither *primary* nor *secondary* to your answer. We will call these *tertiary* considerations. For example, are there hidden features to the essays − features that might enhance your answer if they are included and which might detract from it if they are not? You might think about where they went to; you might also think about those who left home but did not leave Europe − i.e. those who 'migrated' within, rather than emigrated from, Europe.

Remember, if you have studied world migration, you will be aware of (i) the theory of migration (why people generally emigrate); (ii) why people left Europe; (iii) how, say, Germany was different from France or Ireland, etc.; (iv) where these people went to; and (v) why the nine-teenth century was important with respect to population change and movement. Let us juggle with the essay question and formulate a series of questions that might be an essay plan for tackling this question.

Part 1
  (i) **Introduction**: show you know what the question is about and outline how you will answer it.

Part 2
  (ii) **What is emigration**: what causes emigration (general): theory.
  (iii) **The European dimension**: facts and figures; general trends, specific instances.

Part 3
  (iv) **'Push' factors**: things in Europe (social, political, economic) that made people leave; case-studies of different types of migration (political refugees [Russia]; economic migrants [Ireland]).
  (v) **'Pull' factors**: the lure of the 'New World': American and Australasia; opportunity; chain migration (following families and traditions): examples of groups following these patterns.
  (vi) **'Facilitating' factors**: railways, steamships, emigration companies, government schemes; correspondence (letters from families, etc.); returned migrants.

Part 4
  (vii) **Conclusions**: (do not introduce new material): summary: which factors historians think are most important; which you think are most important.

How, then, would you begin to write an essay to answer this question? What would your **introduction** look like? Social science-minded historians seem to prefer a clinical approach: 'this essay seeks to argue... there are four main points to the following discussion', whereas more arts-minded historians prefer to introduce their work with a flurry of quotations, a juxtaposing of views. Perhaps the best thing is to begin with the basics (the social-science approach) and to build up the more creative (arts-based approach) as you grow in confidence. The minimum for the essay, as planned above, is to get these seven key points into the introduction. Thus, it might look something like this:

Emigration was one of the most important human experiences in the nineteenth century. Between 1800 and 1900, the population of the United States, a key recipient of Europe's leavers, grew from 5.3 million to just over 76 million. While this figure was partly the result of natural increase, emigration from Europe constituted a crucial component: in fact, with the exception of China, Europe was overwhelmingly the source of migrants to the USA. What caused Europeans to leave in such great numbers? Historians agree on a number of factors which precipitated mass exodus, but do not accord primacy to one single factor. Therefore, this essay needs to address a range of issues involved in the study of European emigration. First, it considers the theory of emigration to see if the European experience fits any of the key models. Secondly, it considers the scale of European emigration, highlighting key regions of 'leavers' and 'stayers', for this will aid our understanding of the scale and pattern of departure. The essay then goes on to look at circumstances at home ('push' factors) and abroad ('pull' factors) which caused emigration. This section will also look at those developments, such as cheap steam transport, which 'facilitated' migration. Finally, the essay will draw conclusions as to the relative importance of the various factors promoting departure, during what was one of the most significant population movements in world history.

This might seem like a long introduction, but it is well worth taking your time to map out the terrain in some detail. Clearly, you must not write page after page in the introduction, but making your intentions explicit will help you plot a true course. The above is simply an essay plan written out in expanded form. We have an initial statement about migration and then a fact which supports it (see the next section). Then we have a sophisticated listing of the essay-plan points. The final sentence hints that your conclusion will be strong because you already know that emigration is very important.

The main point is this: you do not have to know much about emigration to break the question up as we have done. The detail is added to show how individual paragraphs might be built up to tackle each section. In an exam, you would concentrate much more on the explanatory aspects (parts 1, 3 and 4). The detail from part 2(ii) would be referred to only where necessary. In an essay assignment you have more time and space (sometimes up to 3000 or 4000 words) to discuss facts and figures, as well as ideas.

When you come to writing your **conclusion** do not assume that vague generalisations are required. History students often think that because the range of their question and answer is quite narrow, they need to make grander claims than necessary. With a topic like emigration, it is possible to draw out quite grand comparative themes. Emigration, population growth, urbanisation, industrialisation, democracy –

these are some of the key features of nineteenth-century life. You can say things like 'emigration in a country like Ireland became part of the life-cycle; an accepted and expected feature of growing up'. This is true; it did. For the French, however, emigration was much less a feature of everyday life and culture. So you still have to be careful, even with the general questions.

Problems mainly arise with more focused questions. If you are writing about, say, textile weavers in Lancashire, New England or India, you have to be careful not to draw out excessively broad conclusions: 'their factory conditions were the worst experienced by any workers', for example, would be stretching the case too far. You should, therefore, draw conclusions which can be sustained by the body of evidence which you have promoted throughout the essay. The conclusion should not introduce new material, but encapsulate the most important features of what has gone before. You should write your own views in conclusion, but, again, do not stray from the evidence. Do not suddenly perform a U-turn. Having mediated between the debating parties and having weighed up the reasons for emigration, come down in favour of one or other perspective. Thus, on emigration, we might conclude:

This essay has demonstrated that there were a host of reasons why nineteenth-century Europeans emigrated in such large numbers. Some were political exiles; groups, like the Jews of Tsarist Russia, fled from religious persecution. Others went because their families told them better lives were to be had in America, South Africa or the Antipodes. Perhaps the youth of so many emigrants suggests that a spirit of adventure played a part? New technologies facilitated migration, and the growth of new industrial and urban areas, as well as a concomitant demand for labour, meant that populations became less static in the nineteenth century than they had been before. After all, the lure of work attracted people ten miles to the nearest town as well as across the Atlantic. Overall, we can say that the majority of leavers were economic migrants. Despite the importance of many other factors, this essay has demonstrated that economic considerations were most important. These economic factors are also vital because they tie together the most important 'push' and 'pull' factors, and suggest an integrated approach to the phenomenon of mass emigration – at home, emigrants were driven out by poverty and hardship; abroad, they were attracted by the prospect of opportunity and self-improvement.

You might choose to embellish this with a quotation or two – particularly one where a historian, or a contemporary, supports your conclusion that economic factors are the most important. At the same time, as we have already said, do not use quotations for decoration. This conclusion demonstrates understanding. You know there are many reasons for emigration, yet you are still able to choose the most important one.

The above question is reasonably straightforward. There is a certain corpus of material which must be included and there is also a logical way of approaching that material. At the same time, notice that there are always a number of sub-currents to any essay, and these will be uncovered by the better answers.

Let us think now about a more difficult question, one in which more emphasis is placed upon balancing opinion.

'Nationalism was more important as a product than as a cause of national unification' (J. Breuilly). Discuss.

This question requires the same kind of consideration as the other. In addition, however, it also requires you to show a second level of understanding, concerning debates as to the nature of nineteenth-century nationalism. Thus, your *primary* task here is to highlight the key words and phrases which will be discussed in the essay. The important elements here are:

nationalism, national unification, product, cause, important (importance)

Our essay will have to display: (i) that you understand the difference between 'nationalism' and the 'nation–state'; (ii) that you are aware of the relationship/differences between 'product' (effect) and 'cause'; (iii) that you can attach importance to the parts of the question. Thus you will require a *knowledge* of various features of nineteenth-century nationalism as well as nation–state building; you will also need to be able to *understand* them so that they can be evaluated against each other. This is the essence of good history. Your answer will naturally draw upon differing kinds of nationalism: depending on how your course has been taught/focused, this could include: (i) Italy and Germany as contrasting examples of nation–state building; (ii) South American post-colonial nationalism; (iii) Irish or Indian anti-colonial (i.e. anti-British) nationalism. There are many other instances, but each might be seen to represent different types of national identity/nationalism/ nation–state building.

There is, however, a different level to this question. What Breuilly states is contentious to a certain degree. There were national movements before nation–states; there was national identity before the modern (usually seen as post-1789) era. The question thus tries to elicit a measured approach to the topic, whereby you atomise it and reconstruct it again with the particular question in mind. However, this time it is asking you to discuss an historian's perspective which inevitably leads you to alternative perspectives (including your own). This question asks you to be an arbiter much more than the other, although *all* questions require some degree of judiciousness. The second question also demands you evaluate differing historiographical emphases on nationalism. On top of that, as with the first question on migration, you also need to show some knowledge of the theories of nationalism, of which there are many. Fortunately, any good course teaching an element on nationalism will cover these theoretical issues.

The secret with essays is to answer the question and to show understanding (analysis) as well as knowledge (facts). You also need to show good construction – introduction, main points and conclusion.

STATEMENT AND EVIDENCE

You now have an idea about how to tackle the essay question. The best way to improve your skills is to look at old essay questions and try your hand at planning them. Remember, you do not need to know anything about a topic to begin with the mechanical task of breaking the question down into key words/phrases. What you now need, as you prepare to write, is confidence that your essay will be balanced and well written. You also need to be able to balance statement and evidence: to show you know the importance of each and their necessarily linked relationship.

You have to make sure that the essay marker feels that you have (i) made the right case; (ii) made a strong case; or, preferably, (iii) both. For this purpose, one of the key features of a good essay is the balance between statement and evidence. Let us consider what is meant by these two terms. Here is a simple historical statement:

Hitler's childhood was marked by impoverishment.

This statement is weak, both because it has no supporting evidence and because it is wrong! Hitler himself chose to portray his early life as hard and unyielding because it suited his self-justificatory purpose. It is not unreasonable, however, that a student reading Hitler's autobiographical *Mein Kampf* (*My Struggle*) would believe Hitler's own claim to poverty and privation. Not only does this incorrect statement challenge our historical judgement, it also asks 'have you read enough sources?' If we have only Hitler's view, then the answer is no. However, if we add Alan

Bullock's *Hitler: A Study in Tyranny* (1952) to our reading, contrary evidence becomes apparent. Thus a rewritten statement, supported by evidence, might look like this:

> Hitler stated in *Mein Kampf* that his childhood was one of poverty and hardship. (*statement*) However, as Bullock argues, his father had a comfortable pension and Hitler benefited from a good education, at both primary and secondary level. (*evidence*) His schooling included a period at a commercial and technical school in Linz. (further *evidence*) Even after his father died, Hitler's mother had a pension to keep the family in a measure of comfort. Thus, Hitler's education was to continue until he was sixteen. (further *evidence*)

In history, the presentation of other writers' work is part of the procedural norm, for it is impossible for you always to quote primary material. For English, however, the primary texts – for example, the plays and poems of Shakespeare – are readily available. Unless we go to Linz in Austria to check the school records on Hitler, we cannot do other than rely on historians. The answer, then, is to use a number of historians to see if they differ in interpretation of evidence. These historians, moreover, must be ones who have made a notable contribution to the particular field you are scrutinising: in other words, steer clear of using only very general texts.

For the above passage on Hitler's early life, we know that, because Bullock's line flies in the face of Hitler's own myth-making, that Bullock is likely to be right. In addition, our knowledge of history tells us that anyone still in education at the age of sixteen in 1906 was significantly removed from the lower orders of society. However, because different criteria apply to history at different times, education to the age of sixteen is wholly unremarkable today.

Essays, of course, tend to be constructed of more complex material than a few sentences on an historical character's life. As your studies progress, you will see that questions are more contentious in that there is no right or wrong answer and that historians have debated the topics you must address. In these instances, your writing will need to balance counter-arguments; to plot a course through often turbulent waters. The key point, however, is that you need evidence to support your statements. Consider this statement:

> In the eighteenth century, social theorists were concerned about population growth.

This phrase is true enough, but, without evidence, it is meaningless. Of course they *were* concerned about population; but in what ways? This statement needs further discussion and also evidence to show what is meant. Thus:

> In the eighteenth century, social theorists were concerned about population growth. (*statement*) However, while earlier writers were concerned that population was not growing quickly enough, later observers expressed the opposite opinion. (*qualifying statement*) In 1748 Montesquieu wrote, in his *Esprit des Lois*, that 'Europe is still today in need of laws which favour the propagation of the human race', (*evidence*) whereas in 1798, Thomas Malthus published his *Essay on the Principle of Population* which made bleak forecasts of the impact upon precious natural resources of a growing population, much of which, he claimed, was redundant. (*evidence*)

Here is another, more complex paragraph. Again, notice the balance of statements and evidence; notice also the fact that a paragraph can contain more than one statement:

> Irish immigration, in the generation around the Famine years, has to be seen as part of the wider social problems which Carlyle dubbed the 'Condition of England' question. (*statement*) A host of contemporary literature addressed this question; while many textbooks on the period habitually dwell on passages from Disraeli's *Sybil*, for its portrayal of unionisation and Chartism, or Dickens's *Hard Times*, for its witty yet disturbing portrayals of political economy and the bleak industrial landscape of Coketown. (*evidence*) In the context of these social problems, and in the literature about them, perhaps no place features as visibly as does Manchester, the cotton metropolis which contemporaries saw as the very symbol of their changing world. Many social reformers took the horrors of Manchester life as their theme. (*statements*) These included Dr J. P. Kay-Shuttleworth, whose *Moral and Physical Condition of the Working Classes Employed in the Cotton Manufacture in Manchester* (1832) is a classic of the social-comment genre. (*evidence*) Kay was followed by a host of like-minded investigators, not least Friedrich Engels, whose *Conditions of the Working Class in England* (1845) contains one of the most biting assessments of Irish migration. (*further evidence*) Although Kay and Engels are known to all those with an interest in Irish settlement, their works must be seen as part of a growing body of Victorians – government officials, professionals, journalists and local amateurs – who exercised similarly troubled consciences. (*statement which leads to next paragraph*)

See the way that an idea develops in this paragraph? It starts with a statement about the 'Irish problem' of the 1830s and 1840s being part of a set of wider issues; it goes on to look at those issues; singles out a classic example (Manchester); and ties the Irish in again, near the end. Finally, a hint as to the content of the next paragraph is given by the final statement. The next paragraph *must* now be about some other aspect of the growing tradition of Victorian social commentary.

CONCLUSIONS

The essence of writing a history essay is in organisation, analysis and argument. The essay demands that you understand the question, that you answer it (and not some other question you would prefer), and that your statements are supported by evidence. The essay also requires you to prepare meticulously; to know what you will write and in which order. You must present your plan in the introduction; you must work methodically through the evidence; and you must conclude crisply and with an answer. Try to see yourself as a lawyer arguing a case. It not for nothing that history graduates often go on to study law! In many ways law and history require the same approach. You have conflicting evidence to marshal, and you have to balance the claims for historical truth of different historians. You are an arbitrator between competing views of the past. As a result, your first aim has to be an understanding of what those views might be. Essays thus demand reading. At undergraduate level, a bibliography of five or six books/articles is the minimum requirement. Your bibliography must comprise only those items you have actually used to write the essay. Do not pad out the references.

Practise the things we have outlined here, for they are relevant to every piece of written work you will submit. Basic writing skills also have a utility beyond history, for prospective employers will covet your ability to communicate above most other skills. We move on now to look at two further areas of specific interest: writing a dissertation and preparing for an exam. As you read what follows, remember the content of this chapter underpins everything that we go on to discuss. The rules of writing history, outlined here, apply to all history assignments.

8

Writing history (ii):
the dissertation

INTRODUCTION

THE dissertation is the longest piece of work you have to write for a degree in history. Dissertations vary in length, up to 15 000 words, with 10 000 being the norm. For the dissertation, unlike other written assignments (such as essays and reviews), you will be asked to choose the topic and define the question(s) answered. Most institutions require students writing dissertations to work on primary material. These might be reasonable criteria for a dissertation:

An original piece of work which demonstrates the student's:

    (i)   Understanding of relevant secondary material;
    (ii)   Ability to evaluate a small but significant body of primary evidence;
    (iii)   Ability to bring the primary evidence and secondary material to bear on a question of historical importance.

More recently, university teachers are appreciating the difficulties associated with finding primary evidence. With overseas history, of course, this problem is particularly acute. Thus some institutions will say that the dissertation should be *either* like that mentioned above *or* a rigorous re-examination of an important historical controversy *or* the application of theoretical insights to a problem to give it a new focus. These last two options (i) increase the scope for historians studying overseas history; and (ii) allow for historians concerned with perhaps more sociological (theoretical) history rather than the traditional, empirical type of history. You must check this with your institution, as some will tend towards the empirical, evidence-based dissertation because it demands that you show the full range of the historian's skills. Also note that the examination of primary evidence does not preclude theoretical exposition. This chapter, therefore, assumes that an element of primary material will be demanded of you.

The actual content of your dissertation – paragraph by paragraph – should follow the same format as the essay (see previous chapter). This chapter, therefore, presumes that by the third year you will have found an acceptable style of writing, and concentrates on the things which students find difficult with the dissertation.

CHOOSING A TOPIC AND PRELIMINARY WORK

This will happen towards the end of your second year (perhaps May or June), at the end of exams. You must give thought to your dissertation before the summer recess. It is vital you do not go away not knowing what your topic is.

This is difficult. It is imperative that you do not tackle something too broad. Your history department will probably have a named dissertation tutor: make sure you see that lecturer and ask for advice. Before you think about the topic, however, find out what the assessment criteria are for your department. Have an initial chat, and go away and think about the topic. Your library or department will probably run special workshops for students undertaking dissertations. These will give you advice about literature searches, timetabling your work, and should inform you what primary sources are available. Once you have an idea of the limitations imposed upon you, think seriously about a question/topic.

If you want to study a topic on your own country, primary sources should not be a problem. If you are, say, an American, and want to study the French Revolution, you need to ask three questions:

(i)   Can I get hold of primary material?
(ii) Is that material in a language I can read?
(iii) Is it possible to look at the American dimension of the French Revolution?

If your library holds English translations of French documents or if you can read French (and your library holds French language materials), you should be all right. If not, you might think about a topic like 'American radical politics and the French Revolution'. Even then, you still might have to ask:

(i)   Is my question focused enough?
(ii)   Is it too broad?
(iii) Is there anything original I can say about the topic?

The secret is to focus on a topic and then be prepared to focus down still further. Make sure that the topic has not been, as historians say, 'done to death'. At the same time, you must not overstretch yourself. If you do this, two things can happen: first, you never get beyond the secondary literature because there is too much; (ii) you do not see patterns in the primary material because there is also too much.

Initial supervision.   This should occur before you break up for the summer. You will know your topic and will have been allocated a supervisor who will work through your project with you.

Once you have decided on 'gender and working-class politics', 'Ireland before the Famine', or whatever, it will become apparent to you, and your department's dissertation co-ordinator, who should be your supervisor. You will be strongly advised against, and possibly be prevented from, working on a topic which has no relation to any staff specialism. There are two reasons why this might be the case: first, no one can offer you expert guidance or, secondly, because you will not have studied a related subject at first or second year, so your own background might be shakier than you think.

Your supervisor will arrange an initial meeting to discuss your proposal. Make sure you have done some initial preparation. Show you have done a little reading by preparing a short bibliography of crucial secondary material and also have ideas of where you think primary material will be. Your supervisor will then say if your topic is fine, or if it needs a clearer focus. If your topic is not viable, your supervisor will say so. He/she will also make suggestions as to where primary holdings can be found. These might involve travelling, say, to London, so it may be you want to re-think at this point. Bear in mind, then, that the majority of students work either (i) with library holdings (for example, printed primary records); or (ii) with material held in the archives of the town or city in which they are studying.

The case-study.   Once you have left your supervisor, you should have a better idea of the viability of your dissertation proposal. You will probably have been advised to write a case-study of some sort. However, do remember that any case-study must say something of wider importance, and be located in a more national historiography. Thus, you might examine, say, the Labour Party in Ayr (Scotland), but only so as to find out whether the members in Ayrshire were different from/

similar to other members, and to see what kinds of local/regional issues impacted upon this particular branch of the Party. Moreover, you will still be expected to have read important works of the Labour Party, such as Duncan Tanner's *Political Change and the Labour Party, 1900-1918* (1990). The dissertation is *crucially* concerned with context as well as case-study.

Initial plans. Early on in the process of researching and writing a dissertation, you must prepare three things: (i) a skeleton of the chapters; (ii) a one-page abstract of the topic; and (iii) a plan of execution. Let us look at these now.

Conceptualising the chapters can be difficult at first: you have done little research and only have a passing acquaintance with the topic. However, it is worth thinking about a plan in abstract terms. This will naturally change as you proceed, but that should not be seen as a cause for concern, but as a sign of your development.

Skeleton of the chapters. Here is an abstract plan for a dissertation on 'Chartism in the 1830s and 1840s: two case-studies'. (Topics like 'Chartism' or 'The Labour Party' are good for dissertation work because they operate on both national and local levels, and the interplay between these levels is crucial.) This outline could be applied to the study of *any* organisation.

A.	Preface	Why study Chartism/Acknowledgements.
B.	Introduction	Key issues in Chartism and why your study is important.
C.	Chapter 1	Overview of the historiography/theoretical factors important in studying Chartism.
D.	Chapter 2	Case-study one: Chartism in a mining area.
E.	Chapter 3	Case-study two: Chartism in a textile town.
F.	Chapter 4	Comparision and contrast: the two case-studies.
G.	Conclusion	How your studies specifically accord with/ deviate from received wisdom on Chartism.
H.	Appendices	Issues of methodology and sources which are too dense for the text and too long for footnotes.
I.	Bibliography	Primary and secondary works cited.

As you will see, this plan does not require a great knowledge of Chartism, but is instead based upon a theoretical notion of what is a case-study.

One-page abstract of the topic. A one-page abstract of your proposed dissertation might easily be based upon the above skeletal outline. It needs to include the title, the themes addressed and the main secondary and primary material to be examined. It does not have to be exhaustive or polished; nor does it need concluding comments. You will be asked to write the abstract pretty early on (possibly at the end of your second year or immediately after the third year has begun) for two reasons: first, it offers definite proof that you have thought hard about the topic (there is nothing like having to write for focusing the mind); secondly, the external examiner for your degree has to agree that your topic is viable, and this requires written proof. Again, these are matters which vary among institutions, so check. On the whole, these are matters of good practice and will help you to define your work.

Plan of execution.   The submission of a dissertation seems a long way in the future when you first begin your research. It is likely that the deadline will be some time after Easter in the final year. That is probably a whole year from the time you first begin to talk to your lecturers about a topic. However, time flies, and with other coursework to do, students sometimes put dissertations off for months. This can be disastrous. It is important to work throughout the year. Here is a theoretical plan for completion for someone graduating in 1999:

May 1998	Broad topic decided. Initial supervision.
May/June 1998	Topic refined. Primary material isolated.
June 1998	Skeleton plan. One-page précis. Inter-library loans requests for secondary material not available in your library.
Summer 1998	Most primary research completed (secondary reading all the while).
October 1998	Abstract sent to external examiner for approval. Primary research completed. Most secondary work finished. Plan in greater detail. One page per chapter.
Christmas 1998	First draft of introduction and two chapters.
January 1999	First draft of one more chapter.
February–March 1999	Draft of two further chapters.
Easter 1999	Complete draft, plus some second drafting.
April–May 1999	Final draft completed.
Late May (at the outside)	Final submission.

Notice how much front-loading there is; how much emphasis has been placed on doing preparatory work early and getting primary research finished in the summer. This is very important. By Christmas of your final year, you should only be (i) keeping abreast of secondary material; (ii) tidying up rough edges of research; and (iii) writing drafts.

Second supervision. Your second supervision might not happen until after the summer recess. However, if there is any doubt in your mind, either about your topic or about a programme of research to complete it, you must see your supervisor before you break up.

Supervisions are crucial. You must establish a good rapport with your supervisor and meet them regularly. One meeting per week is certainly not too frequent, although both parties might prefer to meet every two weeks. Regular meetings make you work; it is vital that you never go to your next supervision without having done more work than for the last meeting. Discipline yourself to work solidly, meticulously and weekly! Do not abandon your dissertation for weeks on end because you have essays to write. Keep half a day (or more) each week free to work at this important, long project. Make sure you give your supervisor material to read. Do not turn up with a first draft the night before submission and ask your supervisor to read it so that you can make hurried corrections: it will be too late by then. Make sure you give your chapters to your supervisor as you write them. Do not put off writing; the longer you leave it, the harder it will become to break the block. *Stay in touch with your supervisor.*

GROUNDWORK FOR DISSERTATIONS

The literature search. Whereas five or six books might do for an essay, a good dissertation will use more than twenty references plus primary evidence and, possibly, theoretical works.

It is important that you undertake a systematic search for secondary literature which is relevant to the field at large of your case-study/topic – whether national or regional, theoretical or historiographical. This means looking at all books which are relevant and keeping in touch with journal articles. It also means looking only at material which is *directly* relevant. Only very important (seminal) general books should be used; works that are standard references. General secondary books, however, must not dominate your work – it is supposed to be original and you must find your own niche. A topic like Chartism, for example (which is itself only one part of the British radical tradition), has generated a huge literature. In this case you will want to find materials which encapsulate the received wisdom and case-studies that complement or contrast with your own. You cannot read them all. Moreover, general social histories (with a chapter or section on Chartism) will not add much to your dissertation.

A literature search requires a systematic trawl of bibliographies, indexes and library shelves. You must make a note of all items you consult. Library catalogues can be scanned by key words as well as by title, so you do not even need to know exactly what you are looking for. The Internet enables you to access other libraries, including the National Library, and this will yield references which can be obtained through inter-library loans. Academic journals often produce indexes and bibliographies of materials in specialist areas, so it is worth checking those. Works of reference, like *British Economic and Social History: A Bibliographical Guide* (1996), edited by R. C. Richardson and W. H. Chaloner, are common. These are worth examination because they include materials, usually compiled under thematic and chronological headings, which might take months to track down. Consult your librarians for sources such as these.

Primary materials are also important for undergraduate dissertation work. Broadly speaking, you will have access to three kinds of primary works:

(i) *Printed sources, produced by publishers, which your library holds.* Examples of this type include books like E. R. Norman's *Anti-Catholicism in Victorian England* (1968) and John Killen (ed.), *The Famine Decade: Contemporary Account, 1841–1851* (1996), both of which contain excellent nineteenth-century documents. It is perfectly possible to write dissertations from this kind of work. They are quite common.

(ii) *Local and regional holdings.* These will be available (i) in your university library (or a nearby university); and (ii) in local records offices, reference sections of local libraries, etc. This is a rich and often untapped vein of material. Here you will find everything from town council minutes and trade union materials to newspapers, burial registers and records of marriage and baptism. Schools records are also available, as are records pertaining to local industry, transport and architecture, etc. Some local libraries will also keep old journals and oral history tapes. Many universities, like Bradford (oral history) and Lancaster (North-west regional studies), for example, have collections dedicated to specific types of history. This is a rich seam for dissertations, but local studies *must* be set into context.

(iii) *National holdings.* These are usually held in the capital, although important collections in England, for example, are also found in Cambridge, Oxford and other major cities or university towns. Many national records are available on microfiche, or are held in facsimile in local records centres (for example, population censuses). The scope of national records holdings is truly immense. Students who look for national records must be careful not to go beyond the scope of what can be done as a part of one year's work (which is what a dissertation is). If you use national records you *must* make sure you are addressing a very specific issue. For example, you might wish to see the government's view on a local riot that you studying. This would mean a trip to the National Archives to retrieve perhaps only a few letters and a couple of Home Office reports. If, on the other hand, you went to London to study British relations with Hungary in the 1950s, you would barely have time to read the Foreign Office records in a year, never mind writing on them. Be judicious and take advice.

WRITING THE DISSERTATION

You must write as you go along (see above). Do not leave it all to the end. With essays, you will be used to writing 1500 words or so with an introduction and conclusion. However, with a dissertation, you are expected to write perhaps 10 000 words, so each chapter might be as long as an essay. It is important that you do not write a dissertation, however, that looks like a string of essays. The key is to have a central developing argument running throughout. If the central theme, you decide, is that politics in the French Revolutionary period in your case-study town was conservative and loyalist rather than Jacobin, two things should be apparent. First, that this thesis runs concurrently through all chapters; secondly, that your reference to wider reading acknowledges that historians have argued both for and against your argument. You will, therefore, draw supporting evidence from, for example, Frank O'Gorman, and will criticise, say, E. P. Thompson. This will give your dissertation an organic and developmental momentum and will prove that you can balance *statement* and *evidence* with reference to historiographical controversy.

If we look at this mechanically, your chapters will not be free-standing structures, like essays. They must not contain introductions that imply nothing has come before or conclusions that suggest nothing comes after. In other words, you will leave each chapter slightly open-ended to lead into the next. Here is an example:

Chapter 3 might conclude with these words:

> Thus, we have seen the importance of *a, b* and *c*. However, these three factors tell us only part of the story. The following chapter continues our discussion by referring to a phenomenon, *d,* which historians traditionally have overlooked.

Chapter 4 might then start:

> The importance of *a, b* and *c* is clear from the previous discussion. The role of *d* requires our attention now because without it, I will argue, *a, b* and *c* lack important contexts.

Can you see how the two chapters are threaded together? Not only have you examined *a*, *b* and *c*, but you have also highlighted the importance of something else, *d*, which you are going on to write about. Stylistically, this shows good organisation; historically, it shows you have uncovered something interesting.

Your discussion of case-study material must be shaped around a continuing thesis – an argument – and must refer to the secondary material, which is most relevant, in a critical fashion. In a sense, you must make your own small contribution to historiography. This is especially important in the introduction, where you must state why your topic is generally important and what you will add to it. During introductions, some history students are tempted to write mini-social, economic or political histories which only vaguely correspond to the substance of their dissertations. This is an error. Choose the elements of the national historiographical picture which are (a) most controversial; (b) most up-to-date; and, most importantly, (c) which are most relevant to your work. Do not simply select historians who agree with you; the secret is to support your work *and* to argue against those who offer alternative perspectives to your own.

During the introduction you must demonstrate what you are doing, why you are doing it, and how it is important. You must set out your stall clearly and methodically. You must demonstrate an awareness of wider historical issues and explain what you will say in that context. If you have found a bundle of new sources you must state clearly – but briefly – what your methodological approach will be, and how those sources can be used. If this is too involved, you should make only brief mention of it in the introduction and write an appendix on 'sources and methods', so that reader can see the rigour with which you have gone about your business. The introduction should also mention any theoretical insights which you wish to offer. If you think existing histories of nationalism fail to address the kinds of findings which you have uncovered on, say, nineteenth-century Italy, then say so; and also point out what new position you will adopt. Finally, as with essays, make sure the introduction of your dissertation explains exactly what the following chapters will be about. Use the introduction to make clear the integrated and rational progression of your thought patterns; also make explicit what is your central argument. The main body of your text can then focus on your advancement of primary evidence.

The conclusion should mark a return to the broader canvas. Having set out what you wanted to do in the introduction, and having done it in, for example, Chapters 2 to 6, now you can turn round and say what it is you have shown. This is the time to set your conclusion back into the wider debates of historians. How is your work different from historian *a*, *b* and *c*; how does it correspond with *x*, *y* and *z*? What does it offer that is different from both sets of historians? What is the value of your findings; can you make broader conclusions about them? Is your local case-study, for example, a warning against the notion that the national picture fits all regions and localities? Have you uncovered something about the nature of local power or culture? These are the kinds of conclusions – rooted in reference to your previous chapters and the wider historiography – that you might want to make. You might also modestly point out the limitations of your findings and say where else work might be carried out to add to your own researches (this could be useful to someone following you in future years).

Presentation.   Your institution will have very clear guidelines as to presentation. Your dissertation will have to be typed, double-line-spaced, on A4 paper. It will probably have to be bound. You will be encouraged to include tables, diagrams, charts and images, but only where they are relevant. It must have a bibliography and use footnotes (see previous chapter). The form for these things can vary, but your department will issue guidelines. By the time you come to write a dissertation you *must* be familar with the requirements of referencing and footnotes, presentation and style.

CONCLUSIONS

Despite the length of time you will be given to write it, doing a dissertation requires more discipline and efficiency than any other

mode of writing/assessment. Use on-line resources and scanning techniques to check a wide terrain for materials. When you are searching
for books and articles, remember to be selective; decide on your
approach at the outset. Define your central argument and shape your
reading around it. Discriminate against texts because they are irrelevant, not because you do not like what they say. If you choose a case-
study approach, make sure you bear in mind the context. Do not
burrow into a specific topic so deeply that you lose the wider meaning.
You must follow a well-regimented plan, and the more you have done
by Christmas the better. You must write up as you go along, and make
sure you submit drafts so that your supervisor can suggest improvements. Above all, make sure with your supervisor that your topic is not
too narrow, too broad, and that there is something worthwhile to say
about it.

9

History exams

INTRODUCTION

PREPARATION for history exams is much like that for any other subject. You are given a task to complete in an allotted time, and you must write the number of answers required to stand any chance of reaching your potential. Exams are less popular with academics than they once were, but historians seem still to think that they are a good way of testing a budding historian's mettle. In certain key respects this is true. The exam makes you think on your feet; you have a body of knowledge in your head and the exam tests if you *understand* it. That means you have to be able to sift, sort and deconstruct material on a given topic, and then reconstruct it to suit a certain question – all in about three minutes flat! – before you begin the answer proper. Once you begin to write, the pressure of the time-constrained environment illlustrates not only how quickly you think but also whether or not you can organise a coherent thread of argument in the circumstances. In this chapter, we will try to give you some tips on preparing for and executing a history exam. As a general rule, there are two kinds of exam in history: the essay paper and the document paper. We will look at both of these in this chapter.

PREPARING PROPERLY

The dedicated literature on study skills, one or two important items of which are included in our Further Reading section, set great store by your preparation and planning for exams. This is right. Exams do not simply happen on a given date at a set time; they are the summation of your year or semester of work and must be integrated into your general study of history. That means, when you make notes, when you write term essays, when you research and read for your degree, you must keep that final exam in your mind. Your focused revision might only begin two or three weeks before an exam, but try to think about 'possible exam questions' as you and your colleagues work through the topics on a history course. Have a clutch of old papers at hand from the beginning (you will find these in your library's xerox collection); they will show where the lecturer is coming from, how he/she frames questions, as well as the scope of possible questions for a particular topic. Link these exam papers to (i) lecture notes; (ii) notes from further reading; (iii) textbooks and articles; (iv) seminar notes; and (v) the feedback which your lecturer has given you.

Think about topics in their entirety throughout the year. Prepare widely in the first instance, and remember, if your paper is going to say 'answer three questions', then you are cutting it fine if you only revise three. You need to revise twice as many topics as questions to be answered, with one extra for safety, making seven for a three-question paper. At A level more topics are needed because of the examiners' habit of selecting only a few questions from dozens of topics. At degree level, you will probably get a question on most topics you have covered. This does not mean you can be complacent. You need to prepare more than the minimum, in case you do not like the wording or angle of one or more of the questions.

TOPIC ASSESSMENT

In readiness for an exam, you need to begin specialised preparation. Divide all your materials into topics or themes and read them as individual units. Then read across them to see where patterns emerge. Remember, unlike with literature, certain themes cannot be understood without reference to others. A good answer on migration is bound to mention population growth, industrialisation and urbanisation, whereas it is perfectly possible to answer three questions on Shakespeare without knowing all his plays or even all the plays which your class has studied. Remember, history is best viewed as an integrated whole; society in the past, just as society today, is not made up of hermetically sealed categories. This makes history difficult, but it also means there is room for the more general reflection, so long as it is rooted in some observable reading. This can be invaluable if you find yourself struggling for a third or fourth answer.

Within a couple of months of the exam you should have decided which themes you will revise. You should then have a collection of material dedicated to that topic. Make sure this material includes photocopies of any crucial articles or chapters, etc. Discuss it with your peers: joint-revision sessions can be very fruitful. See how many angles you can approach the topic from. Assess your own weaknesses (as evinced in coursework and seminar feedback) and work on them. At the same time, do not cut adrift from the wider process of learning: keep checking the current literature in journals and reviews, etc. An exam script with references to a very recent historiographical gem will go down very well.

REVISION PROPER

THIS should begin at least three weeks before the exam; earlier if you are a slow worker. Use your judgement. First, you have to ask yourself this: what is the exam trying to test? Too many students think exams are a test of *knowledge* – that they demand you spiel out some facts, memorised so well you can almost visualise them written on the pages of your lecture notebook. This is not the case. History, like literature and other arts and science subjects, is about *understanding*. Historians want their students to show that they came into the room with a flexible body of ideas (which they understood), sat down and marshalled those ideas, and presented them to answer the particular question on the paper. Too often examiners are faced with work which just rehashes term-time essays in a fashion so badly concealed that they do not even try to answer the question in hand. You will find that the *rote-learning* method never works because the term-time and exam questions are never the same. You must, therefore, develop a *flexible* approach to learning. You will get very few marks if you simply rehash your essays and ignore the question's wording.

During your revision for a history exam, it is important not simply to read and re-read your notes. This approach lends itself to a subconscious, if not conscious, rote learning. Reading on its own is too *passive*. You need to engage with *active* revision. This means making notes all the while. Do not make notes from new material in the critical last two weeks – unless it is a crucial recent synthesis or important new source of ideas – but concentrate on making briefer notes from your existing corpus of notes. Try to break down the notes you have on a topic (remember, there could be dozens of pages) into smaller and smaller chunks, again and again. Use buzz-words and list further buzz-words under those. A good way of revising is to make fewer notes, whereby at the end of your revision programme – say a day or two before the exam – you might have distilled a topic to two sides of notes filled with a list of buzz-words, each of which refers to a sub-theme, event, approach, historian, or whatever. This is a better way of *absorbing* your material than simply reading notes over and over again.

In general, it is sensible if you try to organise each of your chosen themes into sub-themes. You might follow a plan something like this:

1. **Introductory/overview** What are the general issues involved? The issues you would draw out in your introduction.
2. **Historiography** How has the writing of the topic developed? (A list of historians and their contribution.)
3. **Theories** Are there social /political/ economic theories associated with the topic? How useful are they?
3. **Controversies** How and why have historians disagreed?
4. **Sources and methods** Has the topic been approached in different ways by historians; have they interpreted the same evidence differently?
5. **Events and incidents** How do *key* events/incidents/facts help us understand the topic?
6. **Concluding** Importance, perspectives, overview of the topic/ theme.

If you break up a theme in this way, you will immediately avoid the tendency to narrate a story, or to give a blow-by-blow account of facts. By reorganising a topic like this, you will be less attracted to the mono-causal, unilinear 'only one answer' approach. The identification of these key platforms should enable you to answer the question from a variety of perspectives. If the question addresses controversies, you know where to look; if it asks about the historiography, this is where you will begin. In effect, you are organising your material in advance of the exam. This means that you do not have to mess around in the exam. Do not go in hoping for a certain question: go in believing that you can follow any approach on that topic.

PRACTISING FOR EXAMS

You need to practise for exams.   They have to become second nature to you. The better your preparation, the easier you will find them. During the year, why not try practice answers? Collect papers and work over the questions which most interest you. Sit down as though you were in an exam and try to answer the question in the given time, an hour, or whatever. Use these 'dry runs' to experiment. If you have trouble with exams, try changing your approach.

The first point of departure must be to make essay plans. Pull together as many questions on a topic as you can and begin to plan them. Notice how different questions can ask for radically different approaches to what is, basically, the same material. Your plan should consist of a few words or a sentence that encapsulates each paragraph. Each one should be a *statement* (see Chapter 7) which you will defend or criticise with *evidence*. Look at each point in your plan and imagine what comes next. Also think about the kind of phrase which is needed to connect, say, point 6 to point 7. That way, you will begin to imagine in a connected and seamless fashion, whereas too many examinees think in staccato, broken flashes which do not lend themselves to a balanced and contiguous answer. *Always make such sketch plans part of your preparations.* Once you are confident that you can plan an essay like this in two or four minutes, use such a plan and expand it into a timed essay. Read back over your work and see where it is weak and where it is strong.

THE QUESTION

When you look at the exam paper, make sure you read the question that is there and not the one that you wish was there. Let us look more closely at our two kinds of history question: the essay and the document.

The essay question.   This will be familar to you in so far as you have seen essay questions – whether in exams or not – dozens of times before. The key difference between term-time and exam essays is the amount that you can get into them. With the term essay you can craft and style your prose; you can leaf in layers of argument and example; you can write and write and rewrite; you can afford many facts and a number of quotations; you will be required to include footnotes and bibliographies. None of this can be done for the time-constrained test, so do not even try. The examiner will think you are wasting time if you deal in superfluities. For example, do not include footnotes, nor append a bibliography. In exams, weaker students have a tendency to 'pad' things out. It is always curious to read a script in which '1865' suddenly changes to 'eighteen hundred and sixty-five' because the student does not feel their answer is long enough. Avoid this kind of thing.

When you are answering the question, your focus must be on *understanding*, not *knowledge*. The examiner wants to know if you understood the question, if you can answer it and if you have evidence to support your case. He/she does not want to read reams of facts; equally, quotations must only be seen as the *icing on the cake*. No marks whatever are awarded for feats of memory. If you are asked, in your American history exam, to 'compare and contrast Jeffersonian and Jacksonian democracy', the examiner does not want to read endless personal details about the life of these two American presidents, nor read quirky little quotations about them. He/she wants to see whether you know what the two forms of democracy were; what they meant for the two presidents in office; how they impact upon the office of President; how, or if, they reflected the common aspirations of ordinary Americans; how their legacies have influenced later developments in American politics. Similarly, a social science-type history question – say, on population – does not necessarily require you to write reams and reams of statistics. It is more likely to want you to understand: (i) general trends in population history; (ii) what sources historians use to understand past population; (iii) how historians have assessed those sources; (iv) where historians have disagreed; and (v) how population has affected other areas of life (i.e. migration, urbanisation and state policy, or social theory, etc.). You will not perform to your potential if you recite the population figures for a number of countries in, say, Europe. The key to the exam essay is to *analyse*, not to *describe*.

The document question. Documents often worry history students, even though they are the meat and drink of historians, and we all have to get used to them. A true understanding of documents comes with time and experience. Most students will be introduced to documents at A level (or equivalent), and will be tested on them at this stage. At degree level, documents tend to be used in all three years, but are only really examined in a time-constrained environment during the third year in special subject courses.

We have already looked at documents (Chapter 6). However, during exams, documents present a specific problem. The document paper consists of a range of documents, and you are usually asked to comment on a number of them (perhaps two to four). At A level, you may be asked a series of questions about the document; at degree level you are more likely to be asked to 'comment on the following'.

This is the kind of document which might be set for a special subject paper on 'The Great Famine in Ireland, 1845–52':

> THE PRESENT CONDITION OF IRELAND, in the midst of its danger and calamity, has that element of consolation which proverbially accompanies an intolerable excess of evil. It brought things to a crisis. It has converted a chronic into an acute disease, which will either kill or be cured. It has made that singular state of society, which in Ireland is called law, property, and social order, simply a thing which cannot any longer hold together. The sluggish, well-meaning mind of the English nation, so willing to do its duty, so slow to discover it has any duty to do, is now perforce rousing to ask itself the question, after five centuries of domination over Ireland, how many millions it is inclined to pay, not in order to save the social system which has grown up under its fostering care, but to help that precious child of its parental nurture to die easy? Any further prolongation of existence for that system no one now seems to predict, and hardly any one any longer ventures to insinuate that it deserves.
>
> This is something to be gained. The state of Ireland – not the present state merely, but the habitual state – is hitherto the most unqualified instance of signal failure which the practical genius of the English people has exhibited....
>
> Amidst the miserable paucity of suggestions, good, indifferent, or even bad, which the present Irish crisis has called forth, it is a fact that only one has hitherto been urged with any vigor, or re-echoed widely by the organs through which opinions find their way to the public; and that one is – what? A poor law, with extensive outdoor relief to the able-bodied.... That which has pauperised nearly the whole agricultural population of England is the expedient recommended for raising to comfort and independence the peasantry of Ireland.
>
> John Stuart Mill, *Morning Chronicle*, 5 October 1846.

Again, you do not need to know anything about the Famine to know how to answer this question. Effectively, you need to be able to demonstrate that you know:

(i)   who John Stuart Mill is;
(ii) about his long series of articles in the *Morning Chronicle* in 1846–47;
(iii) that Mill proposed answers to the 'Irish problem' and what some of them were;
(iv) (context) something about the calamity that had befallen Ireland;

(v)   something about the subsequent debate over England's role in Irish affairs;

(vi)   what are the important passages of the extract and what they tell us.

In relation to point (vi), it is important that you remember that it is impossible to analyse every word of a document. Indeed, the whole point is that you show understanding of the document by selecting its central points. Thus, in this instance, you have to say something about the texture of the Great Famine of which Mill writes: what exactly had happened by autumn 1846, for worse – the 'Black '47' – was yet to come? What is Mill's assessment of the economy of Ireland? What is meant by the phrase, 'The sluggish, well-meaning mind of the English nation'? The most important aspect of the document, however, concerns Mill's contempt for the then widespread idea that a new poor law would provide a panacea for Ireland's economic and social ills. Mill's concern with the weaknesses of the English Poor Law (as enacted in the reforming Poor Law Amendment Act of 1834), and his fears about an Irish version, represent important elements in the wider debate about classical political economy (as economics was then known).

Thus, in the broadest terms, as well as in some detail, you would need to show you understand context and that you can locate Mill's writings (i) in his own times; and (ii) in the subsequent genre of writing on population, emigration and Anglo-Irish relations. You would also need to texture your commentary by quoting the most important parts of the text, and by discussing those bits in detail, to show that you understood, not just Mill, but also this particular extract. It is essentially the same as writing a documentary exercise during the semester, except that you cannot use footnotes, read around the subject and add a bibliography. The documentary exercise is really the ultimate test of the student historian's ability to think on his/her feet.

CONCLUSIONS

In history you do need to learn facts, but only the ones which are important. *Selection* is vital. When it comes to your answer, examiners are much more interested in your *understanding* – of issues like debates, historiography, theories – than in your ability to cite exact dates. As with literature, historians require their students to appreciate texts and documents. In terms of understanding the past, try to see historians as being similar to literary critics – theirs is perhaps the latest word, but certainly not the only word, on a given subject or theme. Develop an *active* revision programme: this means not simply reading without making notes, but reflecting on your material. Do not try to *rote learn* your material: no examiner is looking for that. Finally, make sure your preparation is good: practise planning essays and practise writing them. Once in the exam, read the paper carefully and highlight all the questions you *can* answer: this is more positive than counting those which you cannot answer. Once you have decided which questions you will answer, cross off the others and concentrate on your chosen areas. Focus and concentration are now absolutely crucial. Then you need to plan your answers quickly, but efficiently, in the way you have practised. Be sure to answer the required number of questions and the right questions. You can survive the odd garbled phrase to get high marks; however, if you fail to answer a question at all, you are immediately taking away one-quarter or one-third of the obtainable marks, which means the other two or three answers have to be perfect to get high marks for the paper: although this will not occur and is thus a very poor strategy. Finally, do not spend too much time on one answer at the expense of others. Research shows that once an essay has taken on a certain shape (say a 'B') it is very hard to turn it into a better grade. You might spend half an hour getting only five extra marks, whereas thirty minutes on the next question might earn 40 or even 50 per cent! This stands as a monument to the need for planning and self-control, which is the essence of a confident exam performance in history and other disciplines.

Afterword

By its very nature, history is contingent. Historians know all too well that the judgements, indeed orthodoxies, of one generation will be challenged in the next. This is certainly true of historiography. It is also the case that, even in the present generation, different scholars will often have sharply contrasting views on what should be studied and how it should be approached. They also analyse current and recent trends differently. What is significant, central and/or welcome to one historian might be unimportant, marginal and unwelcome to another. These differences are often expressed overtly in historical controversies and sometimes covertly in publication strategies of journals and publishers, in course requirements and in academic patronage. Indeed, this book has been written in a fruitful interchange of views with important differences between the two authors: for example, over the nature of positivism; the validity of 'old-fashioned' political history; and the significance of Karl Marx and E. P. Thompson. This is to the good. It is wrong to believe that there is only one approach or, indeed, that there is an unquestionably correct approach. Such an authoritarian schema is unwelcome. History is most valuable if it inculcates a sense of humane scepticism (not cynicism) about explanatory models and, indeed, questions our very ability to understand the past and thus our own world.

That, of course, is a statement of our own time, and one that might not be welcome elsewhere. Other cultures today have different views of the past and of the historian's role in discussing it. The context of historical work in Iran or China in 1997 is very different from that in Britain or North America.

Nevertheless, while accepting that a statement about the contingent nature of all historical judgement is itself contingent and can be placed in a context, such a statement reflects our suppositions. The past can be approached in a number of ways; it is open to multiple interpretations. That is what makes history so interesting and so important. The moral message is not that history conforms to the didactic, self-referencing certainty of overarching, grand intellectual strategies – whatever their political sources of emphasis – but rather that historical inquiry is shaped by the necessity and value of diversity.

Suggestions for further reading

It is impossible to offer a complete reading list for the subject matter considered in this book. The following suggests key texts which you might like to consult.

THE PHILOSOPHY OF HISTORY

THE philosophy of history is a difficult subject but one which is clearly covered in a number of volumes, including W. H. Dray, *Philosophy of History* (1964), W. H. Walsh, *An Introduction to the Philosophy of History* (1967) and P. Gardiner (ed.), *The Philosophy of History* (1992). R. G. Collingwood's imperious statement, *The Idea of History* (1946), and Karl Popper's polemical essay, *The Poverty of Historicism* (1957), are what really got British historians (not least E. H. Carr) thinking about the true worth of history. A good overview of the terrain is provided in D. Le Capra and L. Kaplan (eds), *Modern European Intellectual History: Reappraisals and New Perspectives* (1982). Scott Gordon's weighty tome *The History and Philosophy of Social Science* (1991) is an excellent, though at times complex, overview. Perhaps the most accessible first port of call should be B. A. Haddock, *An Introduction to Historical Thought* (1980).

HISTORIOGRAPHY

There are a range of general studies of historiography which have flowed freely since Popper. Some are more difficult than others. Although rather dated, E. H. Carr, *What is History?* (1987 edn), still provides one of the most challenging defences of history as a social

213

science. G. R. Elton, *The Practice of History* (1987 edn), counterpoints Carr with an elegy to traditional forms of history. A systematic overview is provided by J. R. Hale (ed.), *The Evolution of British Historiography* (1967). A. Marwick, *The Nature of History* (1989 edn), is the most comprehensive synthesis; it is also the fattest. John Tosh, *The Pursuit of History* (2nd edn 1991), provides a clear, thematic overview of the main trends in history. John Vincent's biting book, *An Intelligent Person's Guide to History* (1995), is so politically incorrect that a mainstream publisher allegedly refused to produce it. L. Stone, *The Past and Present* (1981) and *The Past and Present Revisited* (1987), show how quickly historiography changes. Other useful, if somewhat dated, studies include J. H. Plumb, *The Death of the Past* (1969), M. Mandelbaum, *The Anatomy of Historical Knowledge* (London, 1977), B. Tuchman, *Practising History* (London, 1983) and D. Lowenthal, *The Past is a Foreign Country* (1985). Some of the historians themselves are discussed in J. Cannon (ed.), *The Historian at Work* (1980), although bizarre inclusions (such as Mortimer Wheeler) and weird exclusions (such as Lucien Febvre) impinge on the overall quality of this volume. Juliet Gardiner (ed.), *What is History Today?* (1988), is a useful collection of essays. F. Stern (ed.), *The Varieties of History* (1970), looks at history since the Enlightenment through extracts from the practitioners. Hayden White's key works, *Metahistory: The Historical Imagination in Nineteenth-Century Europe* (1973) and *Tropics of Discourse* (1978), are foundation-stones for those who would claim that history is a literary or philosophical discipline rather than a social science. In general, postmodern perspectives are made most accessible in two volumes by Keith Jenkins, *Re-thinking History* (1991) and *On What is History?* (1995), as well as by Beverley Southgate's *History: What and Why?* (1996). The journal *Storia della Storiographia* (*History of Historiography*) is a little-known treasure-trove of worldwide perspectives on historiography and the philosophy of history. It also houses many important debates.

HISTORY AS SOCIAL SCIENCE

In recent years much more attention has been paid to the question of whether history is a social science. This has inevitably led to discussion of the links between history and sociology and other social science subjects. A number of important works address these issues. The clearest introduction used to be Peter Burke, *Sociology and History* (1980), which the author has revamped as *History and Social Theory* (1992). P. Abram, *Historical Sociology* (1982), presents the key considerations with a Marxist hue. More dated, though still useful, is R. Blackburn (ed.), *Ideology in Social Science: Readings in Critical Social Theory* (1972), which contains Gareth Stedman Jones's cutting and polemical essay, 'History: the poverty of empiricism'. Jones's ideas are further developed in his 'From historical sociology to theoretical history', *British Journal of Sociology*, 27 (1976). The journal *History and Theory* has published many useful essays in this general area. In addition, journals such as *Social History*, *Economic History Review*, *American Historical Review* and *History Workshop* have covered many of the key debates in the past twenty years or so.

MARXISM

The influence of Marxism upon post-war historiography has been massive. The simplest introduction to Marx himself is D. McLellan, *Karl Marx* (1976). A good starting point for budding historians is S. R. Rigby, *Marxism and History: a Critical Introduction* (1987), which attempts to bring historians around to reading Marx's own theories. G. McLennan, *Marxism and the Methodologies of History* (1981), is a good overview. As the British Marxist school has been enormously influential over the past fifty years, H. J. Kaye, *British Marxist Historians: an Introductory Analysis* (1984), is a must. It contains excellent syntheses of the works of such writers as Maurice Dobb, Rodney Hilton, Christopher Hill, Eric Hobsbawm and E. P. Thompson, written in clear and uncluttered language.

THE *ANNALES* SCHOOL

Only in the past twenty years or so have the works of the *Annales* historians begun to appear in English translation. Before examining key works of their history, students might like to consider what the *Annalistes* had to say about historiography, methodology and the philosophy of history. The starting point should be Marc Bloch, *The Historian's Craft* (1992 edn) and F. Braudel, *On History* (1980). Also useful is J. Le Goff and P. Nora (eds), *Constructing the Past: Essays in Historical Methodology* (1985). Emmanuel Le Roy Ladurie, *The Territory of the Historian* (1979), includes a brilliant exposition on quantitative history. The essays in R. Chartier, *Cultural History* (1993 edn) and Michel Vovelle, *Ideologies and Mentalities* (1990) examine some of the most pressing issues in French historiography. C. Ginzburg, *The Cheese and the Worms: the Cosmos of a Sixteenth-Century Miller* (1976) and Robert Darnton, *The Great Cat Massacre and other Episodes in French Cultural History* (1984) stand as witnesses to the worldwide appeal of the *Annales* spirit. The best and most accessible overview of the whole *Annales* genre is Peter Burke, *The French Historical Tradition: the Annales School, 1929-1989* (1990).

BRITISH ECONOMIC AND SOCIAL HISTORY

Recent developments in British economic and social history are examined in A. Digby and C. Feinstein (eds), *New Directions in Economic and Social History*, Vol. I (1989) and A. Digby, C. Feinstein and D. Jenkins (eds), *New Directions in Economic and Social History*, Vol. II (1992). More dated, but still very useful, is M. W. Flinn and T. C. Smout (eds), *Essays in Social History* (1974). Also see A. Wilson (ed.), *Rethinking Social History. English Society, 1570-1920* (1993). The best exposition of the philosophy of economic and social development is Sidney Pollard, *The Idea of Progress* (1968). American viewpoints are put across in J. A. Henretta, 'Social history as lived and written', *American Historical Review*, 84 (5) (1979). The chief philosopher of social history is Christopher Lloyd, whose *Explanations in Social History* (1988 edn) provides a brilliant but complex examination of social history. The same author's *The Structures of History* (1993) provides an excellent defence of historical realism and a cutting critique of postmodern influences on historical method. Eric Roll's *A History of Economic Thought* (1992 edn) contains everything one could want to know about the emergence of economics, that vital precursor of economic history. For economic history itself, see D. C. Coleman, *History and the Economic Past* (1987).

QUANTIFICATION AND COMPUTING

Of related interest are works on the use of quantification and computing by historians. Michael Drake, *The Quantitative Analysis of Historical Data* (1974), is a good primer. For those fearful of statistics, D. Rowntree, *Statistics Without Tears* (1981 edn) will prove very comforting. O. Adeylotte, *Quantification in History* (1971), is more a philosophical statement than a practical guide. The best guides to using computers for quantitative analysis are E. Mawdsley and T. Munck, *Computing for*

Historians (1990), R. Lloyd-Jones and M. J. Lewis, *Using Computers in History: A Practical Guide* (1996) and C. Harvey and J. Press, *Databases in Historical Research* (1996).

ENVIRONMENT, GEOGRAPHY AND HISTORICAL CHANGE

On environment, geography and historical change, see W. G. Hoskins's classic study, *The Making of the English Landscape* (1955) and Simon Schama's weighty and much-acclaimed *Landscape and Memory* (1995). For the way past spatiality has been represented through the ages, see Jeremy Black, *Maps and History* (1997).

'OLD' AND 'NEW' HISTORY

One of the most important presentations of the dichotomy of 'old' and 'new' history is found in Peter Burke, *New Perspectives on Historical Writing* (1991 edn). The umbrella of 'new' history covers a disparate range of historiographical styles and inheritances. R. Samuel (ed.), *People's History and Social History* (1981), brings together many important essays on the subject of non-traditional history. The complex question of community is examined by a number of contributors in M. Drake (ed.), *Time, Family and Community: Perspectives on Family and Community History* (1994). The use of personal testimony in history, which has grown rapidly since the 1960s, is one of the most important arenas of 'new' history. The differences between Jan Vansina's classic works, *Oral Tradition* (1961) and *Oral Tradition as History* (1985), are themselves illustrations of the way method and approaches have changed. Oral history is the subject of Paul Thompson's path-breaking study, *The Voice of the Past: Oral History* (1988). Trevor Lummis, *Listening to History: The Authenticity of Oral Evidence* (1987), provides a useful accompaniment to Thompson. The journal *Oral History* is essential reading for scholars of personal testimony. W. G. Hoskins, *Fieldwork in Local History* (1982 edn) and Stephen Caunce, *Oral History and the Local Historian* (1994) bring together two important strands of non-traditional history. Robert Perks, *Oral History: An Annotated Bibliography* (1990), contains a mine of useful information on local archive holdings as well as published matter.

GENDER AND WOMEN'S HISTORY

This is a vibrant area of historical study. No better introduction exists than J. W. Scott, *Gender and the Politics of History* (1988). Although somewhat dated, Sheila Rowbotham's *Hidden from History* is still a lucid statement on the genre.

LOCAL HISTORY

This area is usefully examined in W. G. Hoskins, *Local History in England* (1972) and in Michael A. Williams, *Researching Local History: the Human Journey* (1996). Journals dedicated to local history are manifold.

'HISTORY FROM BELOW'

'History from below', which at once brings together a variety of 'new', *Annales* and Marxist historians has surprisingly few dedicated works of theory and practice. F. Krantz (ed.), *History From Below: Studies in Popular Protest and Popular Ideology* (1988 edn), contains numerous good essays. Jim Sharpe's trenchant essay 'History from below', which appears in Peter Burke (ed.), *New Perspectives on Historical Writing*, is by far the best introductory statement. 'History from below' meets the heritage industry in Raphael Samuel's masterful study, *Theatres of Memory* (1994).

STUDY SKILLS

Finally, the work of any student requires good study skills. The subject of reading and writing is covered in clear and concise fashion by G. J. Fairbairn and C. Winch (eds), *Reading, Writing and Reasoning: A Guide for Students* (1995). A more general appraisal of the techniques of learning and assessment is R. Barrass, *Study! A Guide to Effective Study and Revision and Examination Techniques* (1984). Those studying at university level might like to consult the perennial favourite: Patrick Dunleavy, *Studying for a Degree in the Humanities and Social Sciences* (1986).

Index